To my former colleague, Mike

From Farm to Front:
An Innocent Goes to War

1942-1946

Lawrence E. Breeze

Lawrence E. Breeze

Center for Regional History
Southeast Missouri State University
Cape Girardeau, Mo.

Copyright © 2009 by the Center for Regional History, Southeast Missouri State University. All rights reserved. No part of this book may be reproduced or transmitted in any form or by any means, electronic or mechanical, including photocopying, recording, or by any information storage and retrieval system, without permission in writing from the Publisher.

Southeast Missouri State University
Center for Regional History
One University Plaza
Cape Girardeau, Mo. 63701

Printed in the United States

ISBN: 978-1-890551-16-2 (Hardcover)
ISBN: 978-1-890551-15-5 (Paperback)

Dedication

Dedicated to those who went with me,
especially those who didn't come home.

Contents

Acknowledgments	i
For Alison and Daniel	iii
Notes from the Desk of the Typist/Editor/Wife	v
Chap. 1: Induction: Fort Leavenworth, Kansas, 1942	1
Chap. 2: Camp Beale, California	20
Chap. 3: Basic Training and Beyond	47
Chap. 4: ASTP: City College of New York	73
Chap. 5: ASTP: The University of New Hampshire	83
Chap. 6: Camp Pickett: 903 Field Artillery Battalion	102
Chap. 7: Camp Pickett: 311th infantry Regiment	114
Chap. 8: Overseas: England	131
Chap. 9: Overseas: France and Belgium	143
Chap. 10: The Hurtgen Forest and the Bulge	157
Chap. 11: The Rhineland and Central Europe	193
Chap. 12: Occupation	227
Chap. 13: The 29th Division and Home	242
Picture Gallery: Reunions	250
Picture Gallery: Europe Revisited	252
Epilogue	256
About Larry Breeze	261

Maps

Service in European Theater of Operations	130
The 311th Infantry Area of Action December 9, 1944 - February 9, 1945	156
The 78th Holds the North Shoulder of the Battle of the Bulge	169
From the Roer to the Rhine	192
The 311th in the Ruhr Pocket	216

Acknowledgments

For many years following the war, I was not inclined to say much about that period in my life, offering only infrequent and limited glimpses into it. Being a very private sort of person, it never crossed my mind that in my old age I might reveal much of myself in a written memoir.

When finally I undertook a written account more than half a century later, it was due largely to the influence of a dear friend and former office mate, Dr. George G. Suggs, Jr. In retrospect I am profoundly grateful for his repeated suggestion that I write something for the benefit of my children.

Initially the memoir was revealed only to family and a few friends. That it became anything more and that eventually I would find myself agreeing to newspaper, radio, and television interviews is attributable to the interest and influence of another good friend and academic colleague, Dr. Frank Nickell, Director of the Center for Regional History at Southeast Missouri State University.

Two among the several interviewers who came to me as a consequence of Dr. Nickell's influence I would like to acknowledge by name: Vickie Devenport and Jak Tichenor of WSIU radio and television respectively, Southern Illinois University. Their competence and understanding made it easier than ever expected to talk about some difficult and uncomfortable moments in my army life. And I deeply appreciate their inclusion of me in the profiles of area veterans presented by WSIU in conjunction with the showing of the Ken Burns documentary on the war in 2007.

I am much indebted to Dr. Nickell and the manuscript reviewers for deeming my story worthy of publication by the Center for Regional History. Special thanks are due to Hallie Fieser, Research Assistant at the Center, for her meticulous preparation of the manuscript.

Sadly, since the completion of the original memoir in 2000, I have lost several comrades who helped with information and ideas. I remain in contact with a few of the surviving members of the old infantry company, including the captain now in his 90's and in ill health. Most of us have not seen each other for years. Yet we are held together in an enduring bond of camaraderie, forged by a shared experience that began in a dark German forest many Decembers ago.

For Alison and Daniel

One of the posters used by the British government in an attempt to persuade men to volunteer for military service in the First World War showed a man confronted by his children with this question: "What did you do in the war, Daddy?" You, of course, are aware of bits and pieces of my service in the Second World War, but I have undertaken to reconstruct a more complete picture for you of that period in my life from late 1942 to early 1946.

Out of a total of 1,150 days of service with the army, I spent the first 677 of them in the United States. Thus, although affected by it and sometimes preparing for it, I was far removed from the real war. That lay in distant theaters (to use a proper, however euphemistic sounding, term) of operations: Europe, North Africa, Pacific Islands, and on the seas.

D-Day, June 6, 1944, came and I was still in the States. At the time I was in training with a division, the 78th Infantry, that would take me to the European Theater of Operations a few months later. Committed to front line action in early December, the 311th Infantry Regiment of that division would be credited with 128 days of combat service. Since I was with this regiment, I did get a close look at the real war. That does not sound like many days out of the total service as given above, but it was more than enough. Your mother has remarked upon what a dreadful experience this had to be for me. I have to agree it was bad but remind her that some of my friends had it worse, especially those in the regiment's rifle squads. Whenever I think about the casualty rate of my own squad, I realize that either I was incredibly lucky or Someone up there looked out for me. Why me, however, and not some of my buddies is an inexplicable mystery.

Overall I truthfully can say that I am glad of my wartime experience but as many of my fellow veterans of that war have said, I would not want to repeat it.

While my memory of many things remained quite clear, much more than that was needed to prepare this account. Fortunately some good documentary material was at hand in the form of letters I wrote to my parents. Your grandma lovingly saved all of these. Upon her death, your mother, bless her, rescued the bulk of these when she found me thoughtlessly tossing some of them away. Aunt Georgia saved some of my V-mail letters and returned them prior to her death.

There were other important sources available for my use. Shortly after the war ended in Europe, the regiment began working on a history. Upon completion, *Combat Journal, The Story of the Timberwolf Regiment of the 78th Lightning Division in World War II, 1944-1945,* was printed in Germany and a copy given to me before I left the regiment. Very important also was *Lightning, The History of the 78th Infantry Division,* edited by the Division Historical Association and published by the Infantry Journal Press in 1947.

The 78th Division Veteran's Association publishes a quarterly journal, *The Flash,* and some of its letters and articles have been helpful to me.

In the way of reference sources I have used A *Soldier's Story by* Omar N. Bradley (interestingly, a native of Moberly, about a hundred miles down the Wabash rail line from Chillicothe); and A *Crusade in Europe* by Dwight D. Eisenhower, Supreme Commander of the Allied Expeditionary Force. My most important reference source was *The Oxford Companion to World War II,* edited by I.C.B. Dear and M. R. D. Foot, published in 1995.

Last, but certainly not least, telephone conversations, visits, and letters from friends in the service (both stateside. and overseas) have helped me complete this picture I have attempted to portray for you.

As usual with my writing, your mother has been very helpful. You can thank her for taking my copy, in pencil and on backs of scrap sheets, and transforming it into what you are about to read.

Cape Girardeau, Mo. February, 2000

Notes From the
Desk of the Typist/Editor/Wife

The experience of typing and editing the story of Larry's service years has been a moving and eye-opening experience to me. Typical of many war veterans he has been reticent about them. Over the years I have heard most of the stories of the lighter moments and listened as he (very occasionally) painfully told some of the more somber episodes. But in this running narrative I think I finally and fully appreciate the impact of this army experience on the man I love.

We met in the fall of 1952, my sophomore year at Jacksonville Junior College (JJC) when "Mr. Breeze" arrived to teach history and Western Civilization courses. Tall, slim, knowledgeable, and seemingly very serious, he was soon a very popular teacher on campus. He did not wear his "war experience" on his sleeve as some men I had met. He was 30 years old to my 18, but the difference in our backgrounds and experiences seemed more apparent than the difference in our ages. Beside him, the college boys I knew seemed unfinished, uninteresting, and somehow lacking.

As we grew to know and love each other during the next two years before our wedding in March of 1955, some of these war experiences were discussed and I began to understand their place in the make-up of his personality and outlook on life. My earliest understanding included his gratitude to the army for its encouragement toward an engineering degree (<u>that</u> was quite a surprise to me) without which he might not have attended college at all; never become a history professor; and certainly never come to be my professor in Florida. Along with this story of course there is the family joke about the role the U.S. Mail played in losing 2 different letters one about eight years after the other which, if received by Larry, would have kept us apart.

It would be years before I knew about the combat deaths that affected him so, or the Bronze Star. I was aware of a bit of a melancholy, especially in winter months; and that the smell of a southern pine forest, which I dearly love, brought him entirely different memories. As I reflect upon it, he did not seem to avoid talking about his army experiences; he had other things to do, think about, and discuss. But there were situations that triggered his memory and at those times I would hear a little more.

His experience as part of the armed forces that fought in the European theater certainly influenced his teaching of Western Civilization (the first class in which I saw him in action) and European history over the next three decades. One lingering connection to the army years was the annual exchange of Christmas cards with three men from his unit in Germany: Hildebrand, Parsons and DeFilippo. His interest in this section of his life was heightened with his becoming a member of the 78th Infantry Veterans Association and our attending a meeting in St. Louis. There I met and Larry saw again Parsons, Hildebrand, Rifenberrick, Coolbeth and Gordon (these two from the 4th platoon), and Capt. Gapen. I was fascinated by each encounter: it began as a tentative approach and inquiry as to name; but as the fellows smiled and laughed, the recognition and instant rapport was wondrous to behold.

I do not envy them the experience that brought them together the first time, but do envy their comradeship and this long-standing rapport.

The reunion and the 50th anniversary of World War II, especially of D-Day and certain battles, seemed to open Larry up to more conversation and self-analysis. This in turn led to his laying out a chronological narration of his army service. He has read and researched avidly (of course) and savored lengthy correspondence and telephone calls (<u>not</u> his usual *modus operandi*) with many of his buddies, all of whom seemed genuinely glad to hear from him and talk about the war years and this magical connection between men who had seen combat together.

This is written for his children, but the benefit is shared in the catharsis of spirit it has brought to Larry, as well as in furthering my understanding of this man. When I first saw the title I was curious about his choice of the word "innocence", but as I read, typed and we edited, I realized how correct his choice was. Perhaps the experience was not unique with him, but the truly callow youth that left the Missouri farm was truly a man upon his return.

Alice Breeze

From Farm to Front:
An Innocent Goes to War

1942-1946

Chapter One

Induction: Fort Leavenworth, Kansas, 1942

The gray sky seemed perfectly suited to the somber mood of the group gathered before the bus station in Chillicothe, Missouri, on a day in late November, 1942. Family members and friends were there to witness the departure of Livingston County's monthly contribution to the military draft. The chill in the air was attributable only partially to the fact that winter had descended on northwest Missouri. Twenty-three young men were about to embark upon an uncertain future. The Trailways bus stood ready to take them to their induction center at Fort Leavenworth, Kansas.

My parents and I arrived in their Model A Ford, parked on the courthouse square, and joined the growing crowd. Since the departure time was 12:46 and our farm lay ten miles northwest of town, we had eaten an early dinner. On the farm we never had lunch at mid-day; it was always "dinner," generally a big meal for hard working people. Under the circumstances, this particular meal could not be cheerful, even with some of my mother's good blackberry cobbler (made from summer-picked berries now canned and laid up with the rest of the garden surplus). It had been a quiet meal, with each of us lost in his own thoughts but acutely aware that this could be our last meal together for a long time. In the case of Mother, given her outlook on life, I suspect she feared this might be the very last. My thoughts were never that gloomy, and I knew that some of my older acquaintances, already in service, had received furloughs four or five months after their induction. In my case the first furlough turned out to be much closer to a year in the future.

After eating, I walked out into the yard and wandered to the barnyard taking a sad and longing look at familiar things and some of the farm animals, especially my small flock of registered purebred Hampshire sheep. I said goodbye to my little golden-haired dog, Wooly, who had been my faithful companion since I was five years old. Due to an unfortunate encounter with a mowing machine, he had gone through much of that time on three legs. This never kept him from accompanying me all around the farm and neighboring hills, woods and fields. That November day was to be our last time together. He died not long after I left Leavenworth to begin basic training.

It was not the call to service that worried me that day so much as it was the obvious fact that one had to leave home to do so. I had never gotten far from the security of home. The longest period of time I had ever been away from the farm had been for three weeks, a time of homesickness and loneliness, even though I had been around many other people.

So I worried about my ability to deal with homesickness and the loss of familiar surroundings. Reality would soon show me that I was not unique in this regard and that, in actuality, I could handle it as well as most other homesick soldiers and much better than some of my buddies.

At the time of induction the greater problem seemed to be that the war could go on for years. It was unthinkable that we would lose in the long run, yet at the moment it looked far from winnable. The Japanese were firmly established in eastern Asia, spread through the islands of the Pacific held southeast Asia and threated India. The Germans occupied western Europe and central Europe, part of north Africa, and moved deeply into Russia.

My Aunt Maye's second husband, Paul Mansfield, had come by our house earlier that morning, the 27th. He had served with Uncle Willis, Daddy's younger brother, in the First World War, and he tried to assure me that military service was not so bad; and that the war would be over within a couple of years.

I remained unconvinced of the latter point, and, as I recollect, guessed the war would last at least six years. At the age of 20, I found that an interminable time. Interestingly, the war lasted exactly six years, 1939-1945, for those who had been in it from the outset: continental Europeans, the British, our Canadian neighbors, and many others.

In those days, of course, we did not have televised news with CNN offering a continuous commentary. Many of us had access to a radio, which gave small towns and rural communities some sense of what was going on in the outside world. Most of our information came from newspapers; they really were "news" papers in those days.

For those who could afford it (we could not), there might be a news magazine. An occasional opportunity to see someone's copy of *Life* magazine gave me most of my visual impressions of the war. These were supplemented by a rare visit to the cinema with its news reels and authoritative sounding commentary by Lowell Thomas.

In our small community of Lock Springs (population 209 according to the sign post at the edge of town) my generation got a lot of commentary along with the dispensation of worldly wisdom, from an older generation of men who, in fair weather, sat on the benches in front of the town's two stores (one grocery; the other, hardware). There was also one garage (with a single gas pump out front), one cafe, a post office, and the Masonic Lodge hall. In cold weather, the men clustered around a stove in one of the stores.

The war of 1914-18, the Great War, was a favorite topic of conversation for these men. They told some riveting tales, most probably second hand or hearsay, and embellished as such war stories can be. But they made quite an impression on young and innocent ears. I learned from them, for instance, about the Allied war debt and the ungrateful European nations, with the notable exception of Finland, who refused to repay us after we had sacrificed so much. Later, when I studied history in graduate school, I came to the realization that some of what I learned from my storefront elders had been factually wrong, and much of it was misleading.

With the outbreak of the second war in Europe in 1939, they were quick to offer judgments. They followed the war news on the radio and read the big city newspapers, from either Kansas City or St. Joseph, with avid interest. Then they came to town and distilled the news for any available listeners.

At first they could be wildly optimistic as when they reported a large number of planes allegedly shot down by the Poles in their dismal defense against the Germans in September, 1939. As the Axis forces chalked up victory upon victory, however, the mood began to swing the other way. Finally, with the disastrous Canadian raid upon the channel port of Dieppe in August of 1942, about which I first heard from them, most conceded it would be a long war.

Years later when I became a professional historian with interests in modern Europe and a specialty in British history, I came to appreciate the full significance of the events that transpired against the Germans just as I entered the service. That autumn, Allied navies, after horrific losses, began to gain the upper hand at sea.

On November 4, 1942, Field Marshal Bernard Montgomery's British Eighth Army defeated the famed Afrika Korps at El Alamein. This victory in the desert sand west of Cairo, Egypt, broke one arm of a German movement that had threatened to sever links between Britain and the Commonwealth and to seize the Middle East.

Montgomery began methodically and relentlessly to push the Axis forces of Field Marshal Erwin Rommel westward across North Africa. On November 8, Allied forces landed on the coast of French North Africa. Dwight D. Eisenhower and George S. Patton became familiar names as Americans joined in the effort to squeeze the Axis out of North Africa.

On another front, by the third week of November Russian forces had encircled an entire German army at Stalingrad on the Volga in southeastern Russia. Adolf Hitler made the fatal decision that prevented a breakout, lost his Sixth Army, and allowed the Russians to stop the German move to reach into the Caucasus and toward the Middle East.

But even if I had understood something of the strategic importance of these British and Russian victories, it would have seemed like a long war still in front of us. Dieppe had shown how costly and nearly impossible it would be to break the German hold on western Europe.

Reluctant as I might be to leave home, I never doubted the need to go to war and the rightness of the cause. In fact, the whole nation gave solid support to the war effort. Millions of men and women served in various branches of the armed forces. Millions of others, especially women, worked in defense related industries. Some of the young women of our community, for example, worked in an ordinance plant in the Kansas City area. People worked to produce food products and provide natural resources for the war. Victory gardens were common in urban areas. Scrap metal was collected, and it became very patriotic to purchase a war bond. Rationing of food, gasoline and other products was endured with a minimum of complaining and cheating. One way or another we were all in the war together.

The Japanese attack upon Pearl Harbor, December 7, 1941, followed by reports of bestial cruelty to prisoners of war in the Philippines, united the American nation against them. On December 11, 1941, Hitler, in another fatal decision never completely understood, declared war on the United States carrying his fellow dictator, Benito Mussolini of Italy, with him.

Our fight against fascism, the great political surprise of the post-World War I era when experts thought the choice of the future lay between Wilsonian democracy and Leninism, seemed fully justified to me. Once I got to Europe and saw the effects of fascism in its most virulent form, Nazism, there could be no doubt.

Postwar study and teaching confirmed to me that we had fought against a terrible force of evil. In Germany this force had masked itself as being intensely patriotic. It promised to return the nation to the good values prevailing before the onset in the 1920's of a liberal and corrupted society. In gaining mastery of the minds of people, Hitler liked to affect Christian convictions proclaiming, for instance on February 1, 1934, that his Government would "firmly protect Christianity, which is our moral basis." By gulling the important Catholic Center party and confusing the public mind on fundamental distinctions between the Social Democratic and Communist parties, along with the application of force and intimidation, Hitler was able legally to use democracy to destroy democracy itself.

Fascist elements in several European countries unleashed forces of intolerance, bigotry and hatred; created their own paramilitary units operating outside a nation's lawful police force; and never recognized opponents in the give and take debate of a democratic society but considered them only enemies who had to be destroyed. Once in power they created authoritarian regimes that silenced all who were different and any who might differ with them, the German Nazis physically destroying them.

The unfortunate and unhappy truth is that there are latent fascist tendencies in far too many of us even though we would be outraged in our denial. As an old man it saddens and disheartens me to hear the strident, often militant, tones of the political far right. We can be thankful that to date no charismatic individual has emerged to unite all these disruptive forces into a single cohesive movement.

At the same time it is discouraging to see men and women, in a position to know better, play upon these tendencies to gain political position and promote their own agenda. It is even more frustrating to hear this described as "conservatism." We do have something worth conserving that my generation sacrificed to maintain, and it would be a monumental tragedy to let our needless ignorance of history sweep it all away.

But back to November 27, 1942. From a distance of over half a century later, I am still proud to have been a part, albeit insignificant and largely inconspicuous, of what General Eisenhower called a "crusade in Europe." With the exception of an officer in the Missouri State Guard, however, the Livingston county contingent of November, 1942, bore no resemblance to soldiers, let alone crusaders.

We looked exactly what we were—an assortment of farmers, farm boys, day laborers, a taxi driver, a clerk from Montgomery Ward (in local parlance, "Monkey" Ward), and representatives of a few other occupations. We expected the army would make every effort to find and bring out some soldierly qualities in us. Whether or not we were up to the challenge was still a matter of concern to most of us.

We ranged in age from 20, the minimum draft age at the time, to well into the thirties. We came from all parts of the county and from Chillicothe. With a population of around 9000, Chillicothe was a "big" town to those of us who came from the towns and communities of Sampsel (my RFD address), Dawn, Wheeling, Avalon, Chula, Utica, and Mooresville. Some of these places might round up 150 to 200 or so people, but Sampsel would have been hard pressed to find fifty. It still had a small store with a post office in one corner; but it lost its bank at the outset of the depression, its livestock yards shortly afterward, and the tiny high school closed about the time I entered the one-room country school known as Brookshier.

We lived in the northwest part of the county about a mile from the Daviess County line and a little over two miles from Lock Springs in that county. Lock Springs became more of a community center for us than Sampsel. We belonged to the Methodist Episcopal Church South there, and I walked in to the town's little high school. Consequently most of my friends and schoolmates went into military service through Daviess County.

Shortly after 12:30 that day, an official from the draft board came across the street from the court house and read each of our names from an official list. He designated Clark McCown, the state guard officer, to be our leader. The moment I dreaded was near.

My apprehensions about reporting for service were by no means limited to the certainty of homesickness and the uncertainty of what lay before me. The effect that my leaving would have upon my parents was a paramount concern.

I knew my dad would hate to see me leave and undoubtedly would have some anxious moments in the months and years that lay ahead. Yet I felt confident that he would bear it well and would see me off with little outward show of emotion. After all, he had always been a model of physical and emotional strength to me. And not just to me, but to the whole family; for as the eldest of ten children he had accepted responsibility early, and long after the others had reached adulthood they looked up to him. At the beginning of his teen years he had done a man's work on the family homestead near Spokane, Washington. Even though he was past fifty years of age in 1942 and I was twenty, he surpassed me in physical strength and endurance. Only once could I recall ever seeing him shed tears. That was when he received the news of Grandpa Breeze's death.

In his old age, when I was in my fifties, I came to know and understand this gentle and considerate man a lot better. Looking back I came to believe that the years from 1942 to 1946 had been far more difficult for him than I thought at the time.

Most of my anxiety was directed toward my mother. Unquestionably my leaving for the army would affect her profoundly. She was a worrier of the worst kind. There could be no doubt she would miss her only child, born ten years into her marriage when she was 33, whose health and well-being had often been a cause for concern. Only in my fifties and her eighties, when my heart valve problems had been diagnosed properly, and she talked about some events in my earlier years, did I appreciate that she probably had some basis for her worry.

Few of us in our community had either money or opportunity for medical examination by specialists. Dr. A. G. Minnick of Lock Springs was quite literally a horse and buggy doctor, advancing to a car with a high school boy as driver in the 1930s. He was quite good at delivering babies at home (I was one of many), setting broken bones (my cousin Junior Breeze, twice), stitching cuts (my careless encounter with an ax for example), nursing pneumonia cases (one or more serious ones in the community each winter) and prescribing one of the three kinds of pills he carried for just about everything else. What he might have said to my mother about mitral valve prolapse symptoms, or could have said for that matter, I have no idea.

Nor do I know exactly what was said by Dr. John Timberman, a general practitioner to whom I was taken, as a very small boy, after experiencing a black out on a Chillicothe street. He probably talked about a heart murmur anyway and might have spoken of heart leakage, which, if so, surely frightened my mother and would account for what sometimes appeared to be an over-protective attitude toward me in my younger days.

One thing I do recall quite vividly. He cautioned me against certain activities on the playground. A small boy, especially a sensitive one, never forgets the teasing from grade school classmates when he admits he is not allowed to participate in the popular game of seeing how high one could go on the swings. I expect that partly explains why Mother tried to discourage me from playing basketball later in high school, which I did anyway and with some success.

I knew that in addition to her concern about my physical well-being, whether or not anything dire happened to me, it would be a time of loneliness and sadness for my mother. Background and inclination pointed her that way. Her mother, my Grandma Griner, died nine years prior to my birth; but my impression of her is one of a sad, often lonely and sickly asthmatic woman.

As a bride, Grandma Griner had been brought from Indiana to Missouri and she never saw either her parents or siblings again. Her husband, John Griner, died suddenly and unexpectedly a few years after he had moved the family on to Indian Territory, now Oklahoma. Not long after that, her eldest son Ruphard and eldest daughter Eva, both married and with young children, emigrated to Canada. If Indiana appeared far away to my grandmother, then the prairie province of Saskatchewan must have seemed a world away.

And thus my mother lost her father when she was a teenager and her mother a few years later. She never saw her much admired older brother Ruphard after 1910. It would be nearly thirty years before she was to see her older sister Eva again. There was often an element of sadness about it when Mother talked of her family, and it made me feel sad for her; so I never asked a lot of the questions that should have been asked, for a record of family history. But I did come to understand her great fear of separation from the ones she loved.

But even harder on her than the above considerations was her long held fear of war. How this came to develop in her childhood is not clear to me. Her father had been a soldier in the territories of the Southwest in the 1870s. Whether or not he ever talked with his children about any encounters with the Indians there I do not know. I do know that at the age of nine, she felt great fear that her brother would go to the Spanish-American War.

Again, she was very anxious about the First World War. Neither my father nor her brother Virgil were called to service, much to her relief. Uncle Virgil did not pass the physical examination and my father's draft classification card, which we still have in a family scrapbook, placed him in IV A, but I am not sure of its meaning: possibly farming occupation. In any event I knew that my leaving for the Second World War would be an agonizing experience for Mother.

As it turned out, I should have had more confidence in her mental toughness and determination. She may have cried a lot in private during the next three plus years, but on that day she saw me off with a sad look, but dry eyes.

As I looked around that day, I soon realized there was nothing unique about me. Goodbyes were difficult for most of the group, especially the younger ones. Nearly all of us handled it quietly and without incident. One poor fellow, however, proved less fortunate. Parents, siblings, and other relatives accompanied him to the bus station. Some became quite emotional in their farewells, even crying, and it got to him. While I felt sorry for him, I could not help but be relieved that it had not happened to me.

Once aboard the bus and away from families and friends, we settled in for a long ride. In the days before the interstate highways, and without an expressway through Kansas City, it would take five to six hours to get to Leavenworth, Kansas. A day in late November meant it would be well after dark when we arrived.

This would be my third trip to Leavenworth that year. Soon after reaching my 20th birthday and registering for the draft, I began to think about joining the Army Air Corps. I had never even seen an airplane close up let alone ridden in one, yet the Corps had a certain appeal. An officer in one of the local veterans organizations was promoting the Air Corps so I approached him and arranged for the requisite tests at Leavenworth.

Doctors at the post gave me a pretty thorough physical examination and appeared less than satisfied with the results of the heart tests. Following the physical, an officer interviewed me and indicated they could probably find something for me to do in the Air Corps, but certainly not what I really wanted. And so I returned home to wait for the draft.

My second trip to Leavenworth came on November 18 with the Livingston County contingent of selectees. This time the physical exam was quite perfunctory. Bored-acting doctors and technicians hustled us through a line with less attention than a meat inspector stamping a side of beef at the Swift packing plant a few miles up the Missouri, at St. Joseph. One man in the line said he understood that if you were still breathing, the army would take you. Another man related the story of a one-legged man and a one-eyed man found in the same line, so the army took both to make one soldier.

Leavenworth is home to a federal prison as well as the historic army post. The noncommissioned officer who assembled a large group of us to take the oath of allegiance to the Army of the United States revealed a grim sense of humor. Pointing to a distant hill he said, "You have a choice. Take the oath here, or prepare to go over there." The officer who administered the oath assured us we were bound irrevocably by the swearing in ceremony whether or not we opened our mouths and actually uttered the words of commitment.

Thus I became a lowly private in the AUS and henceforth would be known as number 37242203. Immediately we had been placed in the Reserve and sent home to get our affairs in line, with orders to report back to the Reception Center on November 27.

My departure from the world of innocence began in one respect on the ride to Leavenworth. I had my first close encounter with an inebriated person, and a pretty disgusting experience it proved to be. Prior to this my contact with drunks had been infrequent and more distant.

One of the older members of our contingent of November 27 tried to prepare himself for meeting the army, by having a few drinks before reporting to the bus station. To the rest of us this seemed to be a dumb thing to do, but as long as he was quiet it was simply his problem. Since we would get to the fort after mealtime, we stopped for a break in Kansas City. With one exception we all had something to eat. The exception found a nearby drinking establishment, and by the time our leader had gotten him back on the bus he had become a disgusting drunk. With each passing mile he became increasingly obnoxious and especially hostile toward the bus driver whom he seemed to blame for his having to report to Leavenworth.

Somewhere along the way, either McCown or the bus driver must have called ahead to the fort. When we drew up to the Reception Center and unloaded, we were met by two soldiers wearing arm bands with the letters "MP" on them. These military policemen, as I soon learned them to be, dragged our inebriated colleague off and I never saw him again.

But preoccupied with my own problems I cared little about what might happen to our drunk. The stress and tension of the day had given me a terrible headache. This had been a rather common occurrence in my boyhood, but after I had gotten glasses at the age of fifteen, they had been much less frequent. Unfortunately this type of headache, as well as the heavy sinus headaches, so common during my sophomore and junior years in high school, affected my stomach. From Kansas City onward my headache got worse and I became more nauseated. Trailways buses of that era did not contain a rest room. An awkward and embarrassing experience seemed sure to overtake me.

Somehow I survived the trip and managed to get through the checking-in process and into a bunk for the night without becoming "actively ill," as my mother-in-law would so delicately put it in later years. Either incredible luck or a higher power seemed to favor me. Unbelievable as it would have seemed at the time, during my entire military service I did not have another such headache. I must have had a few minor ones, but if so, they did not make a lasting impression.

Exactly two years later, however, when I began sleeping on the damp ground in France and the frozen ground in Belgium, the sinus headaches of my youth returned with intense ferocity.

My brief stay at Fort Leavenworth was unexciting, largely uneventful, and extremely busy. Processing personnel hurried us from one thing to another as they readied us for shipment to a basic training unit. With a war on, this made good sense.

Later on, as I acquired some grasp of military thinking, I realized the army also had another aim with all the busyness. To me, I might explain, the army became an entity in itself, possessing a mind and personality all its own. This seemed to stand quite apart from the fact that logic said a human mind somewhere, probably in that recently opened maze on the Potomac, lay behind it. Keeping recruits busy all day and dog tired when they dropped into their bunks at night, beginning at the processing center and extending at least through basic training, generally served as a preventative measure for homesickness.

My first full day in the army began at 6:00 a.m., when we were rousted out, given a few minutes for ablutions, and lined up on the street for roll call. This would be the first of many roll calls and before leaving Leavenworth I realized this might demand more alertness, even more guesswork, than would seem necessary. It surprised me what some non-commissioned officers, who handled roll call, could do with a simple name like Breeze. Actually I discovered that a man with a tongue bending name might have an advantage. At least he could guess they were trying to say his name. Many of these non-coms showed little respect for good enunciation and elocution would have been a foreign word to them. One learned early that such non-coms never felt they could afford to admit a mistake or had overlooked a name on the list.

Years later I discovered that apparently I inherited from my father a difficulty in separating sounds. This compounded my difficulty with some people who took roll as well as complicating my later efforts to learn a foreign language.

Following roll call we were marched to breakfast. Herded might be a more fitting term, for teaching us to march would be left to basic training instructors. The Livingston County contingent had been joined by many others from various parts of Missouri, Kansas and I believe parts of Nebraska and Iowa. Several hundred men waited to be fed, and we soon learned that waiting in line was an integral part of army life. It came naturally for World War II veterans to hate lines in civilian life.

Also, we learned that what we were about to eat was chow, the dining hall was a chow hall, and to eat was to chow down. More importantly, some of the reception personnel introduced us to griping, in this case about the chow. Griping and bitching, a more fervent and energetic form of griping, were to become essential to enduring army life.

On this occasion one of our handlers told us the food was terrible, and in nasty sounding tones informed us we were about to eat "s--t on a shingle." This turned out to be my introduction to chipped beef on toast. It really tasted quite good to me, and became more appetizing in basic training when it was referred to as "s.o.s." or if pressed to identify the letters in more polite society, as "stuff on a shingle."

When the Leavenworth cooks also served me an orange for breakfast, I began to suspect that some of the griping about food was form without substance. To one who lived through the depression and in the middle of the country, an orange was a delicacy. It truly was a treat for a youngster in the Lock Springs-Sampsel area to find oranges in the top of the small brown bags of hard candy distributed as Christmas treats at grade school and Sunday School.

As a boy I often developed a craving for oranges when I was sick. Mother thought they were good for me and I remember more than one occasion when Daddy indulged me by walking through winter snow to Lock Springs to bring back oranges that, in retrospect, I realize he could ill afford.

With this background it may be understandable that the army made a good first impression by giving me an orange at the induction center. Actually once I left Leavenworth, the closest I came to an orange was in the marmalade found in gallon sized cans, painted olive drab on the outside, in our basic training kitchen.

From the mess hall we moved to Supply, where we were measured from head to toe. Provided with this information as part of our record, we were sent to various stations to receive uniforms, work clothing (well described as "fatigues"), underclothing, socks, shoes, towels, a razor and a toothbrush. The army was big on hygiene and wisely so! At the end of the line I was issued a barracks bag to serve as repository for all my belongings. To this day, I cannot pack a suitcase and live out of it on a trip without recalling how I came to detest carrying all my possessions in a barracks, or duffel, bag, often living out of it for long periods of time, rooting through it trying to find a needed item (invariably near the bottom), and trying hopelessly to keep uniforms in respectable shape.

At the shoe distribution station I received a rude jolt and learned a hard lesson on the intractable nature of the army once an order had been issued, or a fact committed to writing. Either the fellow who measured me for shoes was incompetent, or more likely, occasionally used cruel jokes to relieve the tedium of what must have been one of the army's more monotonous jobs. Imagine his answer to the old question: "Daddy, what did you do during the war?"

The soldier at the counter looked at my record and shouted out in an amused tone, "Thirteen Annie." A soldier from the back responded by bringing forward the largest shoes I had ever seen. At the time I wore either 11 or 11 1/2 in a work shoe. To my great consternation, the 13A on the written form was chiseled in stone to those fellows.

So I was stuck with shoes that were heavy to lug around, the cause of fierce blisters on a long hike, and the source of a problem spot on my left heel that persists to this day. The best thing to be said for shoes issued in 1942 was that the quality greatly surpassed that of the ones I wore into combat in 1944. On the down side, the quality was so good that, with minor repairs, they lasted a long time. When at last I got replacements a sensible supply sergeant ignored the record and gave me a more reasonable size 12A.

From the last supply station my group moved into a large room where we were ordered to strip off our civilian clothes and don O.D.'s, olive drab uniforms. Superficially anyway, the resulting metamorphosis made us look like a roomful of soldiers. Truthfully, since we still needed a lot of shaping and molding, we must have resembled the "Sad Sack" character depicted in a famous army news magazine.

Before I had any time to worry much about shoes that were too large, I was presented with a more serious problem. What to do with my discarded civilian clothing? Unlike today's army, the World War II soldier was never permitted to wear civies, even off-duty or on furlough. To be caught out of uniform was a serious offense. All service personnel of my acquaintance simply accepted this as a fact of life. After all, a uniform was treated with respect in that war, and wearing it offered some advantages when moving within the sphere of civilian activity. With millions of men in service it was the draft age male in civilian clothes that looked out of place.

Seeing no further need for the clothing I had worn to the induction center, at least not for a very long time, I simply wanted to get rid of it. Unfortunately I did not see any place to dispose of it. Worse, I was handed brown wrapping paper and ordered to make a bundle to be sent to my home address.

I cannot recall anything I have ever done with greater reluctance. To me it was cruel to force us to send our clothing home to already saddened parents. I still cringe when I think what it must have done to my mother when Jim Morgan, our rural mail carrier out of Sampsel, left her that bundle. But like much in army life, there seemed no way to avoid compliance.

Some of the frightening images we develop as youngsters persist into adulthood. One such image haunted me as I was sent to stand before doctors to receive shots or whatever else they were dispensing. I still had my tonsils, that being one thing that had never bothered me in childhood. One of the tales of the Great War that lodged in my mind (incidentally not told by an actual observer which should have been a clue in itself) was of soldiers lined up and ordered to open their mouths while a doctor moved down the line snipping tonsils as he went. Admittedly this sounded a lot less plausible at the age of twenty than it had at ten, but after only two days of military service, I had begun to prepare myself for the implausible.

Although I did not care much about being stuck with needles, it was a relief to discover that the medics simply wanted to begin with the first of a series of typhoid and tetanus shots. I was given an "immunization register" card to carry with me at all times. By the time I was discharged the card was filled with entries of these and other kinds of shots. The card also noted "O" as my blood type. This along with name, serial number and "P" for Protestant faith, was stamped on my dog tags, issued before I left Leavenworth and worn around my neck until my discharge at Jefferson Barracks, St. Louis, in 1946.

Three of us from Livingston County were in this particular group moving through the lines together. Melvin Akerson, Gaylen Kenyon, and I were all the same age, became friends, and went to the same camp for basic training, thus assuring us of our own little support group for the next several months. Several of the inductees in our group had more than just a normal dread of shots. Regrettably one of my new friends from Chillicothe, Gaylen, was among them. He had a real horror of them and when the medic thrust a needle into the arm of the fellow directly ahead of him, poor Gaylen fell to the floor in a faint. Pulled out of the way and revived, he still got the shot. A good part of one day was taken up with written tests. It was not clear, to me anyway, why these booklets were thrust at us, but I had always responded well to tests and determined to take these seriously. Not everyone did and there was some quiet groaning. It became a stimulating challenge to me and, having no idea it could make any difference, I turned in my results with some feeling of satisfaction. Some months later I learned that it was a kind of intelligence test and, indeed, it did make a difference. My score turned out to be more than satisfactory and caught the attention of an officer who was in a position to help me.

Part of our processing included an interview in which we gave information on civilian occupation and any particular skills we possessed. Some of the information became part of our record. My discharge papers, for example, contain information I had given about my farming experience. Since the horse (which we were still using on the farm) had given way to motorized equipment in warfare, my background skills would appear of minimal value to the army.

But experience taught me that the possession of militarily useful skills did not necessarily mean the army would utilize them. Before leaving my basic training unit, I became aware of situations of obvious misplacement that gave way to the farcical. Later, in my own case, after the army helped me develop skills of useful application to the battlefield, these skills were recklessly wasted by the ignorance of a first sergeant and the indifference of his superior officer.

In all fairness, I knew of some cases where the army did make good use of these background interviews. The initial placement of a few of the men interviewed with me and sent to the same training division made good sense. Possessing background experience with trucks, tractors, and bulldozers, they were sent to the more mechanized units of our division, including the tank regiments.

One thing instilled in me during my brief stay at Leavenworth remains embedded in my memory bank to this day. We were ordered to memorize our serial numbers before we left the induction center. Supposedly, not to recall it immediately upon demand was to invite trouble. Seeing no need to test this supposition I simply encoded 37242203 in my brain. Along with name and rank it became an integral part of me, regurgitated when required as effortlessly and naturally as breathing. In civilian life I have gone for years at a time without any occasion to think of 37242203. Still, if summoned, the number comes out as automatically as it did a half century ago. But ask for my social security number and it requires more concentrated thought!

After getting us prepared to ship out to basic training, the non-coms in charge kept us busy with the kind of meaningless tasks we soon learned to expect from the army. I found myself attached to a small detail (the term for a work party) washing windows. The windows did not show any need of washing, but we washed them anyway.

Sometime after evening chow the last day of November, most of us who had come in on the 27th were ordered to get ready to ship out. With our barracks bags slung over our shoulders we were marched to a large building alongside the railroad tracks. There a Santa Fe train of Pullman cars stood ready to take us somewhere. Where we were going we did not know, for the army saw no need to divulge this information to privates in basic training.

Melvin and I, much to our relief, found ourselves assigned to the same car and were able to get seats together. Gaylen was sent to a nearby car and later we learned that another fellow from Chillicothe, Glen Gordon, was somewhere on the train.

Although it had been only a few days since we left Chillicothe, home already seemed like a world away. As we settled back for departure we could not help wondering, even worrying a little, where we were being sent and to what kind of an outfit.

Chapter Two

Camp Beale, California

Snow was falling the night we left Fort Leavenworth. As the train carried us away my feelings wavered between apprehension and excitement. Apprehension because of the unknown: Where were we being taken? What kind of training would I receive? And how would I get along with it? Excitement because of the promise of a longer train journey than heretofore had been possible and the prospect of seeing new scenery and new states filled me.

Many times during the next three years I would experience moments of wishing to be free of the army. But at the same time always there was some gratitude to the army for lifting me out of the narrow geographic confines of my first twenty years and permitting me to see a wider world. The war and the military took hundreds of thousands of us out of a limited setting imposed by the combination of a traditional way of life and difficult economic circumstances. We were deposited in new states, introduced to diverse sections of the nation and, for many, even taken to foreign countries. The America of the survivors of this experience could never be the same.

Of course, not everyone appreciated this great mixing and shuffling, but I did. It meant an opportunity to see places previously available to me only in reading and in imagination.

Two of my favorite books as I was growing up were an American history and a geography that Mother used in the sixth grade at the turn of the century. Today I still have the geography book, the back long gone and some of the pages crumbling. As a boy I pored over that book by the hour, learning the maps, studying the pictures (very dated even in my day), and dreaming of someday seeing these faraway and, to me, exotic places.

In addition to spelling bees and arithmetic contests in grade school, we would have geography matches. The teacher would divide the room, around twenty pupils from first through eighth grade, into two teams, have us open our geography books to a certain map, then pull down a large version of the same map from the wall rack above the blackboard, give us the name of a city or some geographic feature, and award a point to the first team to send someone forward with the correct location on the big map. I had not advanced very far up the grade ladder before the team I was with began to win these contests with what had to be an annoying frequency.

Geography was also a favorite subject in high school where I learned the names and spelling of all state and many foreign capitals. Our teacher opened up a whole new world by revealing that for a penny postcard, yes one cent, we could request pieces of information from chambers of commerce, railroad companies, and other organizations. Through this route I collected much treasured information in the form of maps, brochures, pictures and booklets. I dreamed of someday seeing these marvelous sights. One of my favorite booklets was on St. Louis with its zoo, municipal opera, the Jewel Box, and other wonders. It is a measure of the times that even with three aunts and a great uncle living in St. Louis neither money nor time allowed me to get there before the war years.

In fact, except for part of northwest Missouri, I had seen little of my own state; not the capital at Jefferson City nor any of the Ozarks, the beautiful spring fed streams or other sights south of the Missouri River. I lived approximately 100 miles south of Iowa but had been across the border only once. Uncle Jim Breeze drove a truck, mostly short hauls, but on one occasion he made a trip through southwestern Iowa, across the Missouri River and barely into Nebraska. He took me and three cousins along. In addition to this short trip into two neighboring states, I had my first sight of nearby Kansas on my initial trip to the induction center at Leavenworth.

Thus when I left the induction center on the night of November 30, my dread of the future was tempered with thoughts of exciting possibilities. At the time I could not know that "possibilities" would become realities in assignments at various times on both coasts of the United States, a trip in grand style that would take me from West to East, a crossing of the Atlantic and a look, albeit the hard way, at five European countries.

War was the incident and the army was the institution, but the railroad was the instrument that enabled me to see so much of this great land. My life-long love affair with the railroad began with early memories of looking southward from the farm and watching the Wabash engines puff their way across the Grand River Valley in their journey from St. Louis to Omaha, and, in the still of the night, listening to the lonely but inviting sound of the Burlington's whistle in the distant hills beyond the Grand River. I feel nostalgic as I think of the vital role of the railroad in the Second World War and it saddens me to see it so under-used and little appreciated today.

Due to economic circumstances my previous railroad riding experience had been limited to an occasional trip between Lock Springs and Chillicothe. In my boyhood the Wabash ran a combination passenger, mail, milk/cream, and light supplies train that passed eastward toward Chillicothe around nine in the morning. Another returned westward around four in the afternoon, making it a useful service to anyone who needed to get to the big town of the area. It was an exciting ride for a small boy, but it did not last long enough or go far enough. This particular train was discontinued some time in the late 1930s but fortunately for service personnel and other wartime travelers regular passenger service continued between St. Louis and Omaha.

The Pullman car came as a pleasant surprise, for it did not fit my preconceived notion of troop train accommodations. It was my first look inside a sleeping car. In grade school I had read about George Pullman's invention, but my experience with the local passenger train made it difficult to visualize. When the porter completed his work, however, he had transformed our car into a comfortable sleeping arrangement.

When we awoke the next morning, we were still in Kansas. To one who wanted to see more states, and with a bias rather common to people growing up in the western part of Missouri, it was hoped that our destination lay somewhere beyond the Jayhawk state.

It had stopped snowing during the night and there was some sunshine. Sometime during the morning we made a brief stop at a cold and dreary place identified for us as Dodge City. The reality of the place did not measure up to a boyhood image formed by reading about it as a focal point in cattle drives and gunfights. Still, even stripped of any romantic glory, it was very satisfying to see.

We followed along close to the Arkansas River which, as I would learn through travel in later years, roughly paralleled the mountain branch of the Santa Fe Trail that went to Bent's Fort near La Junta, Colorado. Sometime in the afternoon we spotted large dark images looming above the horizon. For most of us in the car this, probably Spanish Peaks, was our first sight of mountains. One of the more experienced travelers explained that the impression of distance was deceptive, that the mountains were actually a lot farther away than they appeared. Sure enough, we rode for some time before we got into obvious foothills to these mountains. We had gradually, though imperceptibly, been gaining in altitude since way back in Kansas. At one point we stopped for awhile, and the porter came through and explained that another engine was being added to the train for the pull up into Trinidad, Colorado.

Unfortunately darkness had set in long before we got to Trinidad. The porter got us settled for the night and explained that we would go through Raton pass and southward into New Mexico during the night. Several decades later I took a daylight railroad trip from Trinidad to Raton, New Mexico, with quite different traveling companions, and had an opportunity to appreciate fully the scenic beauty missed during that night in 1942.

It was daylight when we got to Albuquerque, New Mexico. The train stopped awhile, as I recall, to give the troops a chance to exercise. Albuquerque had always seemed such an intriguing name for a city and I was delighted with a chance to see it. The day was cold, however, and it suited me just as well that we were to be taken on somewhere else for basic training.

From Albuquerque the train turned westward toward Arizona. The journey across New Mexico and all the way to the western border of Arizona was the most fascinating part of the entire trip. Hardly any of us from the Leavenworth center had been to this area before. To men accustomed to the fertile farmlands, trees and greenery of the Middle West, this was an alien land. Vegetation, if present at all, was totally different from anything we knew. The land did not look fit enough to produce a kitchen garden, let alone farm crops. The areas we went through were sparsely inhabited and an air of loneliness pervaded everything beyond Albuquerque. The attraction of the southwestern part of the Sun Belt lay far in the future.

But it was astoundingly beautiful in a wild sort of way. Rock formations in strange and unusual shapes dotted the land. Colors were varied, often brilliant, and subject to interesting change with the light. Beautiful pink hues, in particular, abounded in one part of Arizona. In later travel, I learned that the troop train had taken me through a portion of the Painted Desert. No wonder it was such a memorable trip!

As we made preparation to spend another night on the train, I learned that we would be crossing the Colorado River and entering California at a place called Needles. This was welcome news, for California sounded like a good place to take basic training. During the depression California came to represent a place of hope and opportunity to many in my part of the country who despaired of the future. I was glad to have the opportunity to see the state with this attractive reputation.

Perhaps it was just as well for some of my preconceived notions that I was asleep for many miles into California. Later I learned that we passed through the Mojave Desert, an area I would hear about from some of the basic training cadre and not with pleasant connotations.

As it was, I woke up in the San Joaquin Valley and California looked worthy of its reputation. Passing through Bakersfield, I looked out the window upon greenery, growing vegetables and blooming flowers. It was a marvelous sight indeed to one accustomed to dreary Decembers in northwest Missouri and who had left snow behind in Leavenworth.

But the train gave no indication of stopping here. Eventually we passed through Fresno and headed northward. Finally, approximately forty miles north of Sacramento near a small place called Wheatland we stopped. We pulled on to one of many rail sidings and it became obvious that other troop trains had arrived recently.

I looked out upon a raw appearing and unappealing place, soon identified as Camp Beale. In following the news about men who had preceded me into the service, as reported faithfully in the Gallatin and Chillicothe newspapers back home, I had become familiar with the names of many army camps across the country, but I had never heard of Camp Beale, and for a very good reason. It was a new camp recently made ready to receive recruits.

The Yuba River ran a few miles to the north of the camp; and a few miles south lay the American River, historic site of the gold discovery in 1848. San Francisco lay about 125 miles to the southwest and Reno, Nevada, was about 90 miles east and slightly north. Two towns located very close together, Yuba City and Marysville, could be reached by a short bus ride westward from the main gate. These towns contained a variety of shops and, of course, the usual lures and snares that spring up around a military base. The latter did not entice either me or the close friends I developed in camp, but we did look forward to utilizing the bus service from Marysville to San Francisco and Sacramento.

The main part of the camp, including buildings, motor parks, and drill fields, was located on fairly level land. Across the road from our outfit was a grove of trees different from any I had ever seen. These were identified to me as olive trees and it seemed that much of the once-large orchard had been bulldozed to make way for buildings and drill fields.

Away from the main camp, the terrain changed to undulating hills, then on to ever rising foothills with woods and immense boulders. To the east lay the Sierra Nevada and looking to the north toward distant Oregon, on a clear day we could see the outline of the lower part of the Cascade Range. All things considered, it was not a bad locale for basic training, once it is accepted that army camps should never be likened to resort areas.

Not only was Beale a new camp, it was the home of a newly formed division, the 13th Armored. With so much attention focused upon mechanized warfare, beginning with the German blitzkrieg in Poland and France, 1939-40, it was quite satisfying to become part of an armored division, December 3, 1942. Those of us from Leavenworth were sorted out and sent to various units. Melvin, Gaylen and I were sent to the 496 Armored Field Artillery Battalion.

Individual units in artillery battalions are known as batteries, not companies as in many other parts of the army. I was assigned to the battalion's service battery. Gaylen went to a howitzer battery situated across the street from my barracks and Melvin to a battery a couple of streets away. Conveniently located, we got together when time permitted, the catch being, we soon discovered, that time was rarely at our own disposal. Later we found that Glen Gordon was in the general area and we saw him occasionally.

Each battery had two barracks, an office and orderly room, a supply room, a mess hall, and a dayroom for classes, letter-writing, and other free time activities. The barracks were long two-story structures of wood painted olive-drab, giving them a dark and inhospitable look.

Fifteen to sixteen beds were ranged on each side of the long room. At one point we had more than the normal complement of men and five or six beds were added in the center aisle. There were doors at both ends of the building with outside stairs at the rear for emergency use by second floor residents. To the left of the entrance was the latrine, wash basins, and a shower room. To the right was a room for non-commissioned officers with the same arrangement on the second floor.

My home, quite literally, for the next six months was a bunk with a small space around it with a shelf and clothes rod above the bed, about midway down the left side of the first floor of the second barracks. Initially I lacked hangers for clothes, but so did everyone else, for like so many other things in wartime they were in short supply. Likewise it was a while before production caught up with need and I was issued a locker for the foot of my bed.

Basic training really began with the basics: making a bed properly with smart looking hospital corners. The top sheet was turned back to make a neat six inch cuff of white just below the pillow. Ideally the blanket stretched tautly enough across the bed for an inspecting officer to bounce a quarter off it. If the blanket had "US" printed on it, this should be read from the aisle. Woe to the careless fellow who got the letters upside down. An extra blanket was folded neatly at the foot of the bed.

It soon became evident that the army liked everything neat and orderly, and not just men drilling with precision or standing in uniform rows at roll call. The cuffs on the bed should show a straight line when viewed from either end of the barracks and no bed should project even an inch beyond its neighbors. In the mess hall the tables reflected this same uniformity of placement. Condiments were to be viewed in an unbroken line from either end of the room. Not surprisingly, all vehicles in the motor pool were parked in uniform rows.

Before we ever got around to serious training about warfare, we were instructed in such important matters as military courtesy. We were taught how to distinguish the different ranks of officers from the single gold bar of a second lieutenant—some of ours new enough from OCS to be alluded to as "90 day wonders" by our noncoms—to the gleaming star of a general. Our division commander, we learned, had two stars thus making him a major general. And we spent a lot of time practicing our salute until a meticulous noncom pronounced it sufficiently snappy to turn us loose.

It struck me that this protocol could be a dreadful nuisance to an officer who might like simply to walk quietly down the street, possibly preoccupied with more weighty matters, and not be bothered with responding to salutes from the numerous enlisted men he was bound to meet. But it was a great ego trip for some, and I know from limited personal experience that this type felt mightily offended at the least suspicion that he had been ignored.

Later when we reached the stage to be reviewed by the division commander, General John B. Wogan, I felt that we had arrived. It brought a stirring feeling, one filled with pride and emotion, to march in full dress uniform behind the United States flag with the 13th Armored Division Band playing a rousing number.

Our eventual ability to march in precision while carrying our rifles really brought a soldierly feeling of satisfaction. Of course it took plenty of instruction, practice, and drilling to reach this point.

First we learned about the rifle: an appreciation for it and how to keep it in good working order. Then we worked on the manual of arms: left and right shoulder arms, present arms, preparing the weapon for inspection, receiving it when the inspecting officer thrust it back, and so on. Some of this required extra practice in the barracks and day room.

In the process a few of us learned something extra, strictly for our own satisfaction, from a noncom with several years of service. He could do some impressive, even graceful, maneuvers which he described as Queen Anne's manual of arms. Enough of what he taught me remained in the immediate postwar years to enable me to pick up my souvenir Mauser and repeat the final bow.

Winter in that part of California in 1942-43 was certainly noticeable, but still relatively mild when compared to memories of Missouri winters. We had hot water for showers and shaving; but the barracks were unheated. Consequently when reveille called me out from under a warm blanket (or two) around 6 a.m., I hated to get up and dress in the cold building. Perhaps I recalled with nostalgia how, on a cold morning in our small farm house, my dad got up early to start a fire in the wood burning stove. I could dress for school or chores in some comfort.

Our first sergeant did not spoil us this way! Instead he whistled us into the street to fall in for roll call and to hear the orders of the day. I came to dislike whistles with a passion. But in all honesty, and especially in comparison with a first sergeant encountered later, I recall this fellow as a decent sort.

He did have one very irritating practice. When a soldier did not respond loudly enough to suit him, instead of bellowing like Gomer Pyle's sergeant "I can't hear you!" he asked in a cutting way, "Did I hear you?" Of course there are some good answers to such a foolish question but they are off limits to the prudent soldier.

We had frequent rain and men familiar with the area said it would continue that way for the next three months or so. Then, they said, the rains would cease, the weather would turn much warmer, even hot, and the ground would become hard and the bare training areas dusty.

In the meantime we spent a lot of time out in the wet weather, and in some training exercises we crawled along the damp ground. The combination of unheated barracks, cool weather and wet conditions quickly gave all of us ferocious colds. Classes and lecture sessions were interrupted by much coughing and sneezing. We were instructed to take the pole from the shelter half we had been issued, secure it upright against the frame at the head of our bed, fasten one end of the shelter half to the pole and stretch the other end along the side of the bed. Supposedly the barrier reduced the flow of germs between neighbors as we slept.

Slowly we got better and within a three week period we were completely free of colds. Apparently the army knew what it was doing in tossing us to the elements to toughen us. I do not recall having another really bad cold until sometime after returning to civilian life. I am thoroughly convinced that this kind of tough regimen enabled me to endure a harsh German winter in 1944-45.

Most mornings we began the day with an hour of calisthenics. This could be quite grueling but it helped us get in shape and stay in good condition. Some routines I regarded as helpful and even enjoyable, but others were tortuous and personally detrimental, especially to my ego.

Wartime newsreels began military news with a scene of soldiers jumping to extend legs apart while bringing arms up to meet overhead, followed by another movement to bring the feet back together and the arms back to the side. Repeated rapidly in unison by a company or battery size group of soldiers, this was an eye-catching and smart looking sight. Because this was a favorite of one of our noncoms, we often did this.

Upper body and certain kinds of arm exercises were extremely tiring for me. It bothered me that I found these and push-ups difficult to do. It frustrated me that dedicated effort and practice improved my ability so little. Years later, when I understood more about my heart problems, it all made some sense. In all likelihood given a good physical examination I would have been restricted by the army to limited service. But at the time, looking big and strong at six feet and around 190 pounds, it was a humbling experience not to be able to get much better with repetition. One of our instructors, a staff sergeant from South Carolina, had great upper body strength. Understandably he concentrated on arm exercises. In particular he liked one exercise where arms are fully extended and moved from large to ever smaller circles. He could hold this position for an interminable length of time and expected us to do likewise. In an effort to bear the agony, I used to look at the tops of the olive trees above Sgt. Pearson's head and try to force my mind to focus on something that would transport me from the torture. At times I thought my arms would drop off before he mercifully ordered them down.

I was not alone in dreading to see Sgt. Pearson in charge of calisthenics the day after we received booster shots in our arms. Tetanus shots (we got two more in basic) in particular left everyone with a sore arm that could ache for days afterward. Sgt. Pearson's assumption was that this soreness could be "worked out" with exercise. It was those days that I practically prayed for my favorite staff sergeant, Morgan from Kentucky, to be in charge. He preferred leg and lower body exercises and that is where my strength lay.

Push-ups were strictly a form of exercise and never meant to be used as an instrument for punishment in the

496th Armored Field Artillery. Naturally Sgt. Pearson liked push-ups and with my problem I could never do as many as I wanted or that he thought a soldier should be able to do. Thus in a painful way, they could be a form of unintended punishment for me.

In all fairness, I must add that away from calisthenics I really did like and respect Sgt. Pearson. He was never deliberately mean to me or anyone else to my knowledge. It simply seemed beyond his comprehension that others could not develop the strength he possessed, especially if they were considerably larger, as I was. As a soldier he was a first rate model and as a weapons instructor he was quite good in everything from sub-machine guns to howitzers. Next to Sgt. Morgan and Corporal Fetter, I remember him as my favorite training cadre instructor.

At the opposite end of the scale we had a buck sergeant for whom I developed an intense dislike. It appeared to be a sentiment shared by many of my colleagues. Physically he was ugly with an unpleasant personality to match. I wondered how much of the latter was developed because of the former. He was mean-spirited, short tempered, and quick to jump on the slightest misstep. And with raw material fresh from the induction centers there were plenty of mistakes for him to catch.

Near the end of our basic training, however, something happened to our nasty sergeant that shows bad guys sometimes get what they deserve. He became a good example of the bad things that could happen to the soldier foolish enough to ignore the message in certain lectures delivered by the battalion doctors. Some time following his return from a weekend pass to one of the nearby towns, the sergeant mysteriously disappeared from view for a few days. He returned as an embarrassed looking private. It seems he had bought the services of one of the women we were warned about by doctors and chaplains. With a venereal disease to show for his encounter, he promptly was stripped of his stripes by the battery commander and thrust into the ranks of the men he had been abusing.

Those of us living in the middle of the country felt a sense of security and a feeling of remoteness from danger not experienced by inhabitants of coastal regions. Most Midwesterners probably accepted this, as I did, without giving it much consideration. The actual war was somewhere off in the distant Pacific or across the Atlantic. The difference in perspective was brought home to me quite sharply almost as soon as I arrived at Camp Beale.

The approach of the first anniversary of the Japanese bombing of Pearl Harbor produced great anxiety all up and down the Pacific coast. The worry that on December 7, 1942, the Japanese might attempt something was not confined to the civilian population. At the camp we were placed on alert and cautioned against using lights.

The passing of an uneventful anniversary by no means removed the fear that Japan posed a threat to the West Coast. Later I learned of incidents that gave a touch of substance to the fears. In February 1942, a Japanese submarine fired on beach front oil wells in southern California.

A major cause for concern came from rumors of a fifth column at work. The term "fifth column" had been coined during the Spanish Civil War in 1936. But it really became well-known and a potential source of mass hysteria when German propaganda used it with some success to undermine the morale of Germany's intended victims in Western Europe. It became all too easy for far too many people to believe that our own fifth column stood ready to act on the West Coast, in this case Japanese-Americans. The overwhelming majority of Japanese-Americans remained extremely loyal and the injustice of uprooting them as a whole group can be understood, not excused, only within some context of the times.

Later when I transferred to the East Coast, first to New York City and then for a longer period in New England a few miles from the Atlantic, I found a similar sense of danger. The use of blackout curtains and the presence of a civil defense organization gave evidence of that. On that side of the country and on the Gulf Coast the great threat was from Germany. Even if Heinkel bombers lacked the capability to reach America, as alarmed civilians first feared, dangers were nonetheless real.

In one operation a German submarine actually landed saboteurs on Long Island and just south of Jacksonville, Florida. Fortunately the *Abwehr* (German intelligence service) was not nearly the efficient organization portrayed by German propaganda and in American imagination. Caught and betrayed by one of its own members, the operation collapsed in failure. Still, the possibility remained that others could be mounted to menace rail lines, roads, and factories.

The greatest danger lay in U-boat capacity to damage vital merchant shipping off both the Atlantic and Gulf coasts. Submarines were sighted close to shore and evidence of their damage washed in with the tide. By the time I got to the East Coast, Allied navies had gained advantage over the U-boats, but danger and fear lingered.

Although Camp Beale might seem closer to the war in the Pacific, it was developments in North Africa that we followed anxiously throughout the winter of 1942-43. Operation Torch, the Allied landings on the coast of French Morocco and Algeria, began about three weeks before my induction. At least two American armored divisions, as well as other armored units, were involved. As I recall some of our cadre may have trained in the Mojave Desert with some of these men. In any case, they considered it likely that the 13th Armored would go eventually for special training in the desert. They described it as a rugged place to train, but essential to preparation for desert warfare. We wondered if we might find ourselves in North Africa in a few months.

One of the noncoms had a radio and sometimes we caught the news of the course of the war in North Africa. I recall spirits buoyed on occasion by Gabriel Heatter, especially those times he seemed compelled to announce, "Ah, there's good news tonight!" Before long, and especially after learning of the terrible American setback at Kasserine Pass, February 1943, I learned to listen to such upbeat intonations with a large measure of skepticism.

Mail call marked the high point of the day for a soldier. This was one time you welcomed hearing your name called. It meant you were about to be put in touch with home, family and friends. Well aware that the more letters we wrote the more we would hear that welcome call, most of us managed to squeeze time out of a busy schedule to write.

Ever conscious of the value to morale, the army made it easy to mail a letter. Just put name, rank, serial number, unit designation and APO number on the upper left of an envelope, and "free" in place of a stamp, and the army and postal service would take care of the rest. Commanding officers sometimes reminded their men of the importance of writing home. General Wogan even went so far as to order the men of the 13th Armored Division to write to their mothers for Mothers Day, May 9, 1943.

It did not take an order from a major general or a reminder from my captain to cause me to write to my mother. My love and concern for her were great enough for me to act without a push from authority. I knew my absence and her worry about what might happen to me were hard for her to bear. To help make it a little easier I tried to write at least a short letter to my parents several times each week. I continued this practice until it became impossible when I went overseas.

In re-reading my letters (Mother had kept most of them) I find that while sometimes it was obvious I missed being home, the overall tone was, as I fully intended, generally upbeat. I detailed many things about my training but carefully avoided those things that were dangerous or caused me some anxiety. I never saw any point in discussing homesickness or any of those things about the army that I particularly disliked.

Mother wrote me several times each week and I welcomed news of home and community. My dad seldom wrote but when he did, I treasured his letters. Grandma Breeze wrote to me, as did several of my aunts and cousins. Uncle Virgil had lived with us when I was growing up, but to my mother's irritation, he never wrote a single letter. On the other hand, Uncle Ruphard, whom I never met, wrote occasionally. With sons in the Canadian Army, I am sure he appreciated the importance of mail to a serviceman. I corresponded with two of my high school classmates, both in the army. I did not have a girlfriend as such, but two girl friends wrote. One was a friend from childhood. The other I met in high school and we were both active in a church youth group. We dated a few times when I was on army furloughs.

Several men in the battery received home town newspapers. Initially my parents sent me the daily paper from Chillicothe and the weekly from Gallatin. Soon I realized that army life left little time for newspapers so I asked that they send only clippings about local servicemen from the Chillicothe paper. The *Gallatin Democrat* carried news items from each town in the county so I asked for a clipping of the Lock Springs column. If I wished to know anything more about Chillicothe, Gaylen was glad to share his copy of the *Constitution-Tribune*.

Early on I became aware that a personable young fellow from the hills of Kentucky seldom received any mail. Whenever he did, one of the noncoms quietly took him aside and read it to him. It came as something of a shock to learn that scattered throughout the division were numerous men classified as illiterates. In my naiveté, I took it for granted that although many of us were poor in the America of the 1930's, we all had some opportunity to learn the rudiments of reading and writing.

To the army's credit, special classes in reading and writing were set up at division headquarters, and these men were given released time to attend. This is one thing the army certainly got right, for within a few weeks my Kentucky friend proudly wrote letters and read his own mail.

Even with a tree and decorations up in the mess hall, December 25, 1942, hardly seemed like Christmas. Ever since my boyhood, both family and community had made Christmas stand out for me as a very special time. It was an exciting time, and not just in anticipation of packages filled with pleasant surprises. Like most of my fellow soldiers I really missed being home for the occasion. Had I known this was but the first of four Christmases I would spend in the army away from home, my morale really would have taken a dip.

As it was I tried to make the best of it: attending a movie on Christmas Eve with a new friend, George Partridge from Kansas; going to church services on Christmas day with

George and others; and spending some time with Melvin and Gaylen, although with a nearly acute case of homesickness, the latter was not a lot of help to me.

Many families tried to help their loved ones through the season by sending packages, mostly of goodies to eat. By this time a small group of us in the barracks had begun to look to each other for support and companionship, and we shared the edibles from our packages

Appropriately, on Christmas Eve I received a box from St. Louis. Grandma Breeze was spending the winter there with my aunts, Cecil, Faye and Georgia. They combined to send a package with things to eat (chocolate and popcorn) and such practical things as army socks (we always needed more than we were allotted and the family lived just a few blocks from the post exchange at Jefferson Barracks) and toilet articles (likewise useful and appreciated). Aunt Faye sent a pocket size New Testament and Psalms. This came to mean a lot to me as I carried it in my shirt pocket throughout my period of combat, 1944-45. My parents sent a nice kit for carrying toilet articles.

With around 145 men in the battery, waiting in some kind of line became an accepted part of army life. Most of the time the chow line was worth the waiting. The army provided an abundance of food, which proved to be a good thing especially for those times when we were served family style from great bowls of food on the table. As a slow eater, partly by nature and partly the result of an enduring lesson from my grade school health class, I quickly learned to take immediately all I was likely to want. There would not be a second opportunity for those who ate slowly and chewed their food. Some of the smallest men had an amazing capacity and practically inhaled their meal. One rather unpleasant fellow from an eastern city appeared to be trying to make up for the lean times of the depression years.

Our cooks generally did a satisfactory job with the food. Some unappealing things do stand out in my memory but not always due to the fault of the cooks. For instance, coming from a background where even in the darkest days of the depression we had good farm-produced food, I found it hard to accept powdered milk and powdered eggs as real food.

And we never ate mutton on the farm; none of us liked it, so a meat dish tasting like mutton definitely was not for me. Actually it was not popular with a lot of my fellow soldiers either, for there was much complaining that it was goat and rather elderly goat at that.

One dreadful concoction was entirely the creative work of our cooks. They called it "chicken à la king" and frequently served it as, in their unshared opinion, a special treat for the Sunday noon meal. It bore scant resemblance to my one prior experience with chicken à la king, the delicious main dish served at my high school graduation banquet. The cadre called it "half-track chicken." They accused the cooks of tossing chickens on the roadway, running over them with a half-track borrowed from the motor pool, and shoveling the resulting mess into large serving pots. With the red of tomatoes mixed in with the bits of chicken and other unidentifiable ingredients, an active imagination could make the story almost believable.

On occasion we were served pancakes, one of my favorite meals for breakfast. Unfortunately certain of the cooks prepared these with batter of mortar-like consistency. Anyone unwise enough to eat more than one or two of them found they lay heavy on the stomach. Immediately following such a breakfast one morning, one of our officers decided we should do something different from the usual calisthenics. He had us doing such playground activities as leap frog and somersaults. The climax came with a run from a starting line to a pole several yards distant, three rapid turns around the pole, and a return to the starting point. It was to be a timed run.

The light eaters got along fine. Those easily made light-headed, myself included, found that after the third turn we could not navigate a straight return. Those who had eaten too generously of pancakes and syrup were in serious trouble. I really felt sorry for one of the motor pool noncoms. Normally a retiring sort who liked to remain unnoticed, he made the turn and promptly lost his pancakes.

We continued to have pancakes and they remained heavy. But more people learned to eat sparingly and the officer allowed us to return to regular calisthenics.

All privates in the battery developed a generally unwelcome familiarity with the kitchen. Several times during the course of basic training we could expect to find our names on the duty roster for K.P., kitchen police. The assignment was welcome only if it coincided with a date when something more unpleasant was scheduled, such as running the obstacle course.

It could be a long hard day. It began early. Men due on K.P. left a towel wrapped around the railing at the foot of the bed. This enabled the cook on early duty to come by and easily identify those he was supposed to roust in the wee hours of the morning.

There were many things we might do in helping the cooks prepare a meal. The thing I remember most vividly is the mound of potatoes that had to be peeled to feed 145 or so men. The simple little potato peeling gadget was such an improvement over the only thing I had known (i.e. a paring knife) that I thought the army quite advanced.

Cleaning in the mess hall seemed to go on continuously, for the army placed great stress on cleanliness. We scrubbed garbage cans. We scrubbed pots and pans, numerous and huge. We washed dishes, knives, forks and spoons. At the end of the day we scrubbed the floors. The absolute worst job, which I drew only once in my army career, was cleaning the grease trap. It was nasty and smelly, and it ruined the appetite.

At the end of a very long day on K.P., we dragged ourselves back to the barracks. If we were lucky, we had time to do the necessary chores to get ready for the next day. And we hoped some authority had not chosen this night for a fire drill.

Because lights were usually turned out at nine (one of the ranking noncoms saw to that), we felt compelled to use precious evening time to best advantage. For many of us this meant fitting in time to write home. Sometimes there was a trip to the PX to get some needed item, perhaps some brass polish for buckles and buttons. And it always seemed to make the trip worthwhile to take time for ice cream or a candy bar. We had a few fellows, mostly from the older group, who acted deprived if time did not allow them to get to the PX for a beer.

Considerable time had to be devoted to preparing ourselves and our gear for the next day. If it had been a rainy day, it took time to clean red mud from our shoes. Polishing followed to make them ready for an officer to see, should he choose, before they were worn back outside into some mud. On occasion I felt so harried that the popular barracks saying seemed appropriate: "You have to make up your mind whether to s---, shine or shave!" Several times after lights out, I went to the shower room to write a letter to my parents.

There was one line every one hated, an appearance before battalion medics. It might be for shots, usually tetanus or typhoid; but it could be a surprise inspection for signs of venereal infection. In this case, we were ordered to strip to the buff, don raincoats, and appear for what, to me anyway, was an embarrassing and totally unnecessary examination. At such times the army offended me mightily.

Once a month, however, came a line liked by all. Pay day, or as I learned early on from a veteran noncom, "the day the eagle s---s", was worth waiting for a turn. Naturally privates did not receive a lot of money, $50.00 monthly if memory serves me rightly. Still, with the army providing for most of our needs, it could be a nice sum. By no means was I alone in not being used to making a lot of money in civilian life.

From my pay the army deducted $6.50 as the monthly premium for $10,000 worth of life insurance. Today that might seem like a paltry sum, but in the early 1940's such a policy sounded to poor people a lot like wealth. Also, something was taken out toward a war bond and eventually I increased this to a full $18.75 for a $25.00 bond. Just as parents were being urged to support the war effort by buying bonds, so were their sons asked to give monetary along with military support.

The officer assigned to address us on the subject pointed only partly to patriotic duty. The investment could have practical value, he stressed, for our civilian future. Though this seemed remote and even questionable at the time, a few years later I looked back with appreciation for his salesmanship. My wife and I used the accumulated war bonds as the down payment on our first house. And I expect we were not the only ones to have done so.

On my first pay day I witnessed an unfamiliar phenomenon: the urge some people have to gamble. When cool weather forced the men back home in Lock Springs indoors, sometimes they sought a place to play cards. But these times remained strictly occasions for socializing, to josh one another and swap stories, never to bet and exchange money.

A group of men from the battery hardly could wait to get through the pay line and bring out the dice to shoot craps. Some of the most enthusiastic did not even interrupt their playing to go for a meal. By the end of the day their pay had changed hands and a few fellows ended up broke. The interesting and, to me, distressing thing was that the same men repeated this pattern, usually with the same results, each pay day.

Very early in basic, one of the cadre told us we could look forward to Friday night, for we would have a GI party. "Oh yes," chimed in another sergeant. "Work hard all week and we will have a great time Friday night." The knowing smiles on the faces of the other noncoms, whenever the subject came up, raised serious doubts about the "fun" nature of such a party.

Sure enough, on Friday evening, buckets, brooms, mops, soap and scrub brushes were brought out. We were ordered to prepare the barracks for Saturday morning inspection by the battery commander. While some of us scrubbed the floor, others cleaned the windows. Still others cleaned the latrine and polished all wash basin fittings.

Once the entire first floor of the barracks satisfied the fussy sergeant in charge, we began to ready ourselves. Brass had to be polished and shoes shined to a high gloss, any loose buttons secured, and, if not done earlier, division patches sewn at the required distance from the shoulder on the left sleeve of uniform blouses and shirts. Every armored division used the same triangular patch of yellow, blue, and red overlaid with the track of a tank, the barrel of a howitzer, and a red flash of lightning running through them. The yellow at the apex of the triangle contained the division number, in our case 13. The Red Cross had given us little sewing kits at the induction center. These proved handy for sewing on insignia or stripes for those fortunate to get promotion, and for limited mending.

The next morning we did our daily ablutions with care not to mess up our careful work from the "GI party." Beds were made with extra care. The sergeant looked us over with a critical eye, noted our bed, the placement of equipment, and checked to see that those with clothes hangers had arranged their clothing properly. Never afterward could I tolerate my shirts and coats hanging in any other than the army way, all buttoned fronts facing the same way, like items together, all hangers hooked on the rod the same way.

We stood at the foot of our beds ready to snap to attention the moment the officer entered the door and someone yelled "Tench-hut!" Both men and barracks passed inspection but never without some minor admonishment. It must have been obligatory that the inspecting officer be meticulous enough to discover some flaw in our cleaning or, more usual, find one fellow who had not shaved closely enough, had a pocket flap unbuttoned, or whose blanket was a bit loose. Fortunately, I was never the chosen victim.

Some men found it difficult to adjust to the army and its ways. We heard reports of men who broke under the strain and committed acts totally unacceptable to the army. Information about some of the worst cases came from authority itself—came because the 13th Armored used these examples as a form of intimidation. More than once at morning roll call, our commander read a directive from division headquarters. We heard the results of court martial cases citing names, charges, verdict, and punishment. The names were unknown to me and the units were elsewhere on the post. Hearing they were dishonorably discharged would have been bad enough; but in some cases sentences were imprinted indelibly in my mind, as surely intended: "ten years at hard labor," "fifteen years at hard labor," etc.

From a social perspective the army was rather like a huge mixing bowl. Several million men were poured in, a rather heterogeneous lot. They came from every state of the union, every section of the country and a few were even foreign born. They differed in ethnic background, religious practice, economic circumstances, and social and class lines. Some were from cities, many from medium sized towns, but great numbers came from small towns and farms. We were still that kind of nation in the early 1940's. A few came from affluence, some enjoyed comfortable circumstances, and still a great many more had experienced the hard times of a depression era. Educational attainments ranged all the way from little or none, through grammar school, high school, some college, to college graduation.

Yet from the resulting mix of such dissimilar elements, the army molded an efficient fighting machine. In the process it helped us move toward a more socially cohesive nation.

Great numbers of us came from a narrow provincial background. Certainly I did. The Lock Springs-Sampsel community, for example, was thoroughgoing Protestant. Lock Springs had three small churches: Christian, Methodist, and Presbyterian. Tiny Sampsel had none, but a mile north of town was a Baptist church and a mile or so east, a Methodist.

There were no Catholic families in the community. When I was growing up, if Catholicism or the pope were ever mentioned it was in tones of disapproval. Later, I was aware of a Catholic presence in Chillicothe, but I am not aware of actually meeting and getting to know Catholics prior to basic training. Likewise, before entering the army I never became acquainted with any Jews.

My community was Anglo-Saxon in background. A perusal of surnames pointed to origins in some part of the British Isles. The few exceptions were most likely from some part of Germany, as for instance my mother's brother Virgil Griner, with the family name of his Prussian grandfather. Again, as in the case of religious diversity, the army threw me into the bowl and enabled me to mix with men of central, eastern and southern European origins.

My community was white. A lone Negro (that's the word I grew up with: not AfroAmerican or Black) lived somewhere in the hills north of Lock Springs. "Nigger Johnny", as he was known, seldom appeared in town. Whenever he did, the men appeared to treat him with a kind of distant acceptance bordering on friendliness. Clearly, however, they did not consider him as an equal. This, plus occasional things said about the race, instilled attitudes in my generation that, while they seemed perfectly acceptable at the time, were prejudicial. Going into Chillicothe to school hardly could have enlightened my outlook. The town had a separate grade school and high school for Negroes. With the exception of one assignment, I had no opportunity to become acquainted with Negroes in the service. The army was not yet ready to add race to its general mix.

Induction centers from all across the nation contributed to the making of the 13th Armored. The division's approximately 14,000 men represented enormous diversity and our battery was a kind of microcosm of the whole. No matter our backgrounds or differences, it soon became apparent that we were all "in it together." We shared much more than the uniforms and fatigue clothes that gave us a common appearance. We developed a common identity and comradeship in confronting and enduring the army's often harsh program to make soldiers out of us. The really fundamental consideration was not a man's background and any differences that might mean, but what he was like as a person, at the moment as a fellow sufferer, and beyond that, as a comrade in arms against enemy forces.

The men in the service battery ranged in age from 20 to the early 40's. There were a few of us at 20 and the early 20's, but the majority seemed to be in the upper 20's and through the 30's. One fellow at 40 plus had served in the First World War, a kind of awesome status to us youngsters, and another in his 30's had army service in the 1930's.

To my knowledge there were only two other Missourians in the battery. One was from somewhere in the southern part of the state and one was from St. Louis. There were at least two fellows from Kansas who had been on the train from Leavenworth. One of them, George Partridge, was my age and became my best friend in basic. I recall knowing men in my barracks from California, Oregon, Colorado, Illinois, Indiana, Ohio, Kentucky, West Virginia, Virginia, South Carolina, Alabama and Georgia. I am sure additional states were represented in the other barracks. When all units with which I served are considered, I served with men from 40 of the then 48 United States, plus the District of Columbia.

In basic I made friends with two men of Slavic origin. Ted Szymczyk, my age, became our bugler. Metro Kuzewchak, one of the "old men" over 30, talked to me about his hard life as a coal miner and swore he would never go back to that. After leaving the 13th I lost contact with him, so do not know what became of him.

Me and my Slavic friend, Metro Kuzewchak. Camp Beale, CA, 1942.

Either there were more characters on the first floor of my barracks than in any other unit of my experience, or my initial introduction to diversity made it seem that way. One was a genial fellow in his early twenties from West Virginia. Ever cheerful and very talkative, his droll stories reflected his background. When working around his bunk and readying for the next day, he could not refrain from singing. His limited repertoire of mournful country songs could be entertaining to a point, then it became annoying. His unfailing good humor in the face of anything the army threw at him was truly amazing. Some of the training cadre found him amusing and likable. Most were quite tolerant of his eccentricities.

Another fellow was in his early 40's and from Chicago. Whenever I recall him I think of one of my favorite actors of long ago, William Bendix. In size, facial appearance, and general demeanor he was Bendix's double. While he became a good friend for a few months, I regret to say I have neither written record nor memory of his name. He had been a soldier in the First World War, a fact that impressed me more than it did him. He did not appear to resent being called upon to serve again. He did find some army practices, such as those involved in inspections, a nit-picking waste of good time. He indicated to youngsters such as George, Ted (who came with him from Chicago) and me, that these matters were taken too seriously. There were more vital things to learn in soldiering.

This was easier for him to minimize, however, than us. He could get away with things, we discovered, that were not tolerated in the rest of us. For one thing he had a certain rumpled look about him no matter how fresh his uniform. Again, this reminds me of Bendix. Our officers seemed to accept that, like it or not, he had a kind of natural sad sack appearance. Had he been younger and not a veteran, I am sure he would have been someone's project for improvement.

He was one of those with a bunk in the middle of the aisle. At one Saturday morning inspection, he looked particularly disheveled: sloppy hanging uniform, unpolished shoes, in need of a shave, and his blanket was loose. Staring at him, but not saying a word, the captain turned abruptly to his right. This brought him face to face with Ted Szymczyk, standing straight and handsome, uniform immaculate as always, shoes polished, and with his blanket tight with perfect corners. The captain peered at him closely, apparently found a wisp of peach fuzz Ted missed in shaving, and chewed him out royally. "Soldier," he bawled, "Don't ever let me catch you like this again." Poor Ted was chagrined, the rest of us dumbfounded, and the cause of it all slightly amused. After all, the captain had just proven his point about the petty things seized upon by some officers.

When the army lowered the draft age and began releasing older soldiers, "Bendix" was discharged. I was happy for him, but sorry to see him go.

Our third character was tall, lean, and sometimes a nuisance. He bunked on the opposite side of the barracks and down near the rear exit. We probably exchanged no more than a dozen words during basic. He went his own way generally ignoring all but a few of the older fellows.

Apparently a day in training was just something to be endured while looking forward to an evening of beer drinking at the PX. This was a nightly ritual. Either he had friends from home in other units or he had found kindred spirits, pun intended, at the PX. Sometimes a few of them would stagger by with him on the way to their own barracks. One night I was awakened by a noise and heard a voice saying: "Put him down easy, boys." Seems this private had taken on too much, could not make it back before "lights out," and his buddies had carried him home, creating an unwelcome commotion in our barracks. One morning at roll call our sergeant had to report that our barrack's drunk was missing. Someone was sent into the barracks in a futile search for him. Then a fellow walked around toward the rear of our barracks, happened to look underneath, and there he lay, sound asleep. Too drunk to make it up the rear steps, he had crawled under the barracks to spend the night.

When he was discharged for age, I may have been envious of his freedom but not sorry to see him go. I never knew where he was from, but I can imagine tavern keepers somewhere welcomed him home.

Chapter Three

Basic Training and Beyond

As I had expected, training in the handling and care of small arms formed an integral part of basic training. Several hours of instruction preceded the actual use of a weapon. A new word, "nomenclature," entered my vocabulary. I became intimately acquainted with the names and functions of a weapon's parts. Model numbers became important and the designated army field manual served as a kind of bible for each weapon.

Although the army had developed a new semiautomatic rifle, the Garand M1, the majority of us in 1942 and into 1943 did not even see these. Instead we trained with old bolt action rifles used in the First World War. Most of these were Springfields, but I received a British made Enfield. This I used on the drill field, on guard duty, and on the firing range.

Our rifle, we were told, was a faithful friend, to be treated with respect and handled with care. True, no doubt, but I would have appreciated less violent reaction (recoil) on its part in our firing range experience. My initial venture on the range was both painful and discouraging. My first squeeze of the trigger brought a kick akin to that of the proverbial Missouri mule. By the end of the firing my right shoulder ached and was sore for days afterward. At 200 yards, the target was just a blur. Three times I saw a red flag "Maggie's drawers" waved across target, meaning I had missed it completely! With 5 points out of a possible 25, I at least did not have to worry about the armored infantry asking me to become a sniper. Each succeeding trip to the range led to some improvement and eventually I qualified for the lowest level badge awarded for marksmanship. Both Springfields and Enfields took a bayonet, but I was relieved not to receive one. As an avid reader of World War I accounts, I had developed a pronounced fear of a bayonet thrust. It made me uneasy to see that the camp had a bayonet training course, but evidently only the armored infantry used it.

On a few occasions I worked in the target pits, lowering a target to mark the shots, raising it for the shooter to see his results, and waving a red flag if no bullet holes could be found in the target. With live bullets whizzing over our heads, we needed no other incentive to stay down. A daring private in the pits once recklessly waved "Maggie's drawers" when he learned the shooter, who actually did rather well, was an unpopular officer. The officer "managed" to do much better with subsequent rounds and as far as I know never knew he had been tricked.

Some attention was devoted to the carbine. This short rifle with a magazine capacity of 15 rounds was, in language heard today, user friendly. It lacked the range of the regular rifle, but it was much lighter to carry and did not abuse the shoulder when fired.

A few artillerymen carried 45 caliber pistols, but all of us received some training with the weapon. We were warned that when fired it would jump upward and be difficult to control. Sure enough, we discovered it was more difficult than it might appear to hit a precise spot on a man sized target a few feet away. In fact, it was an achievement just to hit the target.

The most fascinating of the small arms available for use was a 45 caliber weapon known as the Thompson submachine gun. Perhaps the intrigue of the tommy gun lay in its association with stories heard in my youth about Chicago gangsters. It came as a surprise to learn it was really an army weapon.

We spent as much time with it as with the rifle. Sometimes I carried one on hikes. It was easily taken apart and reassembled. After doing this many times, we practiced it blindfolded in case we had to fix a problem in the dark.

The battery had several light weight 30 caliber machine guns and a few of the heavier 50 caliber guns. While we learned how to handle both, we spent more time with the 30 caliber. Prior to going on the firing range, we loaded bullets into belts. If it were to be a night exercise, every fifth bullet was a tracer. During some nights in 1944-45, I would see our machine gunners using tracers against enemy troops. As I watched, I remembered that between each of those glowing red bullets were several that could not be seen.

The army placed great emphasis upon keeping a low profile. Consequently we did a lot of crawling on the ground with much screaming at anyone with a protruding rear or a head raised noticeably high. We had one course where no shouting was necessary, only a preliminary warning. The course was probably half the width of a football field and probably half a field in length, though it could seem far longer. Barbed wire was strung from one side to the other at a height that allowed us to crawl beneath it without snagging, provided we remembered what we had been taught. Helping us remember were 30 caliber machine guns firing live ammunition above the wire. Firmly fixed in place, the gun barrel could not be swung downward. Nonetheless it was still a frightening experience to crawl beneath all those live bullets. At times I thought the army must be out of its mind to put men at such risk. The later experience in Germany, however, clarified it all for me.

None of our battery ever got hurt on the barbed wire-machine gun course. More risky in some respects was the hand grenade course. A lot of so-called dry run exercises with dummy grenades preceded the handling of real ones. We practiced pulling the pin, counting a few seconds, then hurling the grenade. The prescribed manner for hurling always seemed unduly awkward to me, reminding me of the way we learned to put the shot in high school. But one learned in this as in other matters—the army way was the only way.

On the course we threw from behind a protective barrier. Everyone got down and stayed down as much as possible. But there was always the frightening possibility some fellow would pull a pin and freeze, or drop the grenade, or perhaps the grenade would not clear the parapet on the throw. Reportedly at least one man in our battalion did lose a hand or nearly so with a slip up, undoubtedly lucky it was not worse.

It was with considerable satisfaction that I became part of a six man detail responsible for cleaning and maintaining guns. Each man in the battery being responsible for cleaning his own rifle, these were mostly tommy guns and a few light machine guns. An interesting older private was in charge. He came in the army with the rest of us but had spent six years in the military in the 1930's. According to him, the peacetime army was "really swell." As soon as promotions opened up he was due to get a sergeant's stripes. On occasion he was allowed to conduct close order drill. Sometimes he talked in his sleep and those nearby heard him count cadence as though he were on the drill field. When I left the outfit he was studying hard to go to OCS (Officer Candidate School). I hope he made it, for he had qualities that should have made him a good officer.

In a combat situation the battalion's mission was to provide indirect support to division infantry and tanks. Indirect because unlike guns with a relatively flat trajectory, its 105 mm. howitzers fired a high trajectory. This enabled them to hurl a 4 inch shell ahead of advancing troops or over intervening obstacles to a designated target that could be up to 12,000 yards distant.

As a service battery in support of the firing batteries we did not have howitzers. Still, we were expected to know all about them and were drilled in their operation and maintenance. Unlike the howitzers of World War I that were pulled by horses and those towed by trucks in an infantry division, these were self-propelled. They were mounted on a vehicle with wheels to the front and tracks to the rear enabling it to go places forbidden to trucks.

Many of us in the service battery were required to learn to drive the half-track. By the late spring of 1943, development and production had reached a point where many of our half-tracks could be replaced with a Sherman tank chassis. Developers literally cut the top off the tank to receive the howitzer and its crew. These marvelous new vehicles arrived too late for me to learn to drive them. In retrospect I think driving them could have been an interesting experience, even fun.

An important function of the service battery was to provide the ammunition for the howitzers. Ammunition was stored in magazines located in an open area some distance from the inhabited parts of the camp. The ammunition dumps, placed widely apart from each other in order to minimize the effects of an unexpected explosion, had rounded humps protruding from the earth, greatly resembling overgrown root cellars on a Midwestern farm.

Before ever touching a shell we received extensive information about them. This required a lot of study in the field manual and learning as much as possible about the different kinds of shells, the various charges, fuses, and other vital matters.

Poison gas had been introduced into modern warfare by the Germans in 1915. Although it was not a decisive weapon in affecting the war's outcome, fellows my age grew up on horror stories of gassed soldiers. Mussolini's Italian forces had gassed Ethiopians from the air in 1935. When I entered service in 1942 expectations that gas would be used were still great enough to command a lot of attention.

Every soldier was issued a gas mask and at Camp Beale we were required to carry them during our training. To be caught without a gas mask was akin to a capital offense, for, it was hammered into us, in combat situations it could mean our very lives. My mask, worn beneath my left arm, became so much a part of me that I felt vulnerable without it.

At the battalion theater we watched training films on gas and ways to try to cope with it. In our day room we heard lectures and practiced the identification of some kinds of gas by odor. Some had unpleasant odors but others had the scent of certain fruit blossoms. At the moment I remember only a few names of the various gases. Chlorine suffocated its victims. Phosgene damaged the respiratory system. Mustard was a violent irritant with blistering qualities. Tear gas was momentarily disabling, but unlike the others had no lasting effects.

Earlier I had been curious about a small dark building quite different from all other structures in the battalion area. After receiving my gas mask, I found this was quite literally a gas chamber. One day we were taken there to test our masks. I approached this chamber with as much trepidation as crawling beneath the machine gun fire. The gas released was supposedly harmless, causing only momentary discomfort, but I was skeptical and uneasy. To my immense relief the mask proved effective. On later visits we were ordered to spend a few seconds in the chamber with the mask removed. We survived, of course, but uncomfortably so.

On field exercises we were warned to remain alert for a special signal indicating gas and the need to don our masks quickly. During one evening training mission, gas was released. Due to the effectiveness of my training at Beale I retained a pronounced fear of gas and a great respect for my gas mask.

On the drill field, barracks to the left, at Camp Beale, CA. The gas mask under my left arm was considered essential in 1942, yet I was sent into combat without it in 1944.

Several times during basic I found my name on the roster for guard duty. One Sunday, the Officer of the Day came around to ask some questions about the post and what I would do if certain situations arose. I wrote to my parents (1/17/43) that I answered satisfactorily. In fact that evening the sergeant of the guard told us, as I proudly wrote my parents, "The Officer of the Day said you men in No. 2 relief (the relief that I'm on) are really on the ball and doing all right especially guard No. 5." That happened to be my number.

As indicated earlier the army taught us its own way of telling time. Instead of dividing a day into two twelve hour parts the army made use of the full twenty-four hours. Today this may seem natural given such things as setting the timing on a VCR or any one of the other uses for considering all twenty-four numbers as hours in the day. But in the early 1940's, we never imagined such a need, and initially this seemed no more than another army eccentricity.

Before long, however, it began to make a lot of sense. For instance, an order to jump off in attack at 0500 hours clearly meant five o'clock in the morning. A soldier never confused it with five o'clock in the afternoon, for that would have been given as 1700 hours. Today I regard this method of determining time as one of the most sensible things learned from the army.

Also, the army taught us its own alphabet: Able for A, Baker for B, Charlie for C, and so on. We attended classes in the battery day room to practice both time and alphabet. At first the alphabet, like the time, seemed a bit frivolous, but actually it was very useful. As one who, even then, had difficulty distinguishing between certain sounds, I developed a great appreciation for it.

Fortunately I seldom had any telephone duty. But if I did, the army alphabet proved helpful. Some sounds, particularly on a telephone, are practically indistinguishable to me. "b's" and "d's" for instance can be very troublesome. Army callers might say "that's d as in dog" or "b as in baker" and it would reduce a problem in communication. Unfortunately many people who called a roll or read off duty rosters recognized no problem and never used the army alphabet for clarification.

In an armored division we were all expected to be able to drive the various vehicles in our respective units. A service battery had a lot of trucks of assorted sizes and this necessitated a great many driving lessons. A small number of men started with no driving experience of any kind. The great majority of us at least had some limited experience with an automobile. As I remember it only one fellow on our floor had ever driven a truck of any kind. I learned to drive a Model T Ford and later had driven a Model A Ford some, mostly into Chillicothe or Lock Springs.

By later measure, gasoline was quite cheap in the 1930's. Even so the economy did not permit its purchase to ride around as we would today. I doubt many of my army buddies had driven any more than was necessary for essential errands or to get to work. In short we possessed the basic tools, but it would require a lot of work to turn us into the accomplished drivers needed for a mechanized force.

As with our introduction to weapons, we received extensive instructions about vehicles and driving before ever getting behind a wheel. Then the instructor loaded a half dozen or so of us in back, the number depending upon the size of the truck and available time, put one fellow in the cab with him; and after a nearly always jerky start we went driving. Those in back knew they were in for a rough ride, not entirely due to the truck's hard fold down seats. When we moved from roads to cross country terrain, those in back really got a bumpy and jolting ride.

Few of us started off shifting smoothly so there was much grinding and gnashing of gears. The heavier the truck the worse the experience. None of us looked forward to these sessions, but, with grim good humor on driving days, one of my friends always announced he was off to grind some gears.

Learning to double clutch was the key to success in shifting without the dreadful grinding. After mastering this with the small trucks, I advanced to the big ones, 6 x 6's, six wheels all driving. Down shifting on hills was a challenge with these big trucks. Learning to drive a half-track was even more difficult, somewhat akin to an imagined wrestling match with a huge gorilla.

Once mastered, however, driving a half-track was a satisfying accomplishment. It could be driven across ditches and rough terrain much easier than any of the wheeled vehicles. Half-tracks and many trucks came equipped with winches on the front. Some days we deliberately stuck some vehicles in mud or in soft, spongy ground in order to practice winching them out.

Opportunities were all too limited unfortunately, but the one really fun driving experience was with a small vehicle recognized by many people as a jeep. For reasons I do not remember, armored people at the time called them "peeps." Eventually "jeep" became the universal name for this useful vehicle.

During the rainy season when roads were muddy and fields even worse, no one liked getting caught with a late afternoon driving lesson. All vehicles were to be cleaned before being parked for the night. Washing a 6 x 6 was bad enough, but California mud clung to the bogies and tracks of a half-track with stubborn persistence. On top of all that we had to work on shoes covered with the same stuff before going to bed.

By late March the rains had stopped and a new problem appeared. Tanks and halftracks churned up roads and fields. The resulting clouds of dust made it difficult to see and hard to breathe. To cope with this we were issued goggles and respirators.

Certainly I never wanted to be a truck driver for the army. But as I wrote my parents (1/27/43), the army was persistent with the lessons so I might as well "give in and drive." By the end of basic training I was licensed for all the vehicles I had driven. To my considerable relief the 496th never gave me a truck assignment. Unfortunately the existence of an army license on my record caused trouble later.

In early February 1943, we were separated into different sections. I was assigned to an ammunition section, meaning we provided howitzer shells for the firing batteries. Each shell weighed more than 30 pounds and was at least 30 inches in length. Since they came in clusters of three secured with a clover leaf looking holder at each end, it took some strength to handle them.

Although I had been in the army long enough (six weeks) to expect the unexpected, some of the assignments still caught me by surprise. A big Kansas farmer, my size and probably stronger, seemed a natural to join me as an ammunition handler. Instead this man, in his early 20's, was assigned to the kitchen and sent off to the division's cook and baker's school. A short slightly built fellow in his 30's became one of my buddies on the other end of a 105 cluster. To make these two assignments all the more ludicrous, in civilian life the older, smaller man had been a chef in a Chicago hotel. Perhaps the army was afraid he would ruin the standard for army chow.

On bivouac a few weeks later we had an opportunity to practice some of the things we had been taught about storing and concealing ammunition. The battalion's three firing batteries preceded us into the rolling hills several miles beyond camp. Our section secured the necessary ammunition and established a position some distance behind the howitzers. First, at each designated spot for an ammo dump, we carefully cut blocks of sod and set them aside. Then we dug the dumps and stored the shells. We replaced the covering of sod and carried the excess dirt several hundred yards down a ravine that ran below the dump.

Our concealment was so successful that I had to brag about it to my parents:

> . . . such a good job of it that the Colonel and a lot of officers praised us a lot on it. To prove how cleverly concealed that it was I'll tell you what happened. A Sgt. from a firing battery came over yesterday morning with a group of men. He asked our Sgt. "We have come after some ammunition. Where is it at?" And believe it or not, he was standing on top of enough ammunition to kill hundreds of men and destroy lots of equipment and he didn't know it. What do you think of that? A Lieut. marched a group of men up to show it to them and they didn't notice them until he pointed them out. I was really proud of our work and so was our officers and the 2 Sgts. that supervised the building of them. (3/17/43)

Although by this time the days were quite warm, I discovered that California nights could still be cold. Sleeping bags were not yet available for us but we did have an extra blanket and I put my raincoat beneath me to cut some chill from the ground. Unlike later issue shelter halves, those at that time had a flap only at one end leaving the other end of a two man pup tent open to the elements.

On this and other training exercises planes from an air base near Sacramento flew over us. This caused us to hit the ground as we had been taught and gave the pilots practice in low level flying over troops and vehicles. It offered me a mild preview of the Remagen Bridgehead, except these were friendly planes. "They were a fascinating sight to me and brought back my old desire to be in the Air Corps. They look so graceful and are such a thrilling sight," I wrote. (3/23/43)

On one bivouac we went on beyond the undulating hills riding trucks and other vehicles up into the foothills of the mountains. At dusk we stopped in a rocky area with some big boulders scattered about. It may have been an appealing area for sightseeing, but I found it most unwelcome as a campsite. As I crawled into my pup tent in the growing darkness I worried about snakes. The rocks and tall grass where we pitched our tents seemed a perfect place for them, at least in my imagination. Part of that generally sleepless night I spent in a truck. In truth I encountered only one snake at Beale, but that was more than enough.

Our ammunition section of a dozen men received a challenging assignment one nice spring day. We were ordered to bridge a small stream at a certain spot out in the rolling hills. We were not allowed to take any timbers, planks, steel, or anything of that nature from camp. The bridge was to be built entirely from materials at hand. In order to pass inspection it was to be sturdy enough to carry the weight of half-tracks and large trucks.

Armed with axes, shovels, pick-axes and confidence in our leader, a buck sergeant named Stevenson, the section began an amateurish attempt at bridge building. Already this section had developed a good bond and everyone did his share of any work to be done. Always there was a lot of give and take and good-natured joshing whether we were hiking, lugging ammunition, building ammo dumps, taking driving lessons together, or in this case trying to bridge a stream.

We located trees of varying sizes and straight enough for building material. After much hacking, hewing, heaving and sweating we had long logs in place across the stream as bridge stringers. Then we used a lot of small logs as a floor.

Bridge Building Detail, I am leaning on a shovel, in the center of the picture.
Camp Beale, CA.

Finally some dirt on top of these logs made a relatively smooth passage way. It must have looked rather crude to the uninvolved, but when it supported the weight of a 6 x 6 truck it was a thing of beauty to us.

One of the fellows brought along his camera and the resulting pictures show our section relaxed and happy with its accomplishment. In one I am shown leaning casually on a shovel. Others are leaning on tools or sitting on the bridge. We also parked a 6 x 6 on the bridge and, draping ourselves on it and around it, offered pictorial evidence of the sturdiness of our work. These pictures came to light 50 years later when my wife was assembling things for an all-army album for me.

All through the winter and spring of 1942-43 we continued to take hikes of around 5 miles. Gradually we interspersed these with long ones: 8 miles, 12 miles, 18 miles and finally one 25 mile hike. Always we carried our gas masks, but beyond that, equipment varied from minimal to full field pack. The new type steel helmets were not only better than the old World War One style issued to the older non-coms, but they came with a good looking liner. Usually we were allowed to wear only the liner for hiking and parade ground purposes.

Successful bridge building. I am on the far left. Camp Beale, CA.

I got along well with the hiking and much preferred that to Sgt. Pearson's arm exercises. Naturally, my "13 Annies" caused some discomfort, and on the 25 mile hike they gave me a ferocious blister.

During much of the winter the area around our battery buildings remained bare and desolate. We kept it policed of all debris. That is, regularly we were ordered to form a line and with head down and rump up, to proceed across the ground picking up all bits of trash. I accepted the desirability of keeping the area neat and clean, but highly resented having to pick up reminders of other people's nasty smoking habit. Smokers were taught to field strip, as it was called, cigarettes and wad the paper residue into a small ball. Even so, these were left on the ground where non-smokers had to handle them.

Although it may appear that all my time at Beale was spent in work and training, there were a few opportunities for diversion and recreation. Some Saturday nights I was free to attend a movie with friends. At least once I attended a program presented by the division band. The division encouraged some sports and a few times some of us went to the boxing matches. My interest was less in boxing per se than in an opportunity to see a former professional boxer of some note who often refereed the matches. It was an amusing sight to see heavyweight Buddy Baer thrust himself between two scrappy little flyweight boxers.

The USO brought at least two shows to Camp Beale in the spring of 1943 and I was able to see them. Some of my friends in the know were greatly excited about the appearance of Louie Prima and Keely Smith. Upon attending the performance, I better understood their enthusiasm.

My own enthusiasm was reserved for the stage show "Hellzapoppin." It offered an opportunity to see Lynn Bari whose good looks I had admired on the movie screen. Allyn Joslyn the movie actor also appeared in the production. But the real highlight of the show for me turned out to be a line of dancers with beautiful legs moving in precision: the Rockettes of Radio City Music Hall.

An opportunity to see a high profile military personality came in April when Lt. Gen. Jacob Devers, chief of all the armored forces, came to Beale. After much spit and polish preparation, the entire division marched on to a large field to hear him speak. I was astonished at the amount of space we covered, but then there must have been around 14,000 of us.

At least twice I got into Marysville on short passes. The iniquitous pleasures available near an army post held no attractions for me, but I did appreciate the town for some of its historic and architectural offerings. Also, its stores gave access to some items not always available in the PX.

Upon the completion of basic training, I applied for and received a three day pass to Sacramento and San Francisco. An older friend from Virginia, Marshall Broadwater, went with me. Marshall was a quiet, unassuming, sensible, serious-minded and good-natured fellow who reminded me of what I might be like given a little more maturity. I have never had much of an ear for sounds and accents, but just as I learned from one friend that South Carolinians have a definite accent, so I learned from Marshall that Virginians had their own peculiar way of pronouncing a word with "ou" in it. "Out" from Marshall's tongue, for example, became something like "ooh't." We had no difficulty understanding each other, however, and we were enough alike in thinking and interests that he made a good traveling companion.

We stopped awhile in Sacramento. For me the highlight was seeing the California state capitol. The building and the grounds with trees and shrubs from that state made a great impression. Recently, Alice and I have been collecting sightings of as many state capitals as possible, and have revisited Sacramento. California's capital will always occupy a special place in my lengthening list, for it was the first one I had seen. It would be another half dozen years or so before I would see my own state capitol in Jefferson City.

San Francisco fully lived up to my expectations. It was a fascinating city and friendly to service personnel. The streets were filled with a variety of uniforms representing all branches of the armed forces. The combination of the city and a look at the Presidio and its attractive setting made clear why soldiers considered an assignment there a plum.

My very first look at an ocean was a special thrill to one who previously had seen nothing larger than the Missouri River. The Pacific looked as peaceful as the name implied, but I continued to hope that any overseas assignment would send me across the Atlantic instead.

The Bay with all its ships and boats, and bustling activity, was a lively sight. After all that I had heard about its notorious prison, my eyes were drawn to the small island of Alcatraz. It truly appeared a grim and forbidding place, securely isolating some of the worst elements of our society.

My long time love affair with beautiful bridges began the moment I first beheld the Golden Gate Bridge. In earlier years I had read newspaper articles on speculation as to whether man could actually span this awesome natural gateway to the Pacific; then the progress of its construction, and finally its triumphal completion a half dozen years earlier. Ancient man and medieval man had their majestic building triumphs in pyramids and cathedrals, but for me modern man challenged for a place in history with this spectacular engineering achievement. What could be more satisfying than being a civil engineer and building bridges that were both utilitarian and beautiful? Not even in my wildest flights of fantasy could I have envisioned at that moment that before long the army would dangle before me an opportunity to become an engineer.

In one of my life's more gratifying moments, the next time (actually over a half century later) I had the opportunity to admire this beautiful bridge, I was with Alice in a restaurant on the Bay at a table with an unobstructed view looking directly toward the bridge. The sun went down behind the hills of the Marin Peninsula and for our benefit, or so it seemed to me, a crescent moon appeared with the evening star nearby.

But back in 1943, almost two weeks after returning from San Francisco, I was surprised to receive a letter posted from a camp in that area. It was from my best friend in high school, Cline McQueen. Cline and another high school classmate, Bob Wickizer, had been drafted by Daviess County a month or more after Livingston County called me. Both had been sent to the same place for basic training. I have forgotten the camp's location, but remember it was not nearly as far from home as California. Also, I remember they had not been assigned to a division as I had been. This meant that eventually they would be sent on somewhere else for more permanent assignments. Sure enough now they had been separated and Cline was in the San Francisco area.

This was disturbing news indeed. While he could have had time for no more than the minimum of basic training, his new location was a port of embarkation for Pacific duty. There could be little doubt that he was shipping out, for his letter had been censored, with parts of it cut out.

Cline wanted to see me. He sounded both lonesome after leaving Bob and uneasy about the future. The fact that I had been to San Francisco so recently made it highly unlikely I would be allowed to return right away. I had to hope he would be there for a month or more. Still, I replied immediately and assured him I would try to see him. Regrettably, I did not hear from him again. Soon I learned through home channels that almost immediately after writing me he had been sent on to a war zone in the Pacific. After seeing a lot of action, he was killed somewhere out there.

Mother and others from Lock Springs reported that while Cline's death hurt his mother, his father was utterly devastated and soon began wasting away. I saw his father soon after I got home from the war and was shocked by his appearance. It was quickly evident that meeting him had been a terrible mistake. It was uncomfortable for both of us. To him I had to be a horrible reminder that his son was never coming home. To me it was almost embarrassing to have been spared, and I simply did not know what to say. It was no great surprise when Mr. McQueen died soon afterward. I have no idea what his death certificate read, but if it is possible to die of a broken heart, Cline's father surely did.

Early in the military I heard two bits of alleged wisdom for the smart soldier: never volunteer for anything, and keep a low profile. Whoever passed on the first failed to add that sergeants had heard it already. As a result, when a sergeant needed volunteers, the routine often went this way: "I want three volunteers," and pointing into the ranks, continued, "you, you, and you, step forward; you have just volunteered for . . ."

The second bit of advice seemed more pertinent for one who by nature was introverted and who very early had written with disgust about a few fellows "putting in" with people in authority. Some of my friends, I discovered, found it equally distasteful and explained to me that the army knew the practice by the crudely appropriate term of "brown-nosing."

I did my training routines and duty assignments to the best of my ability but tried to remain quietly unobtrusive about it. Even so I discovered at the end of the first month of basic that at least as far away as battalion headquarters some people knew me as Breeze and not just number 37242203.

Indications of this came from a noncom who lived in my barracks but did something at battalion headquarters. Since he had nothing to do with my training and was seldom seen around the barracks, I was surprised that he even knew my name. But when I went into the washroom one afternoon and found him there shaving, he turned to me and asked,

"Breeze, what did you do before you came to the army?" He followed with other questions about education and what I wanted to do in the army.

Then he said the word at headquarters was that I had made a very high score on tests taken at the induction center. He encouraged me to believe that I had an excellent chance to attend one of the specialist schools such as Fort Knox (armor) or Fort Sill (artillery), perhaps become an instructor and get a good rating.

When I thought about it, one of his statements offered some interesting revelations. "Breeze," he said, "you have an awful high I.Q. for a farm boy and have a good chance in the army." It came as news to me that some of the tests at Leavenworth were considered a measure of intelligence. While I had completed the tests feeling comfortable about the outcome, it came as a pleasant surprise to learn the score was enough to impress some people. If others thought well of me as a result of a written test, fine and good, but I wondered what it really did show other than that I was smart enough to be test wise.

But perhaps the statement was even more interesting for what it revealed about the speaker. Evidently his cultural background, some Eastern city I believe, had not prepared him to equate farming with intelligence. Later I learned that his perception was shared by other men from Northern and Eastern urban areas. When the state of Missouri was thrown in, the equation became even more implausible to some of them. Just as I had a lot to learn about city folks and their ways, so they had a lot to learn about Midwestern farmers. Thanks to the army, most of us on both sides of this cultural chasm eventually made the crossover rather well.

The second indication that my profile was not as low as I thought came in a surprising and mysterious, even to this day, manner. Where the first indication led to optimism and hope, the second was more a cause for distaste and puzzlement. One of the older noncoms came to me one day saying he needed to talk to me about something very important but also highly confidential. Because I never mentioned a word of this in letters home and understandably did not make any notes of it at the time, only a dim outline remains in my memory. The gist of it ran something like this. Someone from higher authority (battalion level I believe) had given him what that officer considered a very important assignment. Furthermore he was directed to bring another enlisted man, one both reliable and intelligent, into the operation. Somehow they agreed upon my name. The assignment seemed totally unnecessary then and appears completely ridiculous now. But as noted in earlier comments about the mood on the anniversary of Pearl Harbor, there was fear of subversion and suspicion that bordered on paranoia at the time.

The assignment was to be alert to any potentially dangerous talk or signs of possible subversion. Henceforth the noncom and I were not to communicate in any way with each other on the subject. I was to give a short response in writing each month, more often if necessary. This went to an appropriately innocuous appearing name (not an individual as I recall) at a post office box in San Francisco.

With considerable reluctance I found myself drawn into this enterprise. In retrospect it is another measure of just how innocent I was in those days. Making it easier, I was quite certain nothing was going on at Beale, at least nothing I was likely to encounter. The noncom, I surmised, felt the same way about it. Information gathering, or spying to put it bluntly, was never my forte. At least after my few empty reports to the San Francisco address there was little likelihood that William J. Donovan, head of the OSS (Office of Strategic Services and forerunner to the CIA), would request my services.

In my last written response, June, 1943, I informed the mysterious unit, person, or persons on the other end that I was leaving Camp Beale. No one ever made contact with me in any way about the matter. My busy life after Beale removed thoughts of it from my mind. Only on rare occasions in the intervening years, such as now as I write this, have I wondered what I involved myself in by my inability to say no to a likable noncom who obviously trusted me.

The third indication that I had been noticed came on April 2, 1943. It was the kind of notice that a soldier could appreciate. Upon the completion of basic training, we understood that some promotions in rank would be awarded. Not expecting any recognition at this point, I thought one of the boys in the barracks was either joking (it was April Fool's Day) or badly mistaken when he claimed I was on the recommended list for private first class. Sure enough, my next letter home informed my parents that: "I was really surprised and thrilled when the captain called my name tonight and gave me my paper and congratulated me."

Only about eight men from the battery were promoted to private first class, about the same number to corporal (they were already in jobs that called for that rank), and one to sergeant (the fellow with prior service). To my disappointment none of my close friends got promoted, but all seemed happy for me and were generous enough to say I deserved it. The four dollar raise attached might buy a hamburger and fries today, but in 1943 it represented real money.

In sewing the single stripe on blouse and uniform shirts I happily anticipated a future in which I would be adding more. Not yet twenty-one years of age, I felt time seemed to pass very slowly and impatiently longed to part the veil of the future to see whether dreams and expectations would be realized. Older and wiser now with the years seeming to rush by much more rapidly than in my teens and early twenties, I know it is best to appreciate each day, to savor any beauty it contains, any delight it holds and any success it may bring to my life.

Sometimes it is just as well not to know what lies down the road. If, in April 1943, I had been permitted to see that upwards of three more years of army service would never give the opportunity to sew on even a second stripe (corporal), it would have clouded my happiness and crushed my spirit.

As it turned out, within a few short months I willingly gave up my stripe for what appeared to be a chance for a college degree and the gold bar of a second lieutenant. Eventually, when the dream of a degree and gold vanished I considered myself fortunate that an artillery captain chose to return my lonely stripe.

In my youth, reaching the age of twenty-one was considered an important milestone. Indeed for many legal purposes it was such, and very significant to me, it meant the right to vote. Chronologically anyway it signified a change in male status from youth to man.

It was something of a letdown, therefore, to have to spend June 3, 1943, not only in the army but in preparation for a bivouac. There was, it seemed, really nothing at all special about turning twenty-one, just another day in the life of a soldier. On the evening of the 4th I received a box from home but did not even have an opportunity to open it.

When opened the following day, the package contained another of my mother's delicious cakes. The realization that she had carefully hoarded sugar rations to make it touched me deeply, and I wrote her so. As usual I shared the cake with several of the boys who only then learned of my birthday. Mother had sent goodies previously so she already had a well deserved baking reputation with them, as did several other mothers. In particular, my mother's devil's food cake made a big hit with my friends.

My parents and I were all looking forward to a furlough as I completed a long six months of service. From the tone of letters around the first of May, I could tell Mother was getting very anxious. As she saw others from the community on furlough, some who barely could have finished basic training, I know she was worried that I might not get home at all. I tried to assure her that in late spring or early summer I would get there. We had been told that upon completion of the current "firing schedule" (howitzers), furloughs would begin.

At last, in the same letter in which I acknowledged my birthday cake, I reported that the first bunch of boys was leaving on the night of June 7 and some were almost counting the hours. Gaylen, Melvin and I might all get to come home together, the way it looked. If so, what a contrast in appearance _that_ would be from our departure the preceding November.

Other developments, however, were about to complicate my anticipation of a furlough. The fourth indication that I had been noticed, this time by a major from battalion headquarters, would play a decisive role in my future.

I may have forgotten the major's name, but I have not forgotten nor underestimated the importance of his interest in me. Other than the name, I can still recall him quite distinctly. At six feet I was considered tall by most of my battery mates, but the major seemed to loom at least three or four inches above me, with a frame appropriate to his height. With his size, his piercing brown eyes beneath dark bushy eyebrows, and rugged facial features, he fairly exuded strength and leadership.

I do not remember his exact position at headquarters but for whatever reason he spent a lot of time with our battery. Frequently when we set off on our routine short hikes, he would appear and stride along beside us. With the gold oak leaves of a major he was the highest ranking officer most of us encountered. Only infrequently did we see our colonel and perhaps an occasional lieutenant colonel. The brigadier general and our major general were distant entities, almost mythical figures.

Unlike some officers I would meet, the major never seemed infatuated with his rank. The barracks news line had it that as a civilian he had been an official with one of the airlines and commanded a lofty (by 1930's and early 1940's standards) salary of more than $20,000 annually. If true, it was an impressive position and a princely income to me and my friends. In any case, from my observation all of us in the battery admired and respected the major.

One afternoon, near the end of the first week in June, I was doing some chore in the barracks when someone came to me with a message. The major, it seemed, was in the battery day room and wanted to see me. Admittedly this gave me something of a start, for why would the major want to see me? From the experience of others, I knew that for an enlisted man to be summoned by an officer could be unwelcome news.

I found him alone in the day room. After I saluted and announced myself, as protocol demanded, he made me at ease, told me to sit down and announced he had something important to discuss with me.

He had been observing me, he explained, and knew I had made an outstanding score on the army test. The army had just initiated a new program, he went on, that he believed offered me a great opportunity. The program represented a cooperative arrangement between the army and leading universities across the land. It was called ASTP, for Army Specialized Training Program. This joint venture grew out of university concern that military demands were draining enrollment from professional schools and the army's recognition of its future need for medical doctors and engineers.

Soldiers accepted into this program would be educated at army expense in either medicine or engineering with a smaller number placed to study certain languages. Medicine held no interest for me and I suspected (our tiny high school could not afford a language instructor) that I lacked the ability to do anything other than to learn to read a foreign language. Engineering, particularly civil engineering, always held a certain fascination but in my economic circumstances seemed completely out of reach.

The major seemed delighted to hear of my interest in building bridges and other aspects of civil engineering, and said the program was perfect for me. The schedule would be rigorous, he cautioned, accelerated so as to accomplish in three years what was normally a four year program. It would demand a lot of hard work and require a lot of determination, but if I really wanted to become an engineer, he was confident I had the capability to achieve the goal. Successful completion of the program would lead to a bachelor's degree in engineering and probably the commission of a second lieutenant.

Along with our discussion of the merits of the program, he acknowledged one immediate drawback and possibly a second longer range one. Most immediately I would have to forego the much anticipated furlough and leave very soon for New York City for testing, some refresher work, final determination of acceptance into the program and assignment to some university. In the long run, having helped me with a degree and given me a commission, the army could demand some extra years of service.

At the moment the latter seemed less a matter for serious consideration than did the more immediate reality of losing a furlough, causing deep disappointment to my parents. It seemed to me the war could go on for years anyway and the prospect for a commission held some allure.

We parted with the major urging me to give it serious consideration and my promise to do so. In a little while I learned that he had brought my favorite lieutenant into the matter. The latter called me into the orderly room to talk about the ASTP. By that time I was ready to agree with the lieutenant's assessment of the program: it could be a regrettable mistake to let such an opportunity pass without some attempt to seize it. Consequently he arranged for the first step in the procedure, an interview before a board of officers at division headquarters.

Battery officers found a second man with the requisite test score for the program as well as some interest in it. Pfc. Eugene McGowan was in a different section and lived in the other barracks, but we were well acquainted. On the designated evening, we polished our brass, shined our shoes, donned our dress uniforms, and joined the other slightly nervous applicants from across the division. No one knew quite what to expect as one by one we were called before the board of five officers.

The interview proved harmless enough, and later in the evening we learned that the division recommended both of us for the program. We were ordered to finalize arrangements with our battery and prepare for an early departure for City College of New York. Our acceptance into the program would be determined there.

Then came the really difficult part, for I had to tell my parents that I would not be getting a furlough. I knew this would be a crushing blow to my mother. Yet in explaining about the ASTP I felt confident both parents would agree with my decision. Neither had more than a grade school education, but both had always been supportive of education for me. Dad had served at least two terms on the Lock Springs-Brookshier School Board. Unlike some fathers of high school boys, he never kept me out of school for planting and harvesting work.

Mother often had talked happily of her school days at Pinkley School, a few miles outside Chillicothe in rural Livingston County. It was a great regret of her life that family circumstances kept her from going beyond the sixth grade. Always she encouraged me and was proud of every step in my education. Had I but pushed for it, I know they would have put themselves deeper into debt to give me an education beyond high school. Even though I knew they would accept my decision in June, 1943, I still worried about the disappointment they were experiencing.

McGowan and I, along with 60 or more other men from the division, were scheduled to leave Sacramento on June 12 for New York City. When ordered to turn in all my field equipment except the mess kit and gas mask, along with some of my division insignias, I knew the army was serious about sending us.

With a little free time on my hands, I went down to the camp library and found some information on the City College of New York. CCNY, I learned, was located in Manhattan and appeared to have a good reputation in the academic world. By enrollment standards of the time, it was large with an enrollment of over 20,000 students. This was where the tests would be administered and my future determined.

I looked forward with excitement to a trip all the way across the country. At the same time I could not help feeling a little uneasy about leaving the familiar and entering what would be another new world for me. In six long months Beale had become not necessarily a happy home, but a place where I had found a fairly comfortable niche. Certainly my horizon had expanded considerably as I mingled with men from many different parts of the land and with varied backgrounds. I learned about ways of living and thinking in other areas and environments.

In six months I had learned the basic essentials of soldiering and a great deal about howitzers and their shells (most of the latter willingly forgotten long ago.) The worst thing about departing was the thought of leaving good friends. We had endured so much together—homesickness, worry, apprehension, fear, discomfort, even pain and challenging assignments. But we also shared successes, "care" packages from home, and some happy moments. I would feel very close to some of these men and that has never been an easy thing for me to do.

Some of my friends were already on furlough and surely would be surprised to return to find me gone for good. Unless the ASTP rejected me and returned me to the 13th Armored, I knew that in all likelihood I would never see these men again. As usual the army allowed only a moment for such sad reflection and soon we were hustled off to Sacramento and a new chapter in my life as a soldier.

Chapter Four

ASTP : City College of New York

At the Sacramento rail station those of us from the 13th armored joined men from other camps, all of us on our way to the ASTP program. It soon became evident that we were to make the trip to New York City in a style seldom accorded enlisted men. The Pullman from Fort Leavenworth had been impressive enough, but this time I was introduced to a train car with compartments. McGowan and I shared a three person compartment with another man from our division.

At mealtime we were called to a dining car. No army chow or eating out of mess kits here; but delicious food brought by waiters to tables covered with linen cloths and napkins, and eaten from china plates with good railway silverware. The more sophisticated among us advised the less knowing, definitely including me, on the practice of tipping for various attendant services.

The cross-country trip fully lived up to my great expectations of an opportunity to see new states and exciting scenery. Most immediately we moved through the mountains I had known to be east of Camp Beale, the Sierra Nevada.

Our first stop was Reno, Nevada. A conspicuous sign proclaimed it "The Biggest Little City in the World." This was the only place in the state that meant anything to me, aside from knowing that Carson City was the capital. The glittering lure of Las Vegas lay in the postwar future. In a day when divorce was less common, less approved, and therefore more difficult to obtain, Reno had become known in the popular mind as the nation's divorce capital.

Somewhere in the mountains of either Nevada or Utah I looked out at a scene imprinted in my memory forever afterward. We were in a valley with the train traveling alongside a small stream of clear water running over rocks. That in itself was a refreshing sight to someone more familiar with the mud colored streams of Livingston County. Grass grew along the banks and in the meadow beyond. There were some unidentified shrubs along with some trees I took to be cottonwoods like those described in my favorite Zane Grey novels. And to make the scene more memorable, a few beautiful horses grazed in this idyllic setting.

We reached Salt Lake City with the setting sun. Color on the Great Salt Lake and its surrounding mountains provided another long-lasting memory. Of all the interesting mountains in the western states, however, I found the Colorado Rockies the most captivating. As a would-be civil engineer I admired the way men had managed to build a railroad on the sides of such fiercely rugged terrain. Some curves offered a view of the roadbed literally carved from canyon walls, with great heights above and dizzying drops below.

Accustomed to the heat of Missouri in June, it seemed strange to find snow in some of the high places. Somewhere in the Rockies we passed through a military installation and saw soldiers walking in the snow. One of the fellows from Beale speculated that it was a place for specialized training in mountain warfare, much as the Mojave was used for desert training.

At Denver it pleased me to get a view of another capital city, even though merely a glimpse from the train. At that point we left the mountains to ride through the plains for many miles and many hours. Detraining for a short time in Lincoln, Nebraska, we had an opportunity to move about and see this state's distinctive looking capitol building. After passing through Iowa, we crossed the Mississippi River into the Illinois prairie. Being asleep at the time, I would not get a look at the great river down the eastern side of my state until my first leave. At Chicago we stopped and had an opportunity to wander around its impressive railway station. Even though cavernous, it was filled with wartime travelers, many of them service personnel. The stop was long enough for McGowan to contact his family.

Moving on from Chicago, I found that the terrain of Indiana and Ohio reminded me of parts of my Missouri homeland. The beautifully painted barns and neat appearance of many Indiana farms, however, gave them a more prosperous look than most farms at home. It made me wonder why Grandfather Griner left this state for a hill and bottom land farm in Missouri. But then I guess he had a restless streak, for he moved on from there to Indian Territory (later Oklahoma).

In Pennsylvania and all across West Virginia into Virginia, we were in mountains again. The Appalachians were appealing in their own way, but quite different from the mountains of the West. In later years I have enjoyed visiting many different parts of this chain introduced to me by the army.

Pittsburgh offered an impressive sight at night with smoke and flame from its mills filling and coloring the sky. Today we might worry about the ill effects of such pollution, but in 1943 we were thankful for the steel produced there to combat the evil of fascism.

The next morning I awakened to look out upon the Potomac river, immediately recognizing a scene that nearly duplicated a picture in one of my history books. We were passing through Harper's Ferry where John Brown staged his raid in 1859.

One of my greatest thrills came when the train pulled into the nation's capital. Time and opportunity allowed only a glimpse of Washington's buildings and monuments, but this was enough to whet my desire to see more. Over a year later, the army would offer that opportunity.

From Washington we moved north and east passing through Maryland, a corner of Delaware, the southeastern edge of Pennsylvania, and into New Jersey. Our long and exciting train journey came to an end in New Jersey across the Hudson from New York City. In another new experience for me, we rode a ferry across to a more usual mode of army transport: trucks took us to City College of New York (CCNY) on Amsterdam Avenue.

In the prewar years, CCNY had a much larger enrollment than most other colleges and state universities. Accordingly it had a large physical plant. But it hardly fit my idea of a college, for it lacked a sylvan setting abounding with trees and spacious lawns. In stark reality, concrete and asphalt surrounded the buildings with an occasional minuscule patch of grass, interspersed here and there with a few shrubs and even a tree or two.

Army cots had been moved into some of the larger halls to accommodate the influx of soldiers. The crowded setting reminded me of the induction center and once again I lived out of my duffel bag, an army practice I came to dislike intensely. The memory lingers on, for as much as I enjoy traveling in my older years, I still hate to live out of a suitcase and unpack as much as possible for any visit lasting more than one night.

We were fed from the college cafeteria where the food was satisfactory; but even better, this arrangement meant no K.P. duty for the soldiers. This proved especially beneficial as I fell into disfavor my second or third day at CCNY. Morning roll call, I soon realized, was a real challenge when handled by certain noncoms. There seemed to be no alphabetical order or any other discernible pattern to their bumbling rush through a long roster. Nothing at all sounded like "Breeze" to me, nor was I able to check with anyone to see if my name was included. Instead, two hours later I found myself standing before a stern-faced captain. Impatiently waving aside my attempt at explanation, he took it for a certainty that I had missed roll call. He knew that I knew that he was in a position to block my chance at a college education. I smoldered then and can still get angry about it now, but saw no recourse.

His problem then was how to find a satisfyingly appropriate punishment. K.P. was out and there was no guard duty. He could hardly order me to dig a 6x6 hole in the asphalt. And if ordered to dig in one of the small grassy areas, college authorities *would* be on his back. Finally he decided to restrict me to quarters for several evenings. He appeared happy with this solution, and understandably I made no attempt to enlighten him to the fact that I planned to be studying mathematics anyway, rather than sampling New York night life.

There were still moments when I wondered about my decision to forego a furlough, for an uncertain venture. I worried about the possible depth of my parents' disappointment. But when finally they had my new address and were in communication again, they managed to cover any disappointment quite well. Clearly they were proud of this opportunity for me and agreed fully with my decision.

Results of tests taken in algebra and plane geometry would determine whether I had a chance at admission to the program. I completed the tests feeling comfortable and confidant about the algebra, less so with the geometry. In the spring of 1938, I had won a gold medal in plane geometry at the Daviess County academic contests which included eight high schools. But I had not touched the subject since and could only hope that enough had stayed with me to pass the tests.

Fortunately I did not have long to remain anxious about test results. Within twenty-four hours I appeared before a special two-man board, a civilian and an army officer (thankfully not the captain.) After some questions and discussion about my interest, they agreed to recommend me for ASTP in basic engineering. Both advised me to attend mathematics review classes while awaiting assignment, which I did. Also, I followed the civilian's suggestion to purchase from the college book store a copy of *The Blue Book of Plane Geometry.*

Judging from the numbers attending review classes in both algebra and geometry, I was not the only fellow whose skills had rusted. A number of men failed to score high enough on the tests and were rejected from ASTP and regretfully McGowan was among them. After spending a few more days together, we had to part as the army sent him and others back to Beale and other camps.

With the exception of early morning calisthenics, a little drilling, an occasional hike and Saturday morning inspection followed by a parade, the army did not intrude upon our time with military training. We were allowed plenty of time to attend classes and study. Sports were encouraged and I played softball and volleyball.

After the wide open space of Camp Beale, it seemed strange to hike the confining streets of Manhattan. But I welcomed this as an opportunity to see a lot more of the area. Sometimes we hiked down to where I could admire the George Washington bridge spanning the Hudson. Moving along the New York side of the river, I could look across to the cliffs of the Palisades in New Jersey. Walking down Riverside Drive offered some real treats, among them the imposing tomb of General Grant. Nearby I recognized the magnificent Gothic tower of Riverside, the church of the well known clergyman, Harry Emerson Fosdick.

On hikes farther down the way I could appreciate the greatness of New York as a port city. Even in the San Francisco area, I had not seen so much activity and so many ships. Standing out in my memory is a view of the once great French liner, *Normandie*. Built to compete with the *Queens* of Britain, there it lay on its side, just as pictured in the newspapers, following a disabling fire.

My initial impression of New York City was that of a place much too overpowering for a country boy. To begin with there was far too much *of* it. Even with an occasional grassy spot and the oasis of a park, there seemed to be no getting away from the city. It was everywhere. And there were too many people crammed into it. As I explained to my parents:

> In all the time I've been here I've seen only one or two houses and those were unsightly things down near the river. Everyone must live in an apartment house for that's all you see. They sure have some large beautiful ones along Riverside Drive, but I'd take a little farm home somewhere in Missouri. (7/5/43)

When I looked at the apartments on Amsterdam Avenue and neighboring streets and thought of the cramped space, the June-July heat (pre-air conditioning days, of course), the obvious lack of privacy, and the constancy of a city all about, I felt deeply sorry for the inhabitants. Later, upon reflection, I realized these people would feel as lost in the freedom of the country as I felt trapped by the confines of their city. I recall one particularly hot July day when policemen closed down part of the avenue to all but pedestrian traffic, while firemen opened a hydrant and little children poured out of the apartments to run and play in the water. They were as happy and carefree as I had been at that age when, with two cousins, I ran barefoot through the grass and waded in the shallow stream on my parent's farm.

To my pleasant surprise Manhattan was "not so hard to get around," I wrote my parents, "once you learn that the streets that run east and west are numbers such as W. 137th St. where we are and the avenues such as Amsterdam, Seventh, Eighth, Broadway, etc. run north and south." (7/5/43) Fortunately my sense of direction had not yet deserted me, as it would in a year or so, and the sun came up in its proper place and went down beyond the Hudson as nature intended.

As long as I remained above ground I had no problem. The subway, however, was altogether another matter. Perhaps my initial approach was conditioned by an awareness of an earlier experience of two fellows in my sleeping quarters. Venturing into lower Manhattan one evening, they got confused on the return trip and ended up in Harlem, leading to a rather uneasy walk in the darkness (blackout!) across a park to get to the college. I managed to use the subway a few times (once by myself) without misadventure but it remained confusing. In fact, its intimidating effects long endured, and on an initial visit to London nearly two decades later I dreaded my first venture on the underground or "tube." It was therefore, a joy to find that the well-marked system and colorfully distinctive map/diagram of the London Underground enabled one to get anywhere with ease.

On Sundays we were free to do what we liked. A few men in my quarters had heard so much about the resort at Coney Island that they went to see it. One fellow made the dreadful mistake of swimming and then falling asleep on the beach while his companions spent much of the day on rides and other amusement offerings. The next day he had the worst case of sunburn any of us had ever seen. Unable to bear the touch of a top sheet or clothing, he remained thoroughly miserable for several days.

Baseball appealed to me a lot more than Coney Island, and with three teams in the area I hoped to see at least one big league game. Long an avid fan and familiar with names and exploits of many players and their teams, I had never seen a major league game. Learning that the Giants were in town, I was determined to see them. Although the Chicago Cubs would not be the opposing team, McGowan also wanted to see a game. Together we negotiated the subway through Harlem and to the Polo Grounds, where we discovered that men and women in uniform were given free admission. It was a genuine thrill to see my first major league park and first game, truly one of the highlights in my stay in New York. On my last Saturday there I attended another game. To my considerable delight, Mel Ott, one of the great stars of that era, hit a home run.

On Sunday July 4th, I was able to attend services at Riverside Church, something I had wished to do since my first sight of it. A man from the YMCA took nine of us to church and it was a memorable experience. The spacious interior with massive columns supporting a dome shaped ceiling and the stained glass windows full of religious symbolism more than fulfilled my expectations of awesome beauty. The carillon of 65 (according to the guide) bells made beautiful music.

The usefulness of the church as far more than a religious sanctuary impressed me. Between the sanctuary and the belfry, the Gothic style tower contained nine floors of offices and study rooms. The basement held a gymnasium with basketball goals and an assembly hall seating several hundred people. I had never seen anything like this magnificent church. All three of our small churches in Lock Springs, plus the country churches near Sampsel, could have been tucked into a part of it and hardly be noticed.

One Monday, when I had neither classes nor army activities, I explored the heart of Manhattan. This gave me a chance to see Central Park, Times Square, Radio Center, the New York Public Library and to gawk at skyscrapers including the Empire State building.

Without a doubt, New York was a fascinating place and in my three weeks there I barely touched upon the opportunities it offered. Yet to be seen of major importance were theater offerings, concerts and marvelous museums. Even so, I was getting eager to move on and anxious to learn where I might be going to school.

When I returned from supper on the evening of July 5, my name was on the bulletin board to be ready to leave the next morning. Since a group had just been sent to Fordham in the nearby Bronx, it seemed unlikely that I would remain in the New York area. This suited me fine, for I knew I would feel more comfortable in a much smaller setting. I rather hoped it might be a midwestern or border state university as that would give more of an opportunity to get home between terms.

With all my belongings in the duffel bag slung across my back, I reported for assignment early on July 6. Soon I learned that we were going to the University of New Hampshire. Momentarily I was disappointed at the thought of going even farther away from home. But the idea of attending a New England university had a certain appeal. Also it would enable me to see several new states and allow acquaintance with a quite different section of the country.

This time my rail journey was by coach. As distances across New England states are relatively short and we would reach our destination in late afternoon, no sleeping arrangements were needed. I sat back and enjoyed the trip across the lower part of Connecticut with an occasional view of Long Island Sound. Crossing Rhode Island gave a quick glimpse of another state capitol building at Providence.

After all the history I had read about Boston and neighboring parts of Massachusetts, I was delighted to pass through that area. Boston, I learned, had two railway stations. We left the train at one and marched through the streets to the other. Subsequently I became more familiar with both stations and the often narrow twisting way between them. On the march I saw something not seen in the traffic of Kansas City, San Francisco, or New York City. Instead of traffic signals, a policeman stood in a traffic box in the middle of one busy intersection and with precise movements of his white gloved hands directed the flow of traffic around him.

At the second station we boarded the Boston and Maine Railroad for the last leg of our journey. The B & M would play an important role in our lives at New Hampshire. To us it was the important link with the world beyond the university.

Traveling north from Boston I recognized the names of some important old factory towns. Once into New Hampshire, towns became fewer and smaller. The countryside was an inviting green, with many trees. We reached our destination at a railway station marked "Durham."

Getting off the train and lining up to march down a street that stretched ahead for several hundred yards, I looked back across the tracks to our right and saw a gymnasium, a great expanse of open land with ball fields and grassy areas, and beyond that a line of trees. On the immediate left side of the street ahead of us was a large outdoor swimming pool. On the right side, and still near the tracks, were numerous buildings and a power plant.

As we marched away from the station and down the street, the campus stretched out on our right. Many red brick buildings were scattered here and there with spacious green lawns and many trees. After CCNY it looked cool and inviting. On a, slight rise an impressive building with a tower stood out from the others. It, I learned, was Thompson Hall, the administrative center of the university. A newer looking building on beyond turned out to be the library.

On our left a large house, set in the midst of attractive grounds, was the president's home. Beyond it, again on our left, were dormitories for women. Farther along on our right stood another group of red brick dormitories and dining hall. Here we halted. This was to be my new home for the next school term, and, if all went well, quite possibly for the next two to three years.

It was a long way from California where I had started, but here lay the promise that a major in the 496th Armored Field Artillery had held out to me. Thanks to him and courtesy of the United States Army I was about to become a university student.

Chapter Five

ASTP : The University of New Hampshire

Durham, a fittingly English sounding name for a university town, certainly met my desire for a smaller setting. It was the polar opposite of New York City. Take away the university and it was little more than a small sleepy village. Its quiet setting provided the ideal place for one who had to work hard to succeed in a challenging program.

The town's few businesses were clustered diagonally across and down the street from the men's dormitories. Among them were a small eating place, a drug store, a barber shop, a cleaning establishment, and across a narrow intersecting street a clothing store that, in addition to the usual apparel and university materials, carried items of military clothing. The Franklin, a movie theater located off the main street, was the town's only concession to distraction from study. Actually, after a week of rigorous mental activity and some physical exertion, it served as a useful diversion.

Looking beyond the business area and toward rising ground on my dorm's side of the street, I could see what I learned was a typical sight in a small New England town. A small white church thrust its impressive steeple high into the sky. It was Congregational, and being in an area where Methodists were scarce, this became my church home and comfortably so.

Beyond the church and out of town, Durham's main street became a winding road and six miles to the northeast lay Dover. This larger (by New Hampshire standards) town offered more shopping and other opportunities. South Berwick, Maine, lay across the Piscataqua River ten miles to the east of Durham. Boston was an hour and a half away on the B & M. Portsmouth on the Atlantic Ocean lay about ten miles east and slightly south of Durham.

Because it had been the site of a conference ending the Russo-Japanese War in 1905, Portsmouth was one of the few New Hampshire towns to mean anything to me. The use of blackout curtains at the university served as a reminder of the presence of important naval shipyards at Portsmouth, thus a potential enemy target. People in this area seemed as sensitive to the threat from Germany as West Coast people had been from Japan,

We were to be housed in Hetzel Hall. A contingent of soldiers from another center had arrived earlier, and they hailed us with the normal greeting to all newcomers: "You'll be sorry!" We did not expect to be, of course, nor were we.

As rooms were assigned, I was pleased to recognize one of my roommates as a fellow visitor to Riverside Church. His name, I soon learned, was Frank Galloway and he was from Beaumont, Texas.

A second roommate wore a 13th Armored patch and the red braid of field artillery. We were not acquainted by name but had been on the same train from California and then separated at CCNY. Both of us had been in the 496th, but in different batteries. He was James (Jim) Fankle from Pittsburgh, Pennsylvania.

We were given a corner room for four on the second floor. The fourth man, a quiet and pleasant appearing fellow, was another Jim, James Burkhardt, from New Jersey. Admittedly I had been a little anxious about roommates hoping to get companions both congenial and possessing a dedicated work ethic. It could not have turned out any better, for the four of us were compatible and became good friends.

ASTP students at New Hampshire must have numbered well over 300, perhaps as many as 400. We were organized into companies (I was in C) and divided into sections for class programs. We marched to and from classes in orderly fashion, no streaming in and out of classrooms or wandering about as in the case of civilian students.

All ASTP students were equal in rank, all buck privates. The only stripes to be seen on campus were on the arms of men in the unit placed in charge of us. Once again I was Pvt. Breeze. Jim Fankle had been a corporal at Beale. In the smaller corner room adjoining ours, one man had been a corporal and the other thought the program worth surrendering the stripes of a staff sergeant. Some consideration was given to calling us "cadets", as in the service schools. While the term was sometimes used, for official purposes we remained "privates."

Until manpower needs drained away most of the male students, the university had maintained a ROTC (Reserve Officers Training Corps) program. Once again the campus had a small complement of officers and non-commissioned officers, this time in charge of ASTP students. In addition to a heavy academic load, we learned that we were to take work in military science. With the eventual possibility of our earning a commission, this made some sense. But it was easy to resent this intrusion upon study time.

Some of the non-coms, I believe, were holdovers from the ROTC program. Among them, an old master sergeant had seven or eight stripes on his lower sleeve, each representing three years of service. A large unlikable fellow, another holdover I believe, became our first sergeant. Someone coined the apt term for him: "Sgt. Dumbo." As we were leaving Durham in 1944, one of my roommates discovered that he was really a T/4 who had been made acting first sergeant. Perhaps his jumped up status accounted for the apparent need to flaunt his authority. In any case, I still remember his distinctive pronunciation of the word "film." As part of our military science work, he would stand in front of us and bawl out "Now you men are going to see a training fill-um!"

Our captain and a first lieutenant were decent officers and good to me personally. On the other hand a second lieutenant was so taken with his gold bar that he could be a real bother. One evening, for instance, Frank was returning from an errand and met the lieutenant. With more important thoughts on his mind and in a blackout area, Frank did not recognize and salute the lieutenant. Whereupon the offended officer called him back and chewed him out for this terrible breach of military courtesy.

Sometimes the lieutenant liked to prowl around the dorm during required study hours (1900-2100 hours), hoping, we surmised, to find something amiss. One evening he appeared at our closed door, knocked loudly and announced his presence. We pretended to think him one of the pranksters from down the hall pretending to be the lieutenant and told him loudly and rudely to get lost. Finally, we opened the door and, feigning surprise, apologized profusely. He accepted it and went away, but I think that was the last time he bothered our end of the hall.

Returning to college after the war, I learned that 15 hours credit was considered a normal course load. Our load at New Hampshire stood out in sharp contrast. In looking at my weekly schedule in an old notebook and checking a transcript of credits, I find that we averaged 21 hours per term in addition to physical education and military science.

It was most fortunate that I had a good high school background in English, history, and geography. Two very good teachers of history and geography, as well as my poring over books in these fields from an early age, had prepared me to handle these subjects with little study. Later on I would learn that one of my UNH history professors had been a friend and classmate of my future graduate school mentor, Dr. Charles F. Mullett. Regrettably, I simply lacked the time to do justice to Dr. Partridge's class.

Again, two excellent teachers had prepared me well to handle college English with a minimum of effort. New Hampshire English professors placed great stress upon writing, much of it done in class under supervision. Although not fully appreciative at the time, later I would recognize my indebtedness to these men.

The engineering oriented side of the program was quite another matter and at times threatened to overwhelm me. It would have been difficult enough in any case, but the accelerated pace made it worse. There simply were not enough hours in the day nor days in the week. Given my total lack of background preparation, courses in physics and chemistry taken simultaneously loomed before me like a big mountain with a craggy peak. At the same time, add a half term of algebra to be followed by a half term in trigonometry and the mountain appeared nearly unclimbable.

Fortunately I had one tool that enabled me to get a foothold and slowly begin to climb. Two courses of algebra with a great high school teacher gave me a good command of that subject and it, in turn, helped me with the physics. It might take valuable time to do all the algebra homework problems, but at least I could do them. It was fortunate that the algebra came at the beginning of the term. That gave me confidence and a bit of breathing room. Having the trigonometry, new and much more demanding, might have kept me from ever getting off the ground.

By chance I found myself in a physics section with a considerable number of the best prepared fellows in the program, all with at least high school physics and some with college work. Test results from all sections were posted on a bulletin board and several fellows in my section consistently made the highest marks on the board. Not surprisingly, the instructor moved briskly along, leaving me to sink or swim. There can be little doubt that he expected me to drop quickly out of sight. In fact, no one familiar with my situation at that point could have given much for my chances of survival.

One who understood my situation was Jim Fankle. After a year and a half of preengineering study at the University of Pittsburgh, he had dropped out in discouragement and in danger of failing. Now, with more maturity and greater enthusiasm, he was making 80's and 90's on physics tests. Quite candidly he warned me at the outset that my chances were not at all good. Still, he wanted to throw me a lifeline and did so by coaching a lot in the early going.

By dint of much hard work, some help from Jim, and surely a lot of luck, I finally climbed into the low C range and managed to cling there. In high school, scores of 70 and 71, as I was making, would have been humiliating to me. My first term at UNH they were rough cut gems. My morale lifted some when the captain came along and said that good work in the physics lab, which I had, would solidify a grade for people like me. It helped also that in the ninth week some of the sections were shuffled. Fankle went with the "smart" boys, and I dropped into a more comfortable mediocre class. I never would have thought that a solid C would look as good as did my final grade for physics at the end of that first term.

Chemistry, as fully expected, also caused many anxious moments. One hopeful note came early when, discovering that some in my section had little or no high school chemistry, the young instructor promised to "start at the beginning." But even with his patient and, I believe, competent instruction, I still had an extremely difficult time. The course objectives and the time frame for their attainment, set by military authorities outside our instructor's classroom and even beyond the university, came perilously close to being beyond my reach. Even a limited acquaintance with chemicals, their properties and reactions, would have helped significantly. But when I entered high school in 1936, Lock Springs no longer employed a science teacher. Some unused bottles of chemicals and an old Bunsen burner, relics from an earlier era, remained intriguing mysteries to me and my classmates. Sometimes my natural insecurity made me feel an outsider among so many men who were products of large high schools with extensive offerings. And this, one should remember, was at a time when large public high schools generally were respected, not maligned as they are today. What business did a fellow from such a tiny school have, I asked myself, in the same classroom with so many boys from Eastern cities? Sometimes that question caused me to forget my great indebtedness to the teachers mentioned previously and to regret that I had been unable to attend the high school in Chillicothe.

The first chemistry test was a disaster. My grade of 33 seemed too far from the passing requirement of 60 to offer much hope. The fact that some companions in misery made even lower scores was no comfort. From this devastating experience, however, I learned something about preparation for future tests: master formulas thoroughly and there might be enough applicable problems to pass.

Usually enough problems solvable by known formulas were included for me to get a passing grade. I wrote my parents about one test problem which, worked by the formula, "gave an almost impossible answer nevertheless I wrote it down." Fankle, encountering the same problem in another section, "thought the formula answer so unreasonable that he worked it another way and I was right." (9/4/43) Jim had bested me by 52 points on our first test. On the test just cited, the gap had been reduced to four.

At term's end I was grateful to get a low C for a course that just as easily could have been a D. I have always believed the instructor appreciated dedicated effort enough to give me the benefit of what had to be doubt. A solid C in Physics, a shaky C in Chemistry, and a solid B in Algebra-Trigonometry (the trig kept me from an A) meant that I could remain at UNH for a second term.

Physical education instructors and coaches had to be pleased with the influx of soldier-students. The dearth of male civilians threatened to make their continued presence on campus unnecessary. Suddenly they had plenty of bodies available for all sorts of classes.

At least three afternoons a week my section marched beyond the academic buildings, through the B & M underpass, to the gymnasium where we had lockers, and then to the spacious area adjacent to the football field. There the physical education staff enthusiastically took over, and we engaged in a variety of exercises along with some self-defense training. Sometimes, to my considerable satisfaction, we divided into teams and played softball. One of the instructors was a brother to my mathematics professor (a twin, I believe) and another had been on the United States Olympic team in the 1920's.

A few times we were taken to the swimming pool. Around Lock Springs the only place with enough water for swimming was the Grand River. But it was uninviting in appearances and I feared it, especially after a friend of my parents drowned in an attempt to save a boy in a stretch of the river near Chillicothe. Along with a half dozen or so other non-swimmers, I was taken to the shallow end of the pool in a futile attempt to teach me to swim.

War had forced UNH to abandon inter-collegiate athletics. Now, to the obvious delight of the football coaches, there was material for the resurrection of their

Wildcat team. Many of the ASTP boys had played high school football and a few had been good enough to draw college scholarship offers. A sufficient number of these fellows loved the game enough to put in the extra hours needed to field a team.

During the second term, they played a limited schedule of five or six games with service teams and college teams from the Boston area. All games had to be played in our stadium, on Saturday, and begin no earlier than mid-afternoon. At that, and with the game underway, it was not uncommon to see a player come running on to the field just having completed some lab work and hurried to get into uniform.

The team was really quite good and, as I recall, won all its games. Even I, seeing my first ever football games, could appreciate that one of our half-backs was, as my more knowledgeable friends informed me, of star quality.

We took our meals in the dining room of Murkland Hall near Hetzel. The university had its own farm and dairy, and it was a real treat to have pitchers of milk brought to the table. In addition to the milk, I have good memories of one other treat. With the onset of cooler weather, our regular Saturday night fare was baked beans and brown bread, said to be a New England specialty. We were spared the duties normally demanded of privates, such as K.P., and to make our eating experience even more pleasant, the serving line was staffed by young women.

When we arrived at UNH, the campus population consisted of several hundred women and only a scattering of males, mostly 4-F in selective service classification, I guessed. It appeared the president had some reservations about letting loose a bunch of soldiers on his campus. In welcoming us, he made it abundantly clear that he expected respect for the womanhood of New Hampshire. There was no prohibition against dating, however, and a few fellows did spend time (as reflected in their grades) hanging around the women's dorms. Under other circumstances one cute woman in the dining hall could have had some of my time, but my priorities were firmly fixed with no space for socializing.

Frank and I attended Sunday morning service at the little white church rather regularly, as did a small number of other soldiers. The minister and ushers made me feel welcome and comfortable with the Congregational service. While a few members of the congregation spoke to us, my overall impression was that small town New Englanders were a reserved lot. Perhaps this was an unfair characterization on my part, for my shyness kept me from making any overtures to them.

One early experience showed, to my surprise, that terminology common to other parts of the country could be different in New England, in New Hampshire anyway. Going into Durham's small eating place, Frank asked the girl behind the counter what kind of "pop" they had. I assumed that this term for a bottled soft drink (no aluminum cans in those days) was known everywhere. But she stared at Frank with a blank look. After he started to elaborate, her face brightened and she exclaimed, "Oh, you mean a tonic!" And in much later years, I discovered that "soda" was the operative word in southeast Missouri.

My ASTP service provided me with a limited acquaintance with a racial minority as well as contact with a different religious-cultural group. Coming from a border state with a long history of prejudice and discrimination, I was surprised to find two Negroes in the program residing in Hetzel Hall. It was interesting to see that my two roommates from the East did not seem to find it that surprising. The overwhelming majority of my acquaintances at UNH were from Northern, Eastern, and New England states and their generally casual acceptance of Negroes was a new and revealing experience to me. Obviously some of them had already been part of integrated classrooms and athletic teams.

In this more enlightened environment my own perceptions began to change. Soon I realized these men were intelligent and likable fellow students. I sometimes wondered how they must have felt surrounded as they were by a sea of white faces. Whatever their inner feelings may have been, outwardly they appeared to fit comfortably into the group. In addition to being a good student, one of them,

Howard Mitchell, possessed outstanding athletic ability. Word filtered through the hall that the he had been a high school teammate of Tom Harmon, the great college football player of the day. Whether true or not, Mitchell was good in his own right and unquestionably the star of the Wildcat team. Also, he was good on the basketball court and it was a pleasure to play with him in pickup games. Knowing both these men was certainly a rewarding and growing experience for me.

On the other hand my first real contact with Jews was less pleasant with a regressive effect upon my attitudes. And just as the positive approach by others helped me overcome bias toward Negroes, a negative attitude by some around me reinforced a prejudice I found myself developing toward Jews. The number of them in my section was small, but pushiness and smart mouth talk made it seem larger. During the first week of our math class, I developed an immediate dislike for a big fellow who set out to see how far he could push rudeness to the instructor. His small following of fellow Jews may have found it amusing, but the rest of us considered his boorish behavior unacceptable. The professor, I was glad to see, made it clear that there would be no more of that behavior. Nor was there, but Abe found other ways to be obnoxious.

No question about it though, they were good students and made top grades in most courses throughout all class sections. Where I struggled to survive in our physics section, they always made top grades. Some of my acquaintances, who disliked them anyway, were sure they had figured out some way to communicate test information from one section to another. I was never certain they could do this or that it was needed. To those Jews in my physics section, I was a non-entity to be ignored. It should be understood that small mindedness arising from this slight was never my incentive to succeed at UNH. Nonetheless it was immensely satisfying when finally, in third term physics, I pulled even with the best of them and on one or two occasions beat them all.

Fortunately I later had an opportunity to see my attitude toward Jews in a more enlightened perspective. In combat I had a good man for a platoon leader, good as a leader and as a man, an officer who also happened to be Jewish. In knowing him, I began to appreciate that one should resist the temptation to judge an entire cultural group by the obnoxious behavior of individuals, for they are just that—obnoxious individuals, period.

During the third week of classes, representatives of the United States Military Academy sifted through our records seeking potential candidates for West Point. It was gratifying to learn that my score on the army tests exceeded the minimum of 135 they sought, but then it turned out that my birth date put me nearly one month beyond the upper age limit. As I explained in a letter to my parents, of the "few boys" otherwise eligible and given the physical exam, only one passed and he failed to meet the minimum height requirement. I knew it would have been pointless for me to take the physical anyway but, I wrote, "it's nice to know that you almost had a chance." (7/29/43)

About this same time I learned of the death of one of my father's younger sisters. Aunt Gladys McIntire left three young children, the oldest no more than ten. I felt sadness for all of them and a surge of homesickness. Except for those of us in military service, all of the large Breeze family got together for the funeral. This was one of those times I really felt the confining nature of army service.

At the end of the ninth week of the term, I got to Boston for a Saturday night and most of Sunday. My roommates and I felt the need for a more expansive break from hard study than a quick movie at the Franklin. One of the Jims professed a taste for Chinese food so we sought out a recommended restaurant. It was a new and interesting experience, but for my taste hardly worth repeating.

On Sunday we saw more of Boston's narrow and crooked streets and some historical spots, including a view of Bunker Hill. In thinking ahead to term's end, we located the other rail station and checked time tables. Schedules looked good, though tight in some cases, to New Jersey, Pittsburgh, and St. Louis, but unfortunately for Frank, not good to Texas.

Army regulations allowed ASTP students one week off between terms. With the first term ending October 2 and our needing to be back on the evening of the 10th, the right rail connections and a lot of hard riding could give me at least three days at home. I considered this well worth the effort and the train fare. Considering the many changes in my life, it seemed like a lifetime ago that I had reported for service. However brief the visit might be, I was ready to go home.

Burkhardt was eager to visit his family in New Jersey. Fankle, who had married just before entering the service, was anxious to see his wife in Pittsburgh. Unable to make it home, Frank, planned to visit a friend who had recently moved to Columbus, Ohio.

On Saturday afternoon the good old B & M carried several coach loads of happily liberated student-soldiers to Boston. There the four of us joined the lively competition for a taxi to the other station.

Unlike my earlier travel which came at army expense, this time I had to make my own arrangements, stand in line for a ticket, stand in a long line of passengers waiting to board, scramble to find an empty coach seat, and then hope to get some sleep while sitting up. The waiting and scrambling was twice repeated on the long trip to St. Louis, as I made changes at Albany, New York, and Cleveland, Ohio. Once settled a soldier could be expected to be disturbed by MP's on the prowl for anyone without proper papers authorizing him to be on the loose.

After a tiring trip I arrived in Chillicothe by mid-afternoon. Then, with impossible telephone connections, came the problem of getting out to the farm. An apologetic taxi driver explained that due to rationing and restrictions, he could get me no closer than a mile or two to home. I do not believe he appreciated that this was not even a good hike to a soldier, especially one anxious to get home.

Not knowing when, where, or even if, she could expect me, my mother was overjoyed when I walked into the yard. She quickly called my dad from work and the only missing ingredient in a joyous reunion was my little dog. It was comfortably satisfying to eat my mother's cooking, sleep in my own bed, spend time with my father, and reconnect with the farm. My parents were very pleased and obviously proud that I would be returning for a second term of school.

But in worrying less about the immediacy of the war for me, my mother appeared to worry more about others. She seemed especially concerned about one fellow, whose parents had learned was going overseas. In discussing it, I realized he was in a unit that would never be near a combat zone. I tried to explain that for every one person at the front, the army had fifteen or more behind him in support services, many of them far removed from any serious danger. This generalized attempt did little to reassure her, and in reckless exasperation I said something I would come to regret: "Now if he were in the infantry, you would have real cause for worry. Infantrymen are the ones who see war close up. As it is, he is safe as wheat in the bin."

Back in Durham, I approached the term with greater confidence. The schedule was as difficult as ever, but chemistry came easier and I moved into a solid B range in physics. Analytic geometry proved very demanding and solid analytic during the last part of the term made me thankful for a B at the end. Geography became a favorite course as the professor worked the war in Europe, especially the movement of Russian and German armies, into our study of political geography.

Military science instructors issued us field manuals to study. Letters home revealed that precious time needed to study for an academic test (analytic geometry in a specific case) had to be shared with military science. At the time this made some sense but proved a terrible waste of time in retrospect. Subsequent to the dissolution of the ASTP, some of us I know (and all of us I suspect) were treated as though we left the program knowing nothing of military matters.

The physical education staff encouraged interested people to engage in a sport at the end of the class day. Around two dozen of us expressed great interest in basketball and we formed teams. As a member of one of these I found it a most satisfying, even therapeutic, way to spend the interlude between the end of classes and the required study time in the evening.

By mid-November we had our first snow which at that point in the season soon became slush. We were equipped with overshoes, a heavy overcoat, and blessed with a steam heated dorm room, so a cold winter held no terror. It becomes a dark comedy when my winter of 1943-1944 is juxtaposed with that of 1944-45. In the latter, I faced a German winter without benefit of either overshoes or overcoat, and with leaky combat boots and uncertain shelter.

My second Christmas away from home was spent in Durham. Since Christmas fell on a Saturday, classes were dismissed for Friday and Saturday. This gave Burkhardt and Fankle time for a quick visit home. In fact, Frank and I were among the few people left in Hetzel, for most everyone else was able to get home. I had packages of goodies from home and St. Louis. Christmas morning, in a striking departure from my younger years, I slept until ten. Frank spent much of the day waiting for an open telephone line to get through to his family.

Completion of the second term coincided with the end of the year. My chances for a trip home diminished when I learned that the army planned to reduce our time off by one day. Reluctantly I prepared my parents for possible disappointment. "That's the only thing I regret about being in the army. It's so hard on you. Sometimes I think they should send us all across and get this war over with without fooling around so much," I wrote, "but then again I'm thankful I've never been sent across and that I'm getting a good education." (12/8/43)

Then just when it appeared I might be able to manage as much as three days at home after all, my hopes were dimmed by a looming railway strike. No matter what the issue, I considered it outrageous to strike during a war when so much was at stake and so many men had been called to military service. My view at the time may have been colored by a personal stake, but fifty-five years later, and though generally sympathetic to labor, I still stand by my 1943 statement:

> If they strike, I say it is a mighty low thing for them to do and still lower for the government to allow it. I hope they send troops out to put the fools back to work and I would certainly

like to be in on it. We should stick a bayonet in the seat of their pants and tell them to get on board and get moving. Maybe I'm a little rabid but it certainly burns me up to think that tonight boys are being shot at (a matter of their lives) while these birds have the gall to ask for something more when they are being paid good and can do what they please. (12/20/43)

The strike was averted. The trains did run and, making good connections (but only minutes to spare a couple of times), I spent three days at home. Poor Frank, of course, still could not get home. He stayed behind and, as I recall, went to Boston later in the week. Probably the most exciting part of the trip took place at the outset. Tired of sometimes losing in the competition for taxis at Boston's B & M station, Fankle got the idea of going to South Berwick, Maine, and claiming a choice spot on the train. This we were able to do. When the train stopped at Durham and a horde of soldiers scrambled aboard, they found Fankle positioned to be first off at Boston. There, the moment the conductor released him he was off in a flash, leaving us to bring his bag. Burkhardt and I emerged to find he had successfully commandeered the first taxi in line.

The driver entered into the spirit of our need for haste with more enthusiasm than caution. A car traveling in front of us stopped suddenly and before our driver could hit the brakes, the bumpers of the two cars had locked. Both bumpers were of the sturdy sort common to that era, so there was no obvious sign of damage to either. But there we were, locked in place with two irate drivers. Finally the three of us were able to lift the taxi sufficiently for the other fellow to drive off, still muttering about our driver. And we caught our trains.

Arriving back in Durham at the end of the first week in the new year (1944), I found even more snow (at least a foot) than I had left in Missouri. My letter reporting safe arrival reminds me that as much as I enjoyed train riding, I always looked forward to washing off the accumulated coal dust. And the smell from a coal burning engine had a special affinity for woolen uniforms. This had to make Durham's dry cleaner a happy man.

As most of us checked out new textbooks and readied for the third term, a few men were shipped out to military units. Under other circumstances I might have envied one I knew, for he was going to Camp Crowder, Missouri. But these men were leaving because of failing grades.

Engineering drawing replaced chemistry on my new schedule. I continued with physics and in mathematics moved on to calculus, getting a textbook that initially was "all Greek" to me. And I continued with English, history and geography, I plunged into the new term with my usual effort but with greater confidence. At the end, I was rewarded with A's in both physics and calculus, and B's in everything else, all in all a very satisfactory way to complete the program in basic engineering.

During the course of the term, I began to understand that I really could become a civil engineer. It was a tremendously uplifting feeling. My good feeling, pride of accomplishment, and confidence in greater things to come were enhanced greatly by a meeting with the dean of the engineering school. In expressing satisfaction with my progress, he complimented me on overcoming obvious handicaps that could have terminated me at the end of the first term.

One of my third term classmates was especially helpful with calculus. Christian J. Gabriel was among the best of several friends I made at the university. From New York (the City, I believe, but I lost his address long ago), he could be described as a whiz in math. A resident of our part of Hetzel Hall, he was a frequent visitor to our room and well-liked by my roommates. Sometimes the two of us studied together. He helped me with calculus and on occasion I could help him with physics. In some of our idle moments we fantasized about being civil engineers in a post war world, going to far off places, perhaps South America, to build bridges.

Members of the ASTP may have been soldiers, but that did not preclude student pranks in the dormitory. Short sheeting a bed was a favorite trick. The army cuff of the top sheet made for easy deception and much fun in watching a victim vainly endeavor to get between his sheets. One learned to inspect before jumping into bed, especially when we all had been out of the room for a while.

More painful was to get caught in the shower when some pranksters flushed all stools simultaneously. I circumvented this by sneaking off to shower on another floor. Uncomfortable too was the "hotfoot." The ease with which a match could be thrust between upper and sole of an army boot made this an irresistible temptation to some fellows. In a classroom one day some of us watched in fascination as one practitioner went to great lengths to administer a hot foot.

On at least one occasion we found water running across our floor. Someone had tipped a bucket just outside our door. This was an acceptable prank, but the night we discovered someone had poured lighter fluid under our door and dropped a match went beyond fun. We warned the suspect (an unlikable pest anyway) that it better not happen again.

Many years later Frank recalled, with great glee, the good timing of the four of us in the corner room. We started some of the water fights then prudently withdrew, leaving late entrants to be caught by the prowling lieutenant or one of his staff.

Just as I had begun to look forward to the advanced engineering program, I began to hear disturbing rumors that it was all coming to an end. Rumor had it that for us the ASTP would terminate with the completion of basic engineering, that is a third of the way toward a degree. We fervently hoped it was like many rumors that swept through the army—without foundation. In this case it was true, and we got the bad news about four weeks before the end of the term. One of my classmates was able to transfer to the medical part of the program (going to Harvard, I believe), but for the rest of us, it was back to active service.

In early March the first sergeant read an order coming from university officials to the effect that we would receive full college credit for all work completed. That was sufficient incentive to work hard through the end of the term.

Later that same week, we had individual interviews with a professor and a first lieutenant. "They had all my grades and service record before them. They both commented on my grades. The civilian marveled that I had no college and only a little math in high school and yet made good grades." (3/7/44) He congratulated me on my record, and the officer asked about my future military interests. I wanted to return to the field artillery, I told him, and work in fire control. My work in mathematics, I explained, gave me advantages in plotting fire charts for the howitzers. He agreed and promised to "give me a recommendation and thought I had a pretty good chance."

We completed our courses and took our last tests on Saturday, March 25. On Sunday Frank and I attended church, and as I sat there I "thought this was probably the last time I'd ever be in the little church. Soon I'll be attending a nice little army chapel. Where that will be, well ?????" (3/26/44) In this same letter I gave my parents a good evaluation of my experience at UNH:

> I can say I've spent a pretty nice 9 months here in Durham. It really doesn't seem like I've been here long now that I'm ready to leave. It seems like only a short while ago that we came up here. It certainly looked lovely then with everything so nice and green.
>
> I remember we went to a few review classes in algebra then they issued us books and we started work in earnest. I looked inside the physics and chemistry books and almost gave up the fight before I began. It all looked so tough and bewildering to me . . . . [Jim Fanklel told me I would have a pretty tough time.] So I started to work. I kept writing you that I couldn't possibly make it, that I just didn't have the background. At the same time I had that inner most hunch of mine that somehow I couldn't flunk out. God seemed to tell me he'd help me and I'd get along. Nevertheless, I had to prepare you for the worst in case I did fail. I didn't want you to be built up too high so I wrote those discouraging letters to you. The law of reason would say I shouldn't have made it through that I should have left the first term or at least that I shouldn't end up the last term by being among the top students. I'm the kind of person I guess that defies the law of reason for back in July when my roommates talked discouraging to me I thought of that little book Gene Mansfield [my high school social studies teacher] gave me, "I Dare You." I thereby determined that somehow I'd come through. To live peacefully with myself I had to, and with the good help of God I came through. I've studied pretty hard especially these last three months but I feel it's worth it. It's a

mighty comforting feeling to know you have a little college education. (3/26/44)

By a quirk of fate I did not get to return to the field of engineering after the war. Attending a small liberal arts college, I changed direction and majored in history, with the ultimate goal of a doctorate and a career in college teaching. But I retained a life long admiration for the work of civil engineers, with a special attachment to those in Victorian Britain, the area of my specialization in history. And I always have kept a warm spot in my heart for the University of New Hampshire, the institution that gave me an opportunity to prove my worth as a college student.

Near the end of the last week in March, 1944, the ASTP unit marched back down the street we had come up in July, 1943. Then we wondered about the academic program confronting us. Now, we wondered what camp was to be our destination and what kind of army units it contained. With a mixture of sadness at leaving and apprehension for the future, I began my last ride on the Boston and Maine.

Chapter Six

Camp Pickett:
903 Field Artillery Battalion

When we changed trains in Boston, I understood immediately how far I had dropped in the army's world. Waiting to take me to my as yet undisclosed assignment was a genuine troop train. There would be no Pullman coach as we rode to Camp Beale or compartment car as to CCNY. Instead, we were herded into a car with a tier of cot-like bunks along the side. And in place of a railway dining car, we would eat from an army mess car.

In Boston we joined the ASTP unit from Boston University. In addition I am sure there were men from other New England universities. Quite possibly we added more unfortunates in New York, for by the time we reached our destination there were a lot of us.

Unlike my previous railroad journeys courtesy of the army, this left me with no lasting memories of new scenery or impressive sights. Frank Galloway remembers we passed through Washington, D. C., for it was his only opportunity ever to catch a glimpse of the Pentagon.

Sometime during our second night out and somewhere in Virginia the train stopped. Getting off, it did not help my morale to learn that my new army home carried the name associated with a fatal charge at the battle of Gettysburg, Pickett. It seemed an ominous beginning.

We were met by soldiers wearing a shoulder patch I had never seen before, a half circle in red with a lightning bolt of white running through it. It signified, they told us with a pride that later I came to share, the 78th Infantry Division. The "Lightning" Division, as it was known, had a distinguished past. In World War I it had earned battle streamers in three hard-fought campaigns: St. Mihiel, Lorraine, and Meuse-Argonne.

Reactivated in the summer of 1942 at Camp Butner, North Carolina, under the command of Major General Edwin P. Parker, Jr., the division had trained between 40,000 and 50,000 replacement troops. These men were serving in both major theaters of war. Several months before I joined it, the division began training for combat duty. From January to the end of March, 1944, it had maneuvered in Tennessee with at least three other divisions. Conditions of terrain and the elements of rain, mud and cold provided a foretaste of what the division would encounter in real battle near the end of the year. It was excellent training for the division's ultimate mission. Both officers and men fully expected upon completion of maneuvers to prepare for departure to a combat area.

But the army can generally be counted upon to do the unpredictable and sometimes the illogical. This was to be a case in point. With casualties expected to be enormous in the forthcoming invasion of Western Europe, men in high places decided that filling the holes in D-Day divisions with replacements would be more advantageous than inserting a new division into battle. These high-level thinkers were willing to write off the ASTP as a loss and use bodies gained thereby to restock plundered divisions, such as the 78th was about to become.

Late in March, 1944, men of the 78th learned that upon completion of maneuvers they would not be going overseas together as a combat unit. Instead, the division would lose most of its privates and privates first class as replacements. This was particularly applicable to the three infantry regiments. But to a lesser degree all other units were affected, especially the four battalions of artillery. The division's remaining elements, consisting mainly of officers and non-coms in many units, would move to Camp Pickett, Virginia. To replace its losses the division would receive hundreds of ASTP soldiers along with many former Air Corps cadets, fliers as well as engineers no longer deemed a critical need. Later, when I learned more about this background, I better understood why our reception at Camp

Pickett matched the chill of the early spring air. Understanding, however, has never lessened my resentment of treatment received from some quarters, and from one non-com in particular.

In any major move the army always sent out an advance party to prepare the way for a main body to follow. Such arrangements had been made for the 78th's move to Pickett. In a touch of irony many units of the division, muddy, weary, and not especially high in morale, arrived at their new home on the same date that some of us arrived from ASTP, April 1! It was a cruel joke on all of us.

We were sorted out to be sent to our assigned units. In the process I was separated from my roommates as well as others I had known at UNH. By now I had come to accept that separation from friends was part of the army way. Upon learning that I was to go to the 903rd Field Artillery Battalion, my spirits improved considerably. They rose higher when the battalion assigned me to Headquarters Battery. Since that battery contained the fire direction center, it appeared the lieutenant at Durham had made good on his promise. It was just as well on that April first day that I did not know my eventual fate lay in the hands of a man of less character and intelligence than the lieutenant.

Meanwhile, I prepared to settle into the barracks. While there were a few other ASTP men, many of the men in the barracks had been with the division for a while. Most of the privates and privates first class among them were to leave on furlough the next day prior to being sent on as replacements.

Before I could make my bed, I got a rude jolt. Clearly some people in authority did not consider the ASTP additions as real soldiers. Someone, most likely the battery's first sergeant, had ordered one of the non-coms to "teach" us how to make a bed army style. Since I had been making a bed army style for at least sixteen months, and my efforts had always satisfied the critical eyes of inspecting officers, I took this as a deliberate insult.

Early the next morning I witnessed a most unpleasant side of the battery. From the early days at Leavenworth through the final days at Durham, I had been accustomed to seeing men hurry through morning preparations to make roll call. But I had never seen anything quite like the unfolding spectacle of that morning. All the older hands scurried as though their lives depended upon it. Then came a piercing whistle and men jostled each other to get out the doors, some practically falling down the front steps in their frantic haste. On the street we lined up at attention before a mean looking first sergeant with a whistle protruding from his mouth. He repeated blast after blast upon it, managing all the while to inflict an even angrier tone. Once we were all in place, he removed the whistle and berated us for not hurrying.

The other batteries, lining up on the street with more military dignity, were treated to this ridiculous exhibition on our part nearly every work day. Even though we departed the barracks as though flames were lapping behind us, we seldom satisfied him. This man who induced such a Pavlovian response in his unfortunate men caused me to hate the sound of any military whistle. Never did I see a man more obsessed by the power of his whistle, and never did I see so many men with repressed desires to thrust that whistle into the most appropriate part of his anatomy.

The sergeant was regular army. Later, in the 311th Infantry Regiment, I would meet another ranking non-com who was regular army. No doubt there were others scattered throughout the division. Joining the army during the hard times of the 1930's, they had several years service by the time the U. S. went to war. The war opened an opportunity for advancement that otherwise never would have been available to many of these career men. They became training cadre for the transformation of a few million civilians into citizen soldiers. On the whole, I believe they must have done a satisfactory job in this mission. My limited experience in combat with the one from the 311th, however, exposed a man out of his element, a man who should have been left as a private down in the ranks with the rest of us. Hopefully the first sergeant of Headquarters Battery proved a much more capable leader in combat. Another non-com, not regular army, who went through combat with him, recently described him as "a good 1st sergeant but," he added, "not many of the guys liked him."

It was readily apparent that the sergeant had no liking for his ASTP replacements. Perhaps his attitude covered a feeling of inadequacy as we served to remind him of his own limited education. Possibly there was resentment, even envy, that the army had chosen us for something unavailable to soldiers who had not scored well on the army tests. Maybe he remembered the misery of maneuvers coinciding with a time when we were sleeping in warm, dry quarters and eating hot meals. For whatever reason, he displayed a kind of mean-spirited satisfaction in finding lowly tasks for the "college boys," as he called us with a sneer. When calling us out as "volunteers" for some unappealing assignment, he could make "college boys" sound as though he had stepped into something unpleasant. Although we might be useful in absorbing a lot of his ill will, our presence did not always shield others of low rank. I recall a few non-ASTP privates and pfcs. who were made to feel his displeasure.

I did not take long to settle into the routine of life in an army camp. Of course I had to adjust to living in barracks with dozens of men in place of a dormitory room for four. It was back to K.P. and guard duty. We were put through a refresher course that amounted to basic training all over again: close order drill, hikes, classes, weapons training, firing range, bivouacs and the works. It was good to become reacquainted with the 105 mm. howitzer. Unlike those of the armored field artillery, these were towed weapons. Emplacement required some heavy lifting by men in the firing batteries.

Before long I could count several men in Headquarters Battery as good friends. Among these were a few holdover privates and pfcs. who had been with the unit a while and a fellow ASTP refugee, in his case from the language school at Princeton. Most interesting in some respects was my friendship with the supply sergeant, liked and respected by all, and his assistant, a graduate of Notre Dame as I recall. It pleased me that they accepted me and seemed to like my company.

Frank had taken artillery basic at Camp Roberts, California, and I was glad to find him assigned to an artillery battalion at Pickett. Jim Fankle, who had been in my battalion at Beale, also got back to the artillery. Although in different battalions, we were all located in the same area of camp and could get together on off-duty hours. We finally found Jim Burkhardt in a rifle company with the 311th Infantry Regiment.

But the army did not leave us all together for long. Within three weeks of our arrival, Frank had been shipped out to Camp McCoy, Wisconsin. This development came as a nasty surprise to him and a great disappointment to me. I hated to see him go, but at the time I naively thought he might find some good in it. Since he had gone to the engineers, I assumed it must be because of his ASTP background. Perhaps in his case the army intended to take advantage of the expensive education the tax payers had provided.

When Frank and I got together again many years later, I learned how wrong my assumption had been. There had been no logical reason, not that the army ever acted from logic, in plucking him from the artillery and sending him to the engineers. He and the other ASTP men in his new outfit were treated rather scornfully as the "school boys", and no attempt was made to utilize their education. Mainly they were expected to carry their share of a heavy panel for a Bailey bridge. As a combat engineer in Belgium and Germany he got plenty of exercise with that but no opportunity to use what he had learned in basic engineering.

Two good things happened about the time I completed the refresher in basic training. First, the battery commander returned the stripe I had given up to attend UNH. It was a far cry from the gold bar of my dreams, but realistically I knew I was probably fortunate to get this. At this point the first sergeant did not yet dislike me enough to stand in the way of my becoming a pfc.

Secondly, I received my first real furlough. Catching the Norfolk and Western at the nearby town of Blackstone, I rode westward through Roanoke and across the Appalachians to Cincinnati. There I got a look at the Ohio River and changed to a train for St. Louis, then one right to Lock Springs.

Me with my parents, Clara and Dan Breeze.
First furlough, October 1943.

Rather than the quick turn around of previous visits, this time I could relax and enjoy being home for several days. Learning that I would have a delay in St. Louis upon the return, I arranged to visit some of the relatives there. The stop at St. Louis helped cushion the letdown of the return to camp.

At roll call on the morning of June 6, 1944, our captain announced that a few hours earlier Anglo-American forces had landed on the Normandy coast of France. This momentous news filled me with hope that we had reached a turning point in the war. Possibly it would loosen the Nazi grip on Western Europe and we could all go on to defeat Hitler's Germany. At the same time I was filled with dread for the men of the invading force. I could not visualize any as specific individuals with faces known to me but only as a composite of soldiers I had known who were already overseas and might be involved. I could not even begin to imagine the horrible reality of what they were facing. I was certain, however, that it would be the nearest thing to hell on earth they could ever experience. This saddened me and I feared for them.

Those early days we spent a lot of off-duty hours listening anxiously to radio reports. We studied newspaper maps of the area and while our forces appeared to have gained a foothold, their boundaries moved away from the coast with agonizing slowness.

Some time later a letter from home put a face to one of the early victims. An older brother of one of the girls in my high school class had been killed on June 10. Bill Lollar and I had worked together on a bridge repair project sometime before he entered service. "We have to suffer some casualties," I wrote later to my family, "but you realize it more when it's a boy you know like that." (8/1/44) The small, close knit community of Lock Springs, already grieving for a flyer lost in a bombing mission somewhere over southeastern Europe and never found, had another reason to grieve. There would be at least two more reasons for sorrow before it was all over.

Both Fankle and Burkhardt got furloughs sometime after I returned from mine. I half expected that Jim B. would come back a married man. But while his girl friend wanted to get married right away, he thought it best to wait until the end of the war. Since service in an infantry regiment posed a high risk of not returning at all, I thought he did the prudent thing. In visiting him in the 311th I found two other good ASTP friends. They had just returned from furlough that afternoon "so their morale needed building up somewhat." (6/25/44)

Camp Pickett was located approximately fifty miles southwest of Richmond. Even though bus service there was reportedly bad, I wanted to see this historic city. Letters home reveal that at least on two occasions I applied for a weekend pass there. Both times I got K.P. instead. In retrospect I suspect this may been deliberate on the part of the first sergeant.

With high hopes of being able to do something that mattered a great deal to me, I had been glad to join Headquarters Battery of the 903rd. In a pre-computer age and before hand-held calculators, a soldier who had some knowledge of certain principles of physics and considerable skill in mathematical computations could be a valuable addition to an artillery fire direction center. In such a role, I firmly believed I could contribute my greatest service as a soldier. From my perspective, the lieutenant at UNH had done well by me and the army had gotten things right for a change. I could not foresee that the ignorance of a sergeant, prejudiced against a "college boy" in such a responsible position, and the indifference of his commanding officer toward his actions would stand in my way as unmovable obstacles.

As part of our basic training many of us were given an introduction to the fire direction center and attended classes in its operation. I enjoyed the challenge of the problems presented, caught on quickly and seemed to impress the instructors, both officer and non-com, with my competence. Thus in the beginning I had cause for optimism. Surely I would be assigned to service with the center.

As the weeks wore on, however, it became increasingly clear that for some reason the first sergeant did not intend to allow me to do more than attend an occasional fire direction class. When we went out on field problems and bivouac, I was never allowed to work with the center in assisting the firing batteries. The sergeant always managed to find something else for me to do. The opportunity to employ my education and ability for a useful purpose with the center was to be wasted.

At an early age I developed an antipathy for waste of any kind. Part of this comes from growing up during the Depression when it was essential to save anything that might be useful. For example, I learned from my dad to save bent nails and straighten them for re-use. Part of it came from family background. I never knew my grandfather Griner, but I know he impressed upon my mother that one never wasted anything. I did know Grandpa Breeze, and he set the same kind of example for his family.

With this background I was appalled at the waste found in the army. At that, it was nothing like the horror stories of post-World War II procurement policies effected after the military-industrial complex, warned against by my wartime commander after he became president, assumed a prominent role in American life. Still, it was often conspicuous enough to bother me.

To be denied an opportunity to serve where I could be most useful was a personal disappointment and remained a sore point. But more than that, it meant a waste of taxpayer money that sent me to UNH. In the post-war period, my work at UNH helped me earn a bachelor's degree in a little over two years, but the experience was wasted as far as the army gaining anything from it. In fact, it deprived the army of active service from me, most probably in armored field artillery, for more than nine months.

The 13th Armored's requirement that nearly all its personnel learn to drive came back to haunt me. Looking in my file, the first sergeant ignored those factors that qualified me for the fire direction center and latched upon the fact that I was licensed to drive a number of army vehicles. I do not want to underestimate the importance of those who drove for the army. I respected their skill and appreciated their role. But I did not consider myself a skillful driver and wanted to do something more suited to my abilities. I could drive in a pinch and that is all the armored field artillery had expected of me.

The first sergeant seemed determined, however, to assign me to driving. On a field exercise I might be sent to drive a jeep for an officer. Other times I drove trucks of different sizes on a variety of assignments. In each case I tried to give a satisfactory performance, but it must have been obvious that I was not enthusiastic about the assignments.

The climax came during the last week of June. Driving one of the light trucks, I was the last driver to reach the motor pool. All vehicles had to be parked in lines as orderly as ranks of soldiers on review. Standing there waiting for me to park was the sergeant and part of the battery. Aware of his menacing gaze I swung into line and realized immediately that the alignment was less than perfect. Reversing, and with the sergeant thundering at me, I tried again with no better result. He ordered me out of the truck and proceeded to chew me out before my battery mates, some of whom I learned later were cringing for me. In his suspicious mind, no doubt, I had messed up deliberately in an effort to get a different assignment.

A day or two later the sergeant called me in and ordered me to report to a bugle training class at division headquarters. Perhaps he guessed I lacked ability here and he could find satisfaction in my failure; or perhaps he knew that, if successful, I would become a candidate for the battery's most disliked man. Reluctantly, and burdened with the depressing knowledge that I had absolutely no musical ability, I reported to the class. Although it appeared that the class was comprised mostly of unwilling conscripts, it gradually emerged that several showed some sign of promise. On the other hand the unfortunate instructor spent much time trying to help a few of us simply to get a sound from the instrument. At the end of the day, I could not even produce a promising squawk from it. With a discouraging feeling that this was beyond my ability, I tried again the next day without noticeable success. Unquestionably I was a hopeless case and the instructor said as much when he asked the battery not to send me back. The notion that I of all people, clueless about music and not even able to sing, could become a bugler had been a cruel joke from the start.

The sergeant dropped the ax on my head the following Sunday. Ordered to pack all my gear and report to the orderly room, I joined five other dispirited individuals. The six of us, complete with gear and accompanied by the appropriate papers, were loaded into a truck and delivered to the 311th Infantry Regiment. My banishment from the field artillery occurred on July 2, 1944. As I reflected on it later, I realized it must have given the sergeant fiendish pleasure to send me to the infantry.

In late July, 1997, I received a telephone call from a man identifying himself as Harry Whitman. This meant nothing to me until he explained that he had been the older man (early 30's at the time) among the six unhappy exiles on that dismal day 53 years earlier. Finding my name and number in the membership directory of the division's association, he had called to renew acquaintance. I was grateful for the phone call from Whitman, not only as a voice from the past, but as someone who confirmed my belief that the sergeant really was "out to get me!" "He thought you were a smart college boy," said Whitman who remembered me as one of the sergeant's targets; I was not paranoid!

The first sergeant got us transferred, Whitman said, because he considered us "foul-ups". I had long since forgotten, but I may have been the only ASTP man in the group. Whitman's own case was interesting. He had been with the 903rd before I joined it. Obviously he had not incurred the sergeant's deep displeasure until sometime after April 1, or he would have been sent out with that bunch of transfers. When an influential officer in the 311th learned of Whitman's experience in artillery and long time service in the 903rd, he said in effect: "You do not belong in the infantry," and sent him back to the battery we had come from! Since Whitman had long established friendships there, he was glad to return. I gathered he got a kick out of this further annoyance for the sergeant. For me the only good thing about it all was that with any luck, I would never see that sergeant again.

Chapter Seven

Camp Pickett: 311th Infantry Regiment

Known as the Timberwolf Regiment with the motto of *Jamais Trop Tard,* Never Too Late, the 311th was one of the division's three infantry regiments, the others being the 309th and 310th. Commanded by a colonel, a regiment consisted of three battalions each led by a lieutenant colonel and made up of three rifle companies and a heavy weapons company. In addition a regiment included an anti-tank company, a cannon company, a service company, a headquarters company, and a medical detachment. When fully staffed, the 311th contained a little over 3200 officers and men.

In the long run I became very proud to be a part of the 311th, but initially I went to it with considerable uneasiness. Fully aware that once in combat members of the regiment would be exposed to many dangerous situations, I wondered if I could measure up to this. I do not mean to minimize the dangers in other units of an infantry division. Reconnaissance, signals, engineers, artillery and others were often at great risk. Artillery, for instance, dreaded the possibility of counter battery fire from the enemy's artillery. And a few artillerymen had to go forward with the infantry as observers to send back information for fire direction.

On one such occasion I saw a forward observer wounded and recognized him as an officer associated with some of my fire direction classes in the 903rd. But while it would be hard to find a safe unit in an infantry division, the lot of the infantry regiment was always hazardous. My greatest source of anxiety in exchanging the red braid of the artillery for the beautiful blue of the infantry had come from my own careless tongue. In a lifetime one utters many words that upon reflection should have remained unspoken. At the top of my list is the foolish attempt to allay my mother's worries by focusing upon the infantry as the greatest source of danger. My words came back to worry me in July, 1944, and in a few months they would haunt me. To my knowledge only a very small number of the several soldiers from the Lock Springs-Sampsel communities experienced infantry service. Circumstances, however, placed me among them. In my misguided effort to stop my mother's rather needless worry about what was really minimal risk to sons of some of her acquaintances, I had set her up with a genuine cause for anxiety about her own son.

The regiment sent me to its anti-tank company. This was my first time to report to an outfit all by myself. As the only new man at the moment, initially I felt like an intruder in the ranks and in the barracks. At least this outfit did not treat me as a raw recruit in need of a lesson in bed making or who could not distinguish a left foot from the right. Among the men I recognized a few familiar faces from the campus at Durham. This helped even though we had not been personally acquainted there as classmates or dorm mates. It helped some also to know that I had several good friends from UNH in nearby barracks: Jim B. in a rifle company, Gabriel in a heavy weapons company, and two or three others in neighboring rifle companies.

On the afternoon of my second day with my new unit I received a most pleasant surprise. One of the men returning from furlough turned out to be a classmate from my third term at UNH, Joe DeFilippo. We had not lived near each other at Durham and so had not become well acquainted. Still it helped a lot that we knew each other and shared something in common. Since I was assigned to his platoon, we would see a lot of each other in the next year or so. His presence certainly helped me and I like to think mine helped him. After I left the company in the fall of 1945, we never met again. But every year since we have kept in touch with at least an annual Christmas card and note.

The company consisted of four platoons each numbering thirty some men. The first three were gun platoons of 57mm. anti-tank guns. The fourth was the mine platoon.

Each platoon, commanded by a second lieutenant with a technical sergeant as platoon sergeant, was divided into three squads each led by a sergeant. I was placed in the first squad of the third platoon.

Before long I felt comfortable in the platoon and found most of its members quite likable. The assistant leader of my squad, Cpl. Carl G. Hill, became my closest friend. A native of Maryland, Hill had been with the company at Camp Butner. He left for the air corps and was sent to the University of Vermont. Even though the air program at Vermont met with the same fate as the engineering one at New Hampshire, Carl regarded the experience as far from a loss: on the campus he met the girl who later became his wife. The army sent him back to the 311th and Captain John Gapen, the AT Company commander, returned him to his squad. As an old hand Carl could fill me in on a lot about the company and some of its personnel.

Our platoon sergeant may have been small in stature but he could make the platoon feel his presence. As with many unemployed men of the early 1930's, he had become a participant in the important work of the CCC, Civilian Conservation Corps. Then he joined the army and upon completion of one hitch re-enlisted, apparently finding that civilian opportunities remained unpromising. Reportedly he made a very unimpressive score on the army test. But with the coming of the war he found his niche, part of the training cadre for the stream of incoming soldiers. There was not a lot for his men to like about him, but admittedly he was good on the drill field and competent enough for basic training. Once in combat, however, several of us fervently wished he had been left on the drill field or at least down in the ranks.

Morning roll call in my new company was mercifully different from my old battery. Naturally the first sergeant had a whistle, but he did not abuse us with it. I served under this man longer than any other first sergeant, and very early he gained my respect and kept it throughout. It began, I believe, with his acceptance of me as a person of worth, and as far as I could tell he behaved the same toward all his men.

My earliest recollection of our company commander comes from my first morning roll call. Capt. Gapen appeared to be about my size and when he responded to the first sergeant's report, I expected to hear a deep commanding voice. Instead it was higher pitched and seemed incongruous with his stature and authority. There was never any doubt, however, that he was in command and fully able to exercise strong leadership. A graduate of Pennsylvania State University and reportedly of its ROTC program, the captain ran a tight company. He took our training very seriously and expected us to do the same. Perhaps that is why he always seemed so satisfied with our platoon sergeant. Both worked us hard in an effort to prepare us for whatever lay ahead.

Army regulations and training practices could become a great irritant to a private in the ranks. It might strike him that some things were carried to an unnecessary, even ridiculous, extreme. To use one of the more descriptive terms, spoken to fellow victims and not for the hearing of his platoon sergeant, these were "chicken s---" practices. To the captain, on the other hand, these were an important part of training and he tolerated no shirking of effort and no evasion of an order. One of my friends in the platoon discovered this the hard way on one of our field exercises.

With our rifles cradled in our arms before us, we were learning to crawl forward toward a designated goal. The idea was to move steadily and keep a low profile. The platoon was spread out over a sizeable area, our goal was a considerable distance away, the terrain was uneven, we were slithering through grass and weeds, and the day was hot. After crawling tediously and uncomfortably for many yards, my friend decided he had gone far enough with this, to him unquestionably "c.s." activity. Rising up and seeing no one watching, he walked closer to his goal before resuming crawling. Unbeknownst to him, the captain had spotted him early on and was waiting as he crawled the final yards to his objective. Roundly chewing him out and reminding him this was an exercise for his own good, the captain ordered him to do it all over again, this time with a continuously low profile.

A few months later I found myself doing exactly what the captain and the sergeant had tried to teach us. This time, though, the weather was cold and I crawled through snow with a real enemy in the vicinity. At the time I doubt there was any conscious recall of the training lesson, but it probably kicked in automatically as a reminder to maintain a low silhouette. That, of course, had been the point of the uncomfortable training under a hot Virginia sun.

Early in my infantry training, instructors introduced me to the much talked about new rifle: the Garand or M-1 as it was better known. The rifles were kept in a rack at the rear of the barracks. As with small arms weapons in the 496th FA, I was taught how to disassemble, reassemble, and clean the M-1. Unlike my old bolt-action Enfield and the more common Springfield, the M-1 was semi-automatic. At more than nine pounds it was slightly heavier than the Enfield, but instructors assured me it would have a much less noticeable recoil and more firepower, making it well worth carrying the extra weight.

A few of us that were rather new to the infantry spent considerable time on the firing range. Targets varied from the regular old bulls-eye kind to the ones that were shaped like a man from the waist up. The range varied from 200 to 500 yards. I was pleased to discover the truth of the instructor's assessment, the M-1 was a wonderful weapon with practically no kick for such a high powered rifle. After some practice I qualified as a sharpshooter. That pleased me for, as I acknowledged, "I hadn't hoped to make expert, anyway." (7/12/44) "Expert" was a higher rank than sharpshooter.

With the introduction of tanks in World War I, land mines were developed as antitank weapons. Then anti-tank personnel mines were developed to keep the anti-tank mines from being lifted. It followed that anti-tank mines would be used to obstruct the advance of infantry. Millions of mines were laid in World War II and mine-laying, detection, and clearance became essential functions. Much of this was done by engineers, but each infantry regiment had one platoon that specialized in this hazardous duty. The fourth platoon of our company drew this unenviable responsibility.

The rest of the company, however, needed to know about mines. All of us attended classes where we received instruction and actually handled samples of Japanese and German mines. We were taught how to use a bayonet to probe for and lift mines. This was followed by a field exercise where we worked our way through a small plot of buried mines. Each mine had been fitted with a small firecracker-like charge and the slightest mistake brought an alarming, though generally harmless, explosion. On our first attempt we had a rather grim chuckle at the expense of the fourth platoon when they set off more explosions than our own platoon. They went on, of course, to undergo diligent training and when confronted by the real thing, performed admirably.

Unlike my old battery, the company had a day room. It was a convenient place to write letters and visit with friends. Books and magazines were available, as well as a radio to catch the war news. Occasionally, well-informed speakers came to talk on the progress of the war. One of these talks was on the developments on the Russian front. By the summer of 1944 the Russians had retaken Minsk, a city destroyed in the German advance in 1941. At the time we had a 35 year old soldier in the outfit for a few days (why the brief time I do not recall) who had been born in Minsk. He had not heard from his relatives there and took it for granted the Germans had killed them. Following the lecture, in broken English he described the Germans as "no damn good" and predicted the Russians would never forget what had been done to them. (7/7/44)

Gabriel Heatter's broadcasts sounded as upbeat in the Pickett day room as they had in the Beale barracks. But this time I found more reason for his optimism. Americans had taken important islands in the Pacific, and B-29's were carrying the war to the Japanese homeland. As the British took Caen, the Americans took St. Lo, Patton broke out of Normandy, and the Allies closed on Paris, I began to see there would be no repetition of the 1914-18 stalemate in France.

My earlier predictions on the length of the war in Europe were revised downward. Always I hoped to stay out of the war in the Pacific but sincerely wanted to get to Europe. In a foolish combination of innocence and ignorance, I wanted to see some action. If I never even got overseas, how could I ever say I had been in the war? "If they don't send me pretty soon," I wrote, "it will be over with before I get there. Maybe I can see where there has been action even if I don't see any. That will be better than spending all my service as a camp soldier in the states." (7/28/44)

This, unfortunately, was hardly what my mother wanted to read. From reading my letters recently, I know that her letters to me surely reflected great worry about my being in the infantry and going overseas. It was true that I came to feel good about being in the infantry and earnestly wanted to get to Europe. My clumsy attempts to ease things for my mother, however, did no good and from the vantage point of age and experience appear embarrassingly naive, if not ridiculous. As one such example:

> Mother, I know you don't want me to go across and worry a lot but I wish you would please change your mind. I want to see a little action some time. How can I ever call myself a soldier if I don't. If I ever go you needn't worry about me getting nervous or hurt. I'm going to be all right and have a great adventure. I'll probably spend my army career in the states though. (8/20/44)

In mid-July two likable young fellows joined the company and were assigned to our platoon. William Sherlock and Louis Kolman were both from Ohio. The draft grabbed them a few days after each turned 18. Upon completion of basic, they had been given furloughs, then sent to Ft. Meade to go overseas. Someone in authority there decided they were too young to go over as infantry replacements and sent them to the 78th. Both were small in size and from my now advanced age of one month over 22, they appeared no more than mere boys. I was glad they had been spared for awhile anyway. Kolman, an outgoing little red head with a friendly disposition, became a squad mate. We remained together until he was wounded March, 1945, and sent home.

Also in mid-July Jim B. made pfc. and a little later Jim F. got the single stripe. He had been a corporal in the 13th armored and now verbally kicked himself for ever leaving the outfit. "He could have had a pretty good rating by now," I wrote. (8/12/44) For that matter I think my own chances for advancement would have been a lot better with the armored force. I do not know that Jim F. ever got his corporal's stripes back. He had not the last time I saw him. We lost contact once the division prepared to go overseas. A remarkably small number of the fellows I knew who had stayed with the ASTP to the end ever made it above pfc. Much later I learned that Frank stayed a pfc. with the rest of us from the corner room at Durham. Rank never mattered nearly as much to him as just getting out of the army. Likewise, I was thankful to get out of the army safely and recognized the three terms at UNH as worth far more than any rank they cost me. Still, I was left with some disappointment and on occasion an embarrassing sense of failure that I had but a single stripe for more than three years service. I wanted more for myself and I suspected that some people who knew me expected more.

Three weeks after I joined the AT Company, I got something that had been denied me in Headquarters Battery, a pass to my choice of either Richmond or Washington. I could not pass up an opportunity to see the nation's capital so I chose Washington. Saturday morning as I waited to buy a bus ticket, a soldier drove up on his way home to Maryland. For some help with gas money, less than the cost of a ticket, he dropped me off in front of Washington's Union Station and picked me up on Sunday evening.

Washington was a bustling place crowded with people and all hotels were full. This was no problem for me. For fifty cents, the United Nations Service Center gave me a bed in a dorm-like room for service men. Service personnel from World War II found several organizations and lots of people ready to help. Probably there never was a better time to be a service man. I spent some time at the USO and ate at the Washington Stage Door Canteen.

Sunday morning I stood in front of Union Station and wondered how best to see the sights. Nearby a lieutenant and his wife (turned out they were from my neighboring state of Iowa) were wondering the same thing. We got a good answer when a man approached and asked if we would like to join a small sightseeing party. He already had a civilian couple from Philadelphia in the front seat of his car. He put us in the rear and for the almost unbelievable sum of

$2.50 "he really showed me the works." Later I excitedly described some of it to my parents:

> We started in at the Capitol and went through it. I'm telling you it's really a thrill to an American to visit our Capitol. If not, then he isn't a very good American.
> We started off in the Rotunda under the huge dome. The guide took us into the Senate chamber and we could look down at the rostrum and their desks. Then we went to the Chamber of the House of Representatives. . . . It's really an impressive sight to look down and think of the great men [I was probably thinking of boyhood admiration for Daniel Webster, Henry Clay, John C. Calhoun and others of their stature] who had sat in those chairs and of the great orations which have been delivered in those Chambers. (7/23/44)

Our guide pointed out the Library of Congress, the Supreme Court, buildings of some departments of government, and the White House. The Lincoln Memorial was a favorite of our driver and we got out for a closer look. It was a thrill to see the Washington Monument even though we did not have time to go up into it. At the Jefferson Memorial we were able to get out for a good look at the statue and a chance to read the inscriptions. We were given a chance to look into the Smithsonian just long enough to whet the appetite for a much longer visit at another time.

Across the Potomac we drove by the Pentagon and into Arlington Cemetery. Our guide pointed out the grave sites of several well known figures in our history. A stop at the tomb of the Unknown Soldier of the First World War was a moving experience for all of us, but especially for me and the lieutenant.

The pass had resulted in a rich and rewarding experience. And it served as yet another reminder that no matter the unpleasantness of the army, it brought opportunities otherwise unavailable to a poor farm boy from Missouri.

Each squad in our platoon had a 57 mm. anti-tank gun. We had lessons on the gun and its different types of ammunition such as armor piercing and high explosive. We spent a lot of time in the field learning to position and dig it in, along with digging fox holes for ourselves. Many of these were night exercises, a type of training that proved especially beneficial once we got into a combat area.

At first impression I thought I might be in a smaller version of the field artillery. Both the 105 and the 57 were towed weapons on carriages with trails that rested on the ground when unlimbered. But I soon learned that any similarities ended there. The 105 was a howitzer with a low muzzle velocity and high trajectory. Thus it could be placed several thousand yards from its intended target, with intervening terrain and other obstructions. The gunner did not have his target in sight, but relied on a fire direction center aided by forward observers on the ground or aerial observers in a light airplane. A large truck with protruding cab and plenty of space for the large clusters of shells could tow the howitzer into place with a minimum of risk from enemy ground observation.

On the other hand the 57 was a gun with a high muzzle velocity and a relatively flat trajectory. The gunner sighted his target directly which could mean it was uncomfortably close to the enemy, and in any case meant that, once fired, the gun came under enemy observation. To minimize detection a small truck, without a cab and with nothing offering a high profile, towed the gun to its position. Ideally the driver then found some cover for his truck while the rest of the squad dug in and wrestled the gun into place. And they dug holes for themselves. Under combat conditions, we tried whenever possible to make these moves under cover of darkness.

Because Camp Pickett was not set up for the actual firing of field artillery and antitank weapons, this part of our training took place elsewhere. Jim F.'s artillery battalion, for example, went to Ft. Bragg and Camp Butner in western North Carolina to fire. Our AT Company went to the A. P. Hill Military Reservation near Fredericksburg, Virginia, to do line firing.

On the afternoon of August 13 our company became part of the 311th convoy to A. P. Hill. The trip of 90 miles north of Pickett took us through the edge of Richmond. That was all I got to see of that city until a few years after the war.

At A. P. Hill we lived in pup tents and I shared a tent with Louis Kolman. We were provided with netting to keep out hungry mosquitoes. It was a challenge to get netting in place and then crawl inside, but somehow we managed with only a rare intruder. "We could hear the old mosquitos [sic] buzzing around outside but they couldn't get in." (8/15/44)

To prepare for the possibility of rain, we learned to trench around our tents. It actually rained once and then we learned something else: touch the inside of a wet tent and it will leak at that spot! These lessons proved of practical value for the short time we stayed in pup tents in France..

Also, at A. P. Hill I learned the practical value of a steel helmet. It made a most useful wash bowl. And it was very handy in gathering apples. The War Department had bought farms to create the reservation, or maneuver area. The farmers were gone but their apple trees remained. One day our platoon stopped briefly before an old farm house and three of us dashed for an apple tree. One man climbed up and started shaking the tree while the other fellow and I took off our helmets, filling them with apples.

Night problems provided experience of a practical kind in learning to dig fox holes in the dark using the small entrenching shovels we carried on our packs. Since the soil in that part of Virginia was sandy and easy digging, this was not a true preparation for, or measure of, the frustration we would encounter with the frozen ground of Germany.

Most evenings a truck was available to take us to the USO in the nearby town of Bowling Green for a shower. By the time we got the gun cleaned some nights, however, it was too late to catch the truck. In that case, I went down to a little creek to bathe.

Some of the company's non-coms, including our squad leader, were on furlough. This meant we had an acting squad leader, and most of the week I served as number one gunner. Since I had never even seen a 57 fired, an experienced man from another squad came over and fired the first round. The gun made a terrific noise and had a lot of recoil and bounce, especially until the trails were set firmly in the ground. When it came my turn, I heeded the advice to get a good sight on the target and then quickly pull back at the moment of firing. Later I watched two fellows forget to do this and get skinned and bruised noses as a consequence.

It gave me a thrill to send a projectile on its way to a target. Obviously both high explosive and armor piercing shells could do a lot of damage. It turned out for the best, I am sure, that I never looked down the sight at a real German tank. The German 88 mm., in particular, had a decided advantage over our 57 mm. In fact, the all-purpose 88 (adaptable to anti-aircraft, tank, anti-tank, and artillery purposes) was the most effective and most feared weapon I encountered in the war.

In addition to the 57, we practiced with a bazooka on some targets. Each squad was equipped with one of these small shoulder-carried anti-tank rocket launchers. This simplelooking weapon could be brought into use more quickly and much less obtrusively than a gun. My guess is that more was accomplished by a few of these than by all of our towed anti-tank guns.

Many of us assumed that upon completion of the training at A. P. Hill, the 78th would soon go overseas. But the army had a different idea. No doubt this was related to developments that occurred soon after we arrived at A. P. Hill. Allied forces opened a new front against the Germans with landings in the south of France on August 15. Now, in addition to Italy and northern France, American divisions were operating in the valley of the Rhone River. Progress on the various fronts came at the cost of many casualties. Consequently the 78th was ordered to provide a considerable number of fully trained replacements for immediate overseas duty.

It was a great relief not to be a part of this group, and I was glad that most of my close friends from UNH stayed behind. Any thought of becoming one of the bewildered new men in an outfit already in the fight could be truly alarming. Even though we were all raw and inexperienced, I much preferred that those of us who had trained together go into combat together. I always felt sorry for the replacements who joined us in combat, especially those who came during and immediately after the Bulge.

With the departure of many of the ASTP and Air Corps men who had been with it for over four months, the 78th received a comparable number of men from the Infantry Replacement Training Centers. Some of these men came to our company and two, possibly three, to our squad. Richard Meade, who became my combat buddy in Germany, must have been among them, for I do not recall knowing him until we were getting ready to go overseas.

Concentrated efforts were made to integrate these men into their units as rapidly as possible. By early September there was no longer any doubt about it, the 78th was going overseas. Just where we were going was not yet made known, at least not to those of us way down in the ranks. Signs pointed to Europe and I entertained high hopes. But I knew one could never count on the army, for it might do the illogical by shipping us out of New York and then through the Panama Canal to the Pacific.

The granting of a furlough in September confirmed that I would soon be on my way overseas. With the exception of two things, the furlough remains a blur in my memory. The first election after I reached the voting age of 21 came in 1944. While at home I prepared an absentee ballot. My parents and I credited Franklin Roosevelt, or his administration anyway, with rescuing us from a near disaster in the mid 1930's. The folks were literally at the end of the financial line. A note at the bank of less than $200 and requiring a payment of $10 could not be met. A life insurance company held a mortgage on the farm that required an annual payment of something over $200. It was impossible for my parents to meet this, and the company initiated foreclosure proceedings. We were to be put out with no place to go. To make it worse, I was ill all summer and there was no way to get proper medical attention. We avoided eviction when one of my dad's friends in Chillicothe contacted a representative of a newly created federal lending agency. This man, a life saver to us, came to the farm and helped my parents make a successful application for a loan. At the same time, he persuaded the mortgage holder to settle for a smaller principal that fell within the limits of the loan. With this background in mind, it should be readily understood why, a decade later, I cast my very first vote in support of President Roosevelt's quest for an unprecedented fourth term. The fact that his vice-presidential candidate was Senator Harry Truman from Missouri made my vote all the more memorable.

The setting for my other memory was the converted railway coach that had served as a station for Lock Springs since the old style structure of wood had burned in the 1930's. My parents waited with me for the midnight train. Except for the man who met the mail train and opened the station for an occasional passenger, we were all alone. This must have appeared a somber scene to him, but I expect he saw many like it during the war. Each of us remained dry-eyed but quiet, not knowing what to say. Each of us had to face the dreaded possibility that this could be our last time together. Once I got on the train and started toward St. Louis, I ached for my parents, knowing it had to be difficult to return to an empty house. Even at the time I knew that it was much easier for me to go than for them to stay behind with worry and uncertainty. Later, with children of my own leaving home and for nothing resembling war, it struck me that as sympathetic as I tried to be to my parents' feelings in 1944, I had not even begun to identify with what they felt that night and for many to come. I had been right in that my role by contrast had been the easier one that night.

Sometime in September the Advance Party left Pickett to prepare a place for the division somewhere overseas. In late September and early October the rest of us busied ourselves with preparations to follow. Company equipment was packed in sturdy boxes for shipment. Personal equipment was checked and new was drawn where needed. New duffel bags of heavy canvas with a heavy shoulder strap were issued. Mine was stenciled with my name in large letters and the identifying 37242203. For protective purposes the barrel and critical parts of our guns were lavishly coated with a thick grease for ocean shipment. Our driver, Terry Millsaps of Tennessee, along with his truck and the gun would take separate passage from the rest of the squad.

One very satisfying experience happened to me in the midst of our preparations. Reporting to the orderly room as directed, 1st Sgt. Coffee astonished me with a greeting to this effect: "You are a good soldier, Breeze, congratulations." Then Capt. Gapen presented me with a Good Conduct Medal and a nice certificate signed by Gen. Parker, division commander. To lessen the chances of information about specific unit movements falling into enemy hands, we removed our colorful shoulder patches and other identifying marks. My well-worn pocket Testament, a gift from Aunt Faye Domahowski, has a mutilated spot inside the front cover. This is where I took a razor blade to remove my unit designation. Rules of censorship were explained to us, and one day in early October we were ordered to leave our letters unsealed for the censor. At the same time everyone was restricted to the camp and the few married men in the company had to say goodbye to their wives living in nearby towns. Shortly afterward we entrained for Camp Kilmer, New Jersey.

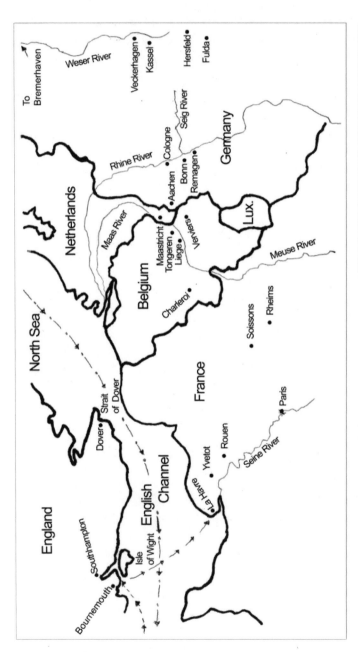

Chapter Eight

Overseas: England

Located near New Brunswick, N.J. and only 30 miles or so from the harbor of New York, Camp Kilmer had already processed thousands of troops for overseas duty. Besides the ever-present "Killroy was here", other penciled markings on barracks' walls gave evidence of the arrival and departure of many of these men. We were there for at least a week and kept busy most of the time. There were medical examinations and inoculations. My "Immunization Register," for example, shows a typhus shot 10-11-44. There were lectures to attend and forms to complete.

New gas masks were issued. Interestingly, in contrast to the heavy emphasis by the 13th Armored in late 1942, the 78th Infantry placed relatively little stress on gas training in 1944. Evidently the fear of gas being used against us had diminished. Possibly so but with my instilled fear from earlier training, I felt much more secure with a brand new mask.

Large box-like structures loomed up on the training field. Standing taller than a two story house, they were draped from top to bottom with heavy nets, simulating landing nets over the side of a ship. The top was flat, about a dozen or so feet across.

Watching others climb this structure, I dreaded the moment when our platoon would be ordered forward. Wearing a steel helmet and weighted by an infantryman's full field pack, I knew this could test my heart and upper body problems to the limit. It did not help any that I had some fear of heights. The climb proved to be as difficult and exhausting as I imagined. Making that first move to start down the other side required a supreme effort of will. My upper body was drained of strength and my palms were sweaty from fear of falling off as I sought a grip on the net. Once safely on the ground, I was greatly relieved not to be ordered to repeat the climb.

With an APO address care of "Postmaster, New York, N.Y.", it now appeared certain that I was going to Europe. Exactly where, of course, I would not know for many days. On what turned out to be the eve of my departure from Kilmer, I wrote a very uninformative letter (no comment on my activities and no name for the camp) and concluded with a totally pointless remark: "I hope you aren't worrying any about me and that you won't in the future." (10/12/44) My infrequent letters of the next several months would be the same tenor and equally uninformative.

Early the next evening my company boarded a train for the short ride to Jersey City. There a ferry took us across the harbor to New York City. Appropriate for the occasion, it was a dark and rainy night. As we waited within sight of a large ship at the dock, Red Cross volunteers handed us coffee and doughnuts. Finally my name was called. Burdened with a field pack, with weapon slung over my shoulder and carrying my duffel bag, I made my way up the gang plank. The date was Friday the 13th of October and after nearly two years in the army, I was on a ship to go overseas and really "go to war."

It took three ships to transport our division. It was late the next afternoon before all was ready. Much of the day had been cloudy and dreary, but as we left the harbor enough sun broke out to cast light on the Statue of Liberty. It was an awesome sight, but still a bit sad as I could not help wondering if I would ever see it again. Our ship joined a convoy escorted by armed craft of the U. S. Navy.

In peacetime my ship, *H.M.S. Carnarvon Castle,* had carried less than 700 passengers for one of the British lines. Making its maiden voyage as a troop transport, it had been refitted to carry the entire 311th (some 3200 men) plus around 1600 men from other units of the 78th. One artilleryman recalls that the ship's swimming pool had been converted into a bunking place for his battery. *(The Flash, vol. XCIX,* January, 1999, p. 98)

Although we were crowded and the space between the bunks, which hung suspended in tiers of four, was cramped, everything was fresh and clean. Once in your bunk (I had a lower one) with some of your gear, it was not bad at all. The rhythmic sound of distant engines, coupled with the ship's movement through relatively tranquil waters, actually made for rather good sleeping.

In common with nearly all of my outfit, this was my first time on the ocean. Remembering how easily I got nauseated as a youngster, I had worried some about seasickness. Happily, unlike a very small number of men including our first sergeant who evidently had a miserable trip, I had no trouble at all. It helped that the weather was pleasant and the water generally smooth. We did calisthenics and other activities up on the open deck. In addition, I spent a lot of free time there, utterly fascinated by the waves and changing color of the water. Looking back, I remember it much more as an exciting adventure than a time of concern about what lay in my immediate future.

Only two things were less than pleasant about the trip. Taking a shower using ocean water (it is soap resistant!) was a novel but far from refreshing experience. And the meals were horrible. It was not the fault of our army, for it provided an abundance of good quality rations. But the ship's British crew included cooks, and they lived down to the reputation that the English are poor cooks.

We were eight or nine days out of New York when I got the good news that we were headed for England. Lectures tried to prepare us to live among the English for awhile. We were cautioned to expect some of their ways to be different from our own. Sometime prior to landing we changed our money into the thoroughly confusing English system of pounds, shillings and pence.

Suddenly one morning there was land to our left. Then we were in a channel, which much later I identified as the Solent, separating the Isle of Wight from England's southern coast. As we sailed slowly along ever closer to land, my eyes were drawn to the sight of a very large impressive looking house back up among the trees. Later I learned the sight was not at all unusual in England. We entered the long approach to Southampton. Many blue-gray colored warships were at anchor in the harbor. Eventually we stopped and tied up at a dock. Around us I could see signs of war damage. As a vital seaport, Southampton had been an inviting target for Nazi bombers.

We got our gear together and then impatiently played the old army game of hurry up and wait. It was long after dark when our company disembarked. Shouldering our gear, we marched through darkened, streets, yet another reminder of war, to the railway station. There I began to see one noticeable difference between the States and Europe. Many things there seemed to be on a smaller scale, including their trains. The passenger cars looked small, and they were divided into several small compartments whose doors opened directly to the outside. A few of us from the platoon shared one of the compartments for what turned out to be a comfortable ride of 25 or 30 miles.

The train stopped at Bournemouth, an important resort city southwest of Southampton on the southern coast of England. This would be the locale for our final training and the inevitable waiting. Thousands of troops had preceded us into this area, and the 50th British Infantry Division had departed from here for D-Day.

After the publication of our division history in 1947, I learned that the original plans had called for the 78th Division to go directly to the Continent. Leaving New York on September 26, the Advance Party landed in Glasgow, entrained for Southampton, crossed the channel on a steamer and transferred to DUKWs (amphibious vehicles) to land at Omaha Beach. After making arrangements for the division to set up in the mud of a place known as "Camp 500", the army changed its mind. Ordered back to Southampton, the Advance Party made housing and training arrangements 30 miles west of the port. No doubt had the original plan been followed, we would have been committed to combat earlier and probably in a different area. My own personal history could have been changed as well.

While I could let my parents know I was in England, I could not reveal the place or area. Seven months later and a few days after V-E Day, however, I began writing lengthy letters home giving them some of the more innocuous details of my overseas experience. For example, I told them what happened when I got off the train at Bournemouth:

> Once again I shouldered my belongings and walked to my new home. The streets, houses, and everything were blacked out. I had quite a long walk and ended up by climbing a very long and steep hill. At an old hotel at the very top of the hill we stopped. The army had taken it over as barracks. Our company was to live on the fourth floor.
>
> In the morning I looked out of the window to see what the surroundings looked like. I was at the top of a very steep cliff with a nice sandy beach and plenty of water just below. The day had that foggy, gloomy look which I later discovered was typical English weather. (5/18/45)

During the days that followed, I spent a lot of time on that beach, very little of it recreational in nature. Most of it was devoted to calisthenics, bayonet exercises, running, and other physical exertions, none made any easier by the incompatible combination of sand and combat boots. In these younger years of my life, and well before I became an ardent Anglophile, I sometimes resented the elderly English bringing out their deck chairs to watch our labors.

We did a lot of hiking, much of this at night. Unless it was some kind of cross country problem, all of this was done on hard surface roads. This was much harder on the feet than our usual hiking areas.

It struck me that no matter how far we hiked we never got completely away from a town or village. The compactness of this part of England I later found common to many parts of the Continent. My midwestern farm boy perception of space, distance and congestion did not translate well to these countries.

One of our night problems turned out to be quite an adventure. Our platoon was divided into a half dozen or so small groups. Each group received a compass and a sheet of directions. Groups set off from different points but eventually we were expected to meet at a common objective. The compass could be read in the dark, but we needed a flashlight under the cover of a raincoat to refer to the instructions. A couple of fellows checked the compass while the rest of us paced off distance. Our first reading took us across what appeared to be some kind of field or pasture. It did not help that the night was very dark, and soon we found ourselves pushing through some kind of brambles. Any confidence we had began to diminish when we stopped just short of plunging into what, in the darkness, appeared to be an open quarry. Surely this had not been part of the course! Any remaining confidence disappeared when our directions took us up to a wall. Scrambling over it, we found ourselves in an Englishman's garden, tramping through what seemed to be heads of cabbage. By the time we realized what we were doing to Anglo-American relations, there seemed little point in turning back.

Knowing we were hopelessly lost, we ignored the instructions and simply sought out a road hoping to find a signpost. We were prepared to go back to Bournemouth, wherever it was, and face the consequences of utter failure. We wandered down different roads for a long time without a clue as to where we were. Finally in the early morning hours, we met a man on a bicycle. I do not know that we questioned why he was out and about at that hour; we were just happy to find someone who might be able to give us directions. Most important of all, he had encountered another group of soldiers a mile or two down the road. They turned out to be from our platoon and were waiting at the pick-up point for all of us. To my knowledge, no one in our group ever admitted we had been lost and wandering around for much of the night.

For the only time in my experience with army chow lines, I remained hungry a lot of the time in Bournemouth. The combination of English sea air and hard work gave me a ferocious appetite. The cooks of the four companies in our hotel took turns preparing and dispensing food. When there was little chance of a cook spotting me as an interloper, I sometimes slipped in with another company to make a second pass through the line. I was not the only one to do this.

On evenings with no assigned work, I often went down the hill to the Red Cross Center, where I usually got a jelly sandwich or two. Nearly always the bread was on the stale side, but I still remember it as satisfying.

At the center and elsewhere I gradually made sense of English money. The mysterious sounding "two and six, please", for example, took on the meaning of two shillings and six pence. The variety of coins seemed endless: farthings, halfpennies, pennies, threepence (pronounced thruppence), sixpence, shillings, florins, half crowns and crowns.

I found it best to get a sense of value in terms of their money instead of trying to compute its equal in our money, as some of my friends did. Some fellows simply handed the clerks some change and told them to pick out what was needed. We received our pay in British money, and I still have a one pound note obtained October 31, 1944. At the time it was worth nearly five dollars. The pound occupied the pre-eminent place among the world's currencies.

Signs of a nation long at war were all around us. Some were conspicuous such as the concertina wire and pillboxes along the beaches where an invasion had been feared in 1940-41, or the heavy curtains that had to be pushed aside to enter a building at night. Some were more subtle such as the shabby appearance of many buildings where maintenance and repairs had been neglected, or the strained looks on the faces of people dressed in well-worn clothing. Things normally taken for granted as readily available to a resort city, such as heat and a variety and plenitude of food, were either in short supply or missing altogether.

In June, 1944, Hitler had launched the first of his revenge weapons against England, the V-1 rocket, called "buzz bombs" by the British. While most were aimed at London, some fell in the Southampton, area. About six weeks before we got to England, Hitler began launching a much more terrifying weapon against London, the V-2. With no defense against this rocket forerunner of the long-range ballistic missile, the British had good cause to be frightened. I wonder today how many people realize how truly fortunate we all are that German science and technology did not reach the breakthrough needed to place an atomic warhead atop this missile. Even with conventional explosives the devastation was enormous. Some men from the 78th got short passes to London and had a close look at some of the effects of the V-2. When we got to Belgium a few weeks later, all of us would become well acquainted with the "buzz bomb", V-1, as we were positioned between the launching site and the intended target, the port of Antwerp.

Terry Millsaps arrived with the truck and the 57. Landing in Liverpool, as I recall, he had driven in convoy to Bournemouth. Once reunited with the anti-tank gun, we began the tedious task of removing all its protective coating of grease, known as cosmoline. It had been a lot easier to smear on than take off. The stack of waste rags issued for the job was about half what we really needed. The day was cold and we had to work without gloves, but after several hours at the miserable job, we finally had the gun in good working order.

Our squad leader at this time was a buck sergeant from Lynn, Mass., Walter Jarzylo. Whether he came from another platoon or another unit in the division, I do not remember. He was a good man and under his leadership the squad worked well together. Cpl. Hill continued as our gunner and assistant squad leader. Our platoon sergeant remained the same too. Our platoon leader, 2nd Lt. Julius Janowitz, from the Bronx, was rather new to me, as I recall. He was a large man and we had a physical characteristic in common. Both of us had larger feet than anyone else in the platoon, a fact that created a serious problem for us when overshoes were distributed.

Becoming acquainted with Lt. Janowitz, a Jew, helped me see a person as an individual rather than as part of a religious culture different from my own. The better I knew him, the more I came to like and admire him. Circumstances in combat put the platoon leader and the platoon sergeant together a lot. Unfortunately the anti-Semitism of the sergeant, who could be a little man in more than size, surfaced in lack of respect for the lieutenant.

With the weather growing colder and no heat in the building, the company's fourth floor quarters provided shelter, but little else in the way of comfort. No doubt this was good preparation for worse to come. My platoon occupied rooms formerly used by the hotel's work force. They were small and double-bunk beds were crammed into every available space. On a lucky day I could find enough lukewarm water to wash my face and shave. But there was absolutely no hot water, not even lukewarm, for bathing.

Unable to tolerate my unwashed state any longer, one evening in early November, by sheer force of will, I went down the hall to the bathroom. Filling the big tub full of water, I made myself step into its icy contents. Once the initial shock wore off and I bathed, I found it was even worse to emerge and expose my wet body to the cold air of the room. No doubt I should have repeated this frigid experience the night before I left Bournemouth. My next bath came upwards of three months later in a quartermaster tent in the Netherlands!

At least I slept warmly. In addition to the trusty khaki woolen blanket, the army issued us sleeping bags while we were in England. This came as a pleasant surprise, for I had no idea the army provided anything this sensible for enlisted men. "That without a doubt," I later wrote my parents, "is the best piece of equipment the army ever issued me." (5/23/45) Although much smaller and lighter than the bag I used years later in camping with my son's Boy Scout troop, it was nonetheless just right for the soldier to carry. The outside was water repellent, and the inside had a lining similar to my blanket. One of the fellows in the platoon promptly dubbed it a "fart sack" and that term was soon adopted by all of us.

The very first time I looked out over the English Channel from Bournemouth, I discovered that a startling and disconcerting thing had happened. My sense of direction had deserted me. My senses told me that I was looking north over the water and that the Isle of Wight loomed up to the west. My intellect knew differently, for the map confirmed that the channel lay to the south and the isle to the east. The sun seldom broke through the gloomy skies, but I doubt it would have made any difference. The truly astounding aspect is that I had absolutely no prior inkling of a problem in orientation. Whether at home, in various army camps, traveling with the army, in New York City, or wherever, directions appeared as they should be. My sense of direction made the trip across the Atlantic in a generally eastward course then turned and went toward the north into Southampton harbor. But for some inexplicable reason, it betrayed me in Bournemouth and has plagued me ever afterward.

Sometimes when we were actually advancing eastward against the enemy in Germany, my sense made it westward. Later, in the 1950's and 60's, I lived in a place where the sun always came up in the west and set in the east. On the other hand, my wife and I have lived in our present home for over thirty years and fortunately the sun behaves as nature intended. Take me out of this restricted setting, however, and I may have trouble elsewhere in the city. I doubt that anyone blessed with a good sense of direction can even begin to imagine what a tortuous thing this is, or the kind of mental wrestling involved in making the mind accept something over the sense's objection. I am an ardent Anglophile, but the loss of a sense of direction seems to be an enduring legacy of my first visit to England.

My introduction to England, suffice it to say, was not a happy one. Thankfully, subsequent visits have always been enjoyable occasions.

In October-November, 1944, I was physically uncomfortable a lot of the time, the skies were dreary, and the general atmosphere was depressing. Knowing we were in Europe for something more than exertions on a sandy beach and a tramp through the English countryside, I wanted to get on with it. Later, writing during the Occupation, I recalled this for my parents:

> I was restless all this time though and wanted to move on or do something. I was wondering all the while just what our mission in Europe was to be. Whatever it was I was anxious to get started on it. Rumors flew thick and fast. Rumor had us doing a lot of things. (5/18/45)

One of the more exciting of these rumors had us becoming a part of the Red Ball Express. Initially this had been truck convoys carrying supplies from the beaches to a depot near Paris. By this time a variant of the express carried supplies from Cherbourg to Namur and Verdun. Supposedly we were to become part of this, some of us as drivers and others handling supplies. To me it hardly seemed likely that an equipped and well-trained infantry division would be diverted to such a task, but such can be army rumor and speculations.

One day it became obvious that we were going to France. I had to change my English money into French invasion francs, money printed by the United States to be used in France. Then we were marched down the hill to a large auditorium in the city. There we were lectured on important matters we should know about on the Continent and in combat. Undoubtedly a lot of important things were discussed, but only two stuck in my memory: one because of cultural shock and the other for its frightening implications.

Europeans, we learned, were less prudish than Americans about such things as the use by both sexes of a common public restroom. Also it was stressed that Germany had signed the 1929 Geneva Convention on the rights and treatment of prisoners of war. Thus if captured, we were obligated to give our captors only our name, rank and serial number.

One rainy night in mid-November I was ordered to pack all my belongings. In a frigid, hard rain we marched to the Bournemouth railway station and by the time I boarded the train for Southampton, I was wet and cold. From Southampton station we marched, more like waded, through rain-filled streets to the dock. There we waited in the rain for our turn to board a channel transport. By this time my gear was wet, my trousers soaked and my feet thoroughly wet.

To this day I remain very unhappy about the combat boots issued to me. To me they were the Second World War equivalent to the rotten meat foisted by greedy contractors and incapable army generals onto Union soldiers in the Civil War. The old style boots I had been issued in 1942 not only took a great shine for dress purposes but were sturdy and left my feet dry even in the worst of the California rainy season. A combination of inept (to put it the kindest way) Pentagon officials and uncaring boot manufacturers had conspired to issue me a new and purportedly better boot! Several months after loading up for the Continent, this is how I described the truth about these boots:

> Some clever individual conceived the idea that if the boot was turned wrong side out with the smooth leather next to the foot it would be more serviceable. So that's the kind they gave us. The rough leather on the outside let great quantities of water inside the shoe and the smooth interior kept it all in. (5/23/45)

Thus it was that—wet, cold and miserable—I finally boarded one of the numerous transports that would take us to France. At the same time motor elements, including our truck driven by Millsaps, were preparing to cross in LSTs.

Chapter Nine

Overseas: France and Belgium

The British Channel transport that took my company to France was neither as nice nor as spacious as the ship that brought the regiment to England. It bore the marks of already having carried hundreds of soldiers. There were no bunks for sleeping and some men simply found a spot on the deck for their bed roll. Our squad got hammocks but the cramped space allotted us made this a dubious advantage. A rack protruding from the wall into a corner of my hammock gave it a tipping motion. There was no heat, of course, and the chilly interior combined with wet clothing to make sleep nearly impossible anyway.

Because of the need to wait for calmer seas, our ship spent the night rocking to and fro in the harbor. It could have been worse for me and was for many. Later I learned that some units of the division had begun boarding their transports much earlier and ended up spending nearly four days aboard.

Having heard that crossing the channel could be much worse than the ocean, I fully expected to be seasick. To my pleasant surprise I was spared this additional misery. Others were less fortunate, among them my first sergeant. The poor fellow became ill almost from the moment he stepped onto the rocking boat. No doubt I could have taken mean satisfaction in such a fate for a first sergeant I had known earlier in the 78th, but I felt genuine sympathy for Sgt. Coffee.

Even though seas remained rather choppy, the next morning we sailed for the Continent. Some six months later, writing to my parents, I recalled what I beheld around mid-afternoon that day:

> ... went up on deck to see what could be seen through the mist and fog. Everyone made speculations as to where we would land. I kept wondering how the boys felt who crossed that same channel on D-Day.
>
> Land was sighted which they said was France. I learned that I was going to Le Havre. As I neared this city the first grim realization of what war does struck me. No matter what you read, what you hear, or what pictures and newsreels you may see, you can never realize just how things actually are. Somehow it is just a story or a picture and doesn't strike you with reality until it is actually seen. Then it comes as a shock.
>
> Before the war Le Havre had been a great French city. The third most important port I believe I've heard. Before me this November day it lay a mass of ruins. Great gaping shell holes peered from the high banks to the left of the city. Buildings were gutted if standing at all. Everywhere was just rubble, more rubble, and twisted steel. (5/18/45)

The docks had been destroyed completely. Le Havre lies at the mouth of the Seine River, and our ship anchored in the big harbor area. Some ships proceeded up the river approximately 50 miles to Rouen and their men disembarked there.

Our unit played the old army game of hurrying to get our gear up on deck and then waiting for further orders. After a tiresome wait, and with dusk approaching, we transferred to a landing craft. It ran up on the beach, dropped its ramp, and we scrambled out onto the rubble. What next, we wondered? As darkness fell we were led through the ruins and up a path to a roadway where trucks waited to take us to a destination still unknown to us.

Many trucks rumbled through the French countryside that night, some from Le Havre and others from Rouen, all converging on Yvetot. This small town, located about 35 miles northeast of Le Havre and some 20 miles northwest of Rouen, had been chosen by the Advance Party as the focal point for the 78th's bivouac area. Bivouac meant tents for us, not the billets anticipated by the optimists among us.

We had a wild ride through the darkness. Our driver showed considerable skill in driving with blackout lights (a small amount of light emitted through narrow slits) and in maneuvering the big truck through the twisting streets of several small villages. Some of these streets were so narrow it seemed we could reach out and touch the walls of some buildings. In one place I got a quick glimpse of people peering out at us as we went by.

Eventually we halted at a grassy field that had been assigned to the AT Company as our home in France. Unloading we were instructed to pitch our tents in four parallel lines, one for each platoon and with space like a small street between each. From a relatively level area near the roadway, the land gradually sloped downward. The more level area provided sufficient space for the big tents needed by the kitchen, a tent for company headquarters, and tents for the officers.

The parallel rows of platoon tents were established at right angles to the roadway. Weather developments soon showed how lucky I was to be a member of the first squad. We pitched our pup tents at the top of the slope, then came those of the second squad and finally the last of the tents of the third squad were at the very bottom of the hill. My position became even better when Cpl. Hill asked me to share a tent. As the assistant squad leader he secured a spot near the head of our line and on practically level ground.

Darkness made it challenging to put our two shelter halves together and get a tent erected, but we managed. A demand that all tents in a platoon be lined up in orderly precision compounded the problem, especially for those below us. To an uninvolved observer it would have been a ludicrous spectacle to see our platoon sergeant running up and down the line with a flashlight, fussing at his men to give him an orderly row. Being located at the head of the line spared me most of this bothersome hassle. The weather obligingly gave us a break, and the company got settled in without the added handicap of rain. A few hours later and we would have been in a dreadful mess. It began raining the next morning and continued for much of the short time we were in France.

Very quickly the ground was trampled into a morass. In erecting tents we had used entrenching shovels to prepare a trench around the outside. These works required almost constant attention. Carl and I maintained a fairly good drainage system, but this action became increasingly difficult to downright impossible as the platoon line dropped down the hill. The poor fellows at the bottom endured the most wretched conditions with ankle deep mud outside their tents and water running through them. An increasing chill in the air added to the misery index for all of us. Lest we get any ideas about gathering wood for a fire, we were given strict orders forbidding this. Not even the sticks and twigs of a nearby orchard were to be touched.

Even with a minimum of gear and in the best of times, a pup tent is barely large enough for two men, especially if one is a six footer. Add our bulky gear plus weapons and rain pouring down, and it became impossible to get into the tent without touching the sides somewhere. Touch a wet tent and water soon drips through at that point. Fortunately we were good enough contortionists to keep all the leaks confined to the lower sides of the tent. My rifle and his carbine, plus the .45 pistol issued to him as the squad's gunner, were placed between us in the most protected part of the tent. My biggest problem came in taking off big, wet, muddy boots so I could slide into my sleeping bag. The ground was, of course, damp and cold, but the sleeping bag proved its worth in repelling water.

Possession of an army driving license had gotten me in trouble at Pickett, but in France it became advantageous. The regiment planned to send eight to ten big trucks to a supply depot in Rheims, in particular to get overshoes for the troops. One of the drivers knew me and asked that I go along as his assistant. Rheims was around 160 miles east of Yvetot, and I considered this a great opportunity to see more of France as well as visit an historic city with its great cathedral.

Although skies remained dark and gloomy, the trip was mostly free of rain. This gave me a chance to see the countryside. As a farm boy I admired the small, neat and generally attractive farms. In one area farmers had just completed the harvesting of a crop unrecognizable to me. It looked to be somewhere between the size of a large turnip and a cabbage. Great piles of these brown colored vegetables could be seen on many farms. Later I learned that they were sugar beets, an important crop in this part of France.

We traveled a roadway that was hard surfaced but very narrow. We saw no motorized traffic, except in a few large towns. On the other hand, we encountered a lot of two wheeled carts and bicycles. Farmers drove their vehicles with a careless disregard for any other users of the highway. The presence of huge army trucks bearing down upon them did not appear to faze either cart drivers or cyclists. Pedestrians in the towns behaved the same way, darting across the street without any consideration for what might be coming at them. As a result, drivers soon learned to drive like mad at the outskirts of a town and close up bumper to bumper in an effort to discourage people from crossing in front of them.

As a schoolboy who found the First World War (still the "Great War" then) both fascinating and appalling, I had read everything available to me on its history. On the road to Rheims I formed a sentimental link to that history as I crossed rivers (Oise and Aisne) and passed through a town (Soissons) made familiar by my reading. Two remarkable sights in the general vicinity of Soissons touched me deeply and remain lodged in my memory to this day. The juxtaposition of the two in my mind demonstrated in a strikingly unforgettable way the tragic side of American participation in two European wars.

The first came as we were admiring a beautiful valley far below the highway. Looking down I beheld the movement of a train bearing the familiar olive drab coloring of the U.S. Army. A large red cross on each car identified it as a hospital train. With a mixture of shock and sorrow I realized it carried wounded men from the battlefront. A few miles further on we suddenly came upon an immaculate field filled with orderly rows of hundreds of white marble crosses. This American cemetery, the Oise-Aisne, had been created for the interment of nearly 6,000 Americans killed in this vicinity in 1918. Brought together in this short distance and time, these dramatic sights of the results of two world wars made a haunting and everlasting impact.

At the supply depot in Rheims I got my first look at a German soldier. As a prisoner of war he certainly did not look like an Aryan superman. I did admire, even envy, his boots for they appeared superior to the sorry pair on my feet.

Observing a Frenchman walking by with an unpackaged loaf of bread under his arm, I asked a nearby soldier how one got such a loaf. He directed me to a bakery. When I confessed my ignorance of the French language, he said, in effect, "no problem." "Just go in and ask for pain" (or so it sounded to me) "and hand the baker some invasion francs. He will pick out the correct amount and hand you a loaf of bread." And so I became the pleased possessor of a delicious loaf of golden crusted bread.

While in Rheims I had time to admire its imposing cathedral. Sand bags had been piled high around the exterior to protect its beautiful windows from possible war damage, but even this unsightly distraction could not detract from the overall air of grandeur about this magnificent structure.

On the return trip I experienced some uneasy moments. Getting sleepy, the driver stopped the truck and asked me to take over. He was soon fast asleep in the passenger corner. Left on my own, I quickly found that the driving skills learned at Beale, including double-clutching, were still with me.

All went well until we got into a more hilly area and the truck's load seemed to pull it down a lot more than the five or six trucks ahead. Gradually, they began pulling away. Eventually, I topped a hill, and the truck I had been following had disappeared. This became a more worrisome problem when I passed through a town. There were neither numbers nor signs on any of the possible roadways and I could only hope that I had chosen the right one in leaving town. After several miles and no sign of any trucks ahead, I began to doubt my choice. At last we got on a straight stretch of road and to my intense relief I spotted the convoy ahead. By the time we reached the bivouac area I had closed up and the driver remained unaware of what had happened.

What the two fellows following me thought, I did not want to know.

When the overshoes were distributed, I was left disappointed, angry, and without overshoes. I was aggravated with myself for trusting the army to get it right. Too late I understood that I should have risked getting into that warehouse to search for large overshoes. Whoever was responsible for getting them for the 311th must have considered size 11 feet as large. Apparently it did not occur to them that the regiment might include a few men with size 12 and beyond. I have no idea of the total number of men in the regiment without overshoes, but two of us in the AT Company were among those left out. While the rest of the company cleaned muddy boots and pulled on new overshoes, Lt. Janowitz and I continued to plod around in leaky combat boots.

It did not help my attitude toward the matter to discover much later that the army could have issued us some waterproofing material for our miserable boots. At least this might have reduced the leaks to minor seepage.

Trying to eat Thanksgiving dinner in France, 1944, was an unforgettable experience. The army provided turkey and all the good things to go with it. We filed through the service tent, filled our mess kits, and then stood out in the pouring rain to eat. Water ran off my helmet liner. Water ran down my raincoat and soaked my trousers. I stood ankle deep in mud. The piece of turkey in my mess kit soon floated in more water than gravy.

One of the regimental chaplains came to hold a Thanksgiving service for our company. It was well attended, much better than chapel services at Pickett. No doubt this could be attributed in no small part to the rapid approach of combat for us. This can have a way of sharply focusing one's thoughts upon a Higher Power. It did not hurt attendance to hold the service in a nice dry shelter. Since arriving in France, I had been admiring a few examples of French skill in thatching. The owner of the estate on which we were encamped let us have the use of a large thatched roofed shed for the service.

Shortly after Thanksgiving, we were ordered to strike tents and prepare to move out. Even though we knew this meant moving closer to a combat zone, there were no regrets at leaving what had become known as "Camp Mud." The regiment's rifle and heavy weapons companies were taken to the train station at Yvetot and loaded on a long line of freight cars. These were like, and possibly even the same in some cases, the cars used to haul American soldiers in World War I and were called "40 and 8's" because they held 40 men or 8 horses. The regiment's cannon, service, headquarters, and anti-tank companies joined a lengthy motor convoy.

It was with some relief that I learned we were headed for eastern Belgium not far from the German border. Rumor had said we might go to the Netherlands. Since I had heard many unpleasant stories about the Canadians fighting in flooded areas there, I wanted to go more directly to Germany. It was just as well that I was completely ignorant of the nature of weather and terrain in that part of Germany I was destined to see.

The move gave me the opportunity to see more of the countryside of northern France. It was something of a thrill to recognize battle sites of World War I in Belgium, such as Charleroi. People were friendly in all the towns and villages that we passed through, both in France and Belgium. They stood along the roadway waving and cheering, sometimes flashing the "V" for victory sign. In several places we saw the results of recent battles, most conspicuously in the form of ugly German tanks that had been destroyed. Occasionally we came across big guns that the enemy had abandoned in the retreat toward the German frontier.

Tongeren, a Flemish town about 30 miles west of Aachen, Germany, became the focal point of the division's bivouac area. Our company went to Jesseren, a small agricultural village about five miles west and north of Tongeren.

Our platoon pitched tents in a farmer's small pasture about 50 yards behind his dwelling. This time tents were erected at random with no one to bother us about orderly rows! Instead of the isolated farms familiar to me, here all the farmers lived in close proximity to each other and went out from this village to work their fields. The family lived in one end of the dwelling and their animals occupied the other. In the case of the farm where my platoon camped, the farmer had paved the area behind the dwelling with cobblestones. Animal stalls were kept surprisingly clean, I noted, with plenty of fresh straw. Just outside the animal entrance he kept a neat manure pile and frequently washed the cobblestones around it. In the springtime the manure would be distributed on his fields as fertilizer.

From grade school days I had always associated wooden shoes with the Dutch people. But I discovered that "our" Belgian farmer kept a pair of wooden shoes at his back door. As a farm boy familiar with the mess of barns and feedlots, I admired his resourcefulness in resorting to wooden shoes. Quickly grasping that American soldiers had a penchant for souvenirs, some enterprising villagers began carving miniature shoes for sale. I put a couple of those in my duffel bag to be sent to my mother and grandmother at some future time.

Belgium had been occupied by German forces for more than four years. Only a few weeks earlier American soldiers had driven German troops from the Tongeren area. The gratitude of the Belgian people toward these American liberators was reflected in the warm welcome extended to the men of the 78th Division.

We discovered immediately that our bivouac area was positioned directly beneath the flyway for German V-1 rockets aimed toward the port of Antwerp and other targets to our west. As light was fading that first evening in Jesseren, I became aware of a noise in the sky. At the same time I glimpsed flashes of light, which were followed immediately by sounds of explosions as anti-aircraft batteries east of us began firing. As the noise drew nearer and grew louder, it reminded me of a noisy and not very well-tuned Model T Ford. Then a cigar shaped object with stubby wings, spewing sparks from its tail, passed right above our tents. Thus I was introduced to the "buzz bomb."

We were told that as long as we could hear the V-1's engine, there was no cause for alarm, but if the engine shut off, it was time to worry. This meant it was ready to glide in for a landing, and with its primitive and unstable guidance system it could hit almost anywhere.

The daily flights of the buzz bombs became such a routine matter that I eventually gave them little thought. But one day as Carl and I were standing near our tent, we suddenly became aware of an abrupt and eerie silence. As I seem to recall, it felt as though I had been hit in the pit of my stomach when it dawned on me that the engine of an approaching buzz bomb had just shut off. There were no holes to get into and no barriers of any kind to protect us from flying metal. All we could do was drop flat on the ground and pray for the best. At the same time we looked up to see our platoon sergeant running across the pasture, frantically yelling "Take cover! Take cover!" To our astonishment, we saw him dive head first into his pup tent.

To our overwhelming relief the bomb hit somewhere beyond the village. As far as I know there were neither military nor civilian casualties, but it was my first really frightening experience. Afterward, Carl and I chuckled at the memory of our platoon sergeant acting as though a thin canvas cover could protect him. Still, on a more somber note, I believe that with that episode we both began to have uneasy feelings about his competency for combat leadership.

The weather turned colder and the chill from frozen ground easily penetrated our light weight sleeping bags. For the first time in several years, sinus problems began to plague me. The bones of my face and above my eyes became painfully sore. Leaning over the least bit caused the top of my head to feel like it would fall off. The intensity of the pain in my head seemed to fluctuate with my pulse, alternately easing and pounding with each heart beat, producing a maddening jack-hammer effect. Unlike the sinus headaches of earlier years which generally eased off at night, this went on without any sign of relief. Regrettably I never deal well with pain, and one day I thought I had just about reached the limit of my tolerance. A couple of friends were commiserating with me. One was James Ford, a man in his upper twenties, possessor of a college degree and widely acknowledged as the most informed and wisest man in the platoon. Impatiently feeling that I could not endure waiting around and hurting so fiercely, I said I wished they would send us on to the front (we were about 40 miles from it) and get it over with one way or another. Ford, in his calm and sensible way, replied: "You can't really mean that, Breeze. You have no idea what we are going to get into."

He was absolutely right, of course, and feeling something of a sense of remorse, I have always regretted my foolish outburst. His words would remain in my mind, indelibly fixed by his death a short time later. Since early 1945 his body has rested at Henri Chapelle Cemetery, located only a few miles southeast of the site of our conversation that December morning. Why I should be spared and Ford taken, remains one of those inexplicable mysteries of my life.

I did get relief from the sinus pain. After the company moved to Jesseren and went into reserve, the division's medical battalion assigned a medic to our platoon. He persuaded me to see one of the doctors and so, for the first and only time in my military service, I went on sick call. Lt. Janowitz's jeep driver took me to see the doctor.

After examining me, the doctor shook his head in discouragement. With a case as bad as mine, he indicated, probably the only real help would be a change to a climate akin to that of Arizona. We both agreed the climate could only get worse for me. But he put drops up my nose and supplied me with a small bottle of the medication. Surprisingly, for I did not have much confidence, the medication provided miraculous relief. This was in the days before the use of plastic containers, of course, and during the winter of 1944-45 I guarded that small glass bottle as though my life depended upon it, fully as much as a rifle or carbine.

It helped that I was able to get off the cold ground and into a warm place for about a week. The good people of the village began to invite us in out of the elements. My squad moved into the loft above the animals of the farmer who owned the land where the platoon camped. We placed our sleeping bags on a pile of straw, and it gave me the most comfortable sleeping arrangement I would have for a long time.

In the evenings the family invited us to come down to their dwelling area for a while, and several of us accepted their hospitality. The medic stayed with our squad and through him we managed some communication with the family. Tongeren was about five or six miles above that invisible frontier that divides Belgium into Flemish and French speaking parts. Jesseren was in the Flemish section. At least some of the family must have been bilingual, however, for the medic used his knowledge of French to talk with them.

In addition to the parents, there were two very attractive daughters, one probably 16 or 17 and the other a couple of years older. I believe there was a son but I have forgotten where he was at the time. Obviously the long period of German occupation had been a grim experience for the family. The parents told us they were fearful for their daughters and tried to keep them out of sight whenever the Nazi officials or German soldiers came into the area.

I remember these evenings with gratitude. Along with more comfortable sleeping quarters, they provided a bright and pleasant interlude in an otherwise dark and dismal period of my life. Later I would regret that I had neglected to write down the family name and the individual names. They have long since faded from my memory.

All too soon the demands of war took me away from this momentary oasis of comfort. Near the end of the first week in December, the 78th Infantry Division was assigned to a corps of the First Army. I believe it must have been the evening of December 8 that Lt. Janowitz came to our loft with orders to prepare to leave for the front the next day. We were to relieve a unit of another division, and our mission would be to participate in seizing an important dam on the Roer River. I tried to visualize an area that the lieutenant described as heavily forested, very rough and hilly.

Each of us already had received a full supply of ammunition. We were told to take a few necessary items in our packs and stow everything else in our duffel bags to be left in storage. Two very surprising items were left behind: overcoats and gas masks. Later on I came to understand why

I was expected to face the bitter cold of a German winter without benefit of my heavy woolen overcoat.

More worrisome as I left for the front was my feeling of nakedness at leaving my gas mask in the top of my duffel bag. The horror of gas, learned so well at Camp Beale, remained firmly embedded in my mind. Interestingly, it appeared that our leadership trusted the enemy a lot more than the latter trusted us, for I soon encountered German soldiers carrying gas masks.

As our squad completed preparations to leave for the front, we knew this surely would be the last opportunity to sleep in a safe and comfortable setting for a long time to come. Even so, I do not think any of us had restful sleep that last night in Belgium.

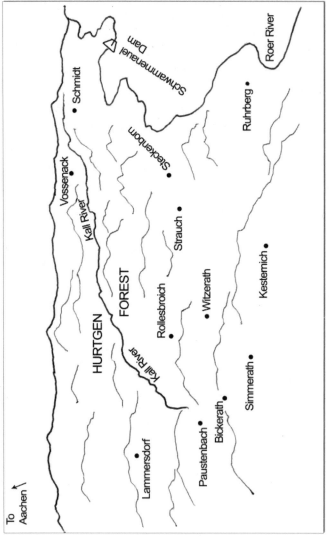

The 311th Infantry Area of Action
December 9, 1944 - February 9, 1945

Entered combat December 9, 1944 in the Hurtgen Forest area around Vossenack. Moved to the Lammersdorf, Simmerath, Kesternich area during the Battle of the Bulge. Beginning January 30, 1945 participated in the push to take Schmidt and the Roer River Dams.

Chapter Ten

The Hurtgen Forest and the Bulge

In order to get to the front from the Tongeren area, we went through the narrow slice of the Netherlands that lies between Belgium and Germany. Although it did not resemble my image of Dutch countryside drawn from *Hans Brinker* and other boyhood reading, I was glad to add another foreign country to my list. We crossed the historic Maas River (the Meuse in France) and passed through the important city of Maastricht.

I did not realize it at the time, but we were near the town of Valkenburg where I would spend two or three days on a rest pass a few months later. And I am sure we passed through the village of Margraten. The only American military cemetery in the Netherlands had been established there in November. The bodies of many members of the 311th would be returned here for burial, among them one of my officers and one of my best friends from UNH.

Just inside the German frontier we arrived at the city of Aachen, which I remembered from history as the capital of the great Charlemagne. It had been subjected to both aerial and artillery bombardment, for German forces had defended it stubbornly before it fell to the First Army in late October. From all I could see, the city had been reduced to a mass of ruin and rubble.

Snow began falling before we reached Aachen. It became heavier as we moved southeastward into a wooded area. Finally, deep in the forest, we stopped and placed the 57 in an assigned spot near a crossroads, or what served as roads in the area. Other units dug in across the road. Temporarily attached to the 8th Infantry Division, the 311th took over a broad front of around seven thousand yards.

Although it was probably no later than four in the afternoon, already it was growing dark, and not simply because of the heavy snow. December days were short anyway, but I had never spent a winter this far north. The heavy forest made it all the darker, and it did not help the mind-set to realize we could expect but a few hours of daylight each day.

The forest was the Hurtgen. Long before I knew much about it, or learned that other infantry divisions had preceded us there with disastrous consequences, I developed a deep dread of it. The gloomy appearance was bad enough in itself, but I soon learned it was one of the most dangerous places to be.

German artillerymen fired shells into the trees, and the shells exploded upon contact, raining shrapnel over a wide area and making it nearly impossible to find protective cover. Shattered trees offered mute testimony that this had been going on for weeks. There is a peculiar smell associated with the combination of explosive powder and the resin from a shattered fir. It permeated the Hurtgen and became enduring in my memory. I can recall it today as a signal representing danger. Even the smell of a freshly broken bough from a pine tree can trigger this unpleasant association.

After the war, military writers were highly critical of the high command's decision to send division upon division to be chewed up in the Hurtgen. Some considered it a battle that never should have been. Casualties taken by some of our predecessors were staggering, and overall the Hurtgen easily became the bloodiest battleground since Normandy.

There really was a very legitimate military objective deep in the forest, Schwammenauel Dam on the Roer River. When Lt. Janowitz first spoke of this river, I found it very confusing. The pronunciation for the Roer is similar to that of the Ruhr, in fact it is sometimes spelled Rur. Knowing that the Ruhr was at the heart of a great industrial district, but east of the Rhine, I could not see how we were expected to get to it.

Once located on the map, the military significance of the Roer could be appreciated. About 130 miles in length, it rises in that border area of Belgium and Germany south of Aachen, runs through Monschau and moves northeastward through the Hurtgen forest. It goes through Duren, east of Aachen, and makes a long arc northwestward to enter the Maas in the Netherlands several miles north of Aachen.

The American Ninth Army and British units under Montgomery would have to cross this arc to get to the Rhine. But at a crucial moment the Germans could cause havoc by releasing billions of gallons of water from the Schwammenauel and a smaller dam on a Roer tributary. Blockbuster bombs had failed to destroy the dams, hence the need for the infantry to capture the town of Schmidt, key to their control.

My mental picture of the area, drawn from the lieutenant's briefing back in Belgium, had been far too simplistic. Once in the Hurtgen we were still a long way from the dams. Between us and Schmidt were thousands of well-armed enemy soldiers, cleverly camouflaged pillboxes, innumerable hidden mines, booby traps, and other devilish devices. To guard against one of the latter (a nearly invisible wire stretched between trees across a narrow roadway) the driver of the platoon's jeep welded, to the front of his vehicle, a vertical bar with a hook on its end to catch the wire before it caught his head or throat. Our company's fourth platoon was called upon to deal with some of the mines.

The 311th took over an area that approached Schmidt from the northwest. It was an area of some of the worst possible terrain. Parts of it were nearly impassable and it limited mobility and nullified any superiority we might hope to claim in firepower. In retrospect it makes no sense to me that earlier at least three divisions had chosen (or perhaps were forced to choose) this approach. Their failure to get through is completely understandable.

Aside from all the problems presented by terrain and clever enemy defenses, December weather became a formidable foe. Some writers have described it as the worst fall and winter weather in decades. Whether true or not I do not know, but I do know that the army had not prepared us for it. I wore my woolen trousers and shirt with a heavy woolen sweater over that, a woolen stocking cap under my helmet liner, gloves and, for outer wear, a field jacket that compared to some developed later was definitely light weight. Note: forty years later my son and army sergeant daughter-in-law gave me a "replacement" that had been declared surplus. It is too much for all but the coldest winter days in Missouri, but it would have been very welcome in the Hurtgen Forest!

Part of the fortifications of the Siegfried Line in the Lammersdorf-Simmerath area included cleverly camouflaged pillboxes.
(From *Combat Journal*)

German soldiers wore long heavy-looking overcoats, and in a place where visibility was often bad, an American soldier's first reaction was to shoot at anyone in a long coat. Under such circumstances, and no matter how bitter the cold, I hardly could regret that my overcoat was somewhere in my duffel bag. My major gripe was that if, as claimed, we were winning the war, how come we were the ones in the light jackets?

The only good thing in this whole miserable scenario was the continued effectiveness of my sinus medication. Even sleeping (stretching a point to use the term!) on cold ground or in snowy holes did not bring back the severe headaches.

On the other hand I worried a lot about trench foot. I do not recall ever hearing the term until I got to the Hurtgen. An inflammatory swelling, even erupting in sores, of the lower limbs and feet brought about by persistent dampness and cold, it caused several thousand casualties that winter of 1944-45.

One very early casualty was a fellow in the platoon whose feet had given him trouble for some time and then had worsened in France and Belgium. Once in Germany he quickly became incapacitated with trench foot. He never returned to us, and I assume he went home permanently crippled.

This is another area where luck (if not a more positive force) surely was with me. With leaky boots, cold feet, and occasional foot discomfort anyway (thanks to my "thirteen Annies" in basic), I seemed a prime candidate for trench foot. Still, when the medic stuck a pin in my feet in his frequent testing for beginning signs of trench foot, I could feel it. Never have I been so glad to feel pain.

Captain Gapen helped us all by having, if at all possible, clean dry socks brought up to us each day. My chances of avoiding trench foot improved later on when one of my squad mates (Gordon Gracey, I believe) found a pair of overshoes that fit me. As I recall he came upon an American tank that had been destroyed and large overshoes had been left behind. The initial snowfall must have stayed on the ground around two months, and about the time it began to melt a lot the army had finally issued me new rubberized boots.

In a grim sort of way, but only long after the fact, an amusing incident happened in the forest. At one point the squad found a rough kind of log shelter about five feet high, with boughs across the top. Four of us claimed it for a sleeping place. One fellow got the bright idea of fastening shelter halves together and securing them beneath the boughs to catch any possible snow melt.

Richard Meade and I were working together as combat buddies. When Meade and I crawled into the shelter that night for our turn to sleep, we found an ominous bulge just above our sleeping bags. Afraid to leave it, yet preferring the log shelter to a hole in the ground, we tried to drain it. Meade carefully eased the water over to one edge where I caught it in a canteen cup. Then the whole thing started to get away from him, and I began bailing and throwing water over my shoulder as fast as I could. Naturally some of it fell onto our sleeping bags anyway. But then, to my disgust, I found that I had thrown almost all the water I caught into my boots over in the corner—about the last thing I needed to inflict on myself.

Our spirits lifted one morning when the sun came out bright and beautiful. We did not have long to enjoy this rare sight before German planes appeared on the scene. When we first became aware of them, I thought the engines sounded different from American planes, less smooth and more rough sounding than the V-1 engines. But a fellow in another squad who had been an Air Corps trainee assured us they were our planes. He quickly changed his mind when they dropped down and began strafing our lines. Then they turned and went after some of the artillery positions behind us, perhaps figuring that more would be gained by destroying them.,

Fortunately, clear skies gave American fighter planes a chance to operate, and after awhile, they arrived in our sector. Confronted by superior numbers, the Germans soon turned and flew away. According to some reports we were getting from home, Germany was not supposed to have any planes left. But several times in the next two or three months many of us were in a position to know otherwise.

At some point our squad was ordered to move to a small town (probably Vossenack, but I am not certain) and to prepare for an attack in the direction of Schmidt. Sgt. Walter Jarzylo, our squad leader, took a man and went forward to scout the area. We were to dig in at the edge of the town, and they found that except for a few scattered trees our assigned position was in full view of Germans on a distant hill.

Once we had some cover of darkness, the sergeant led us back to begin digging holes. The night was very dark, the ground partially frozen, and our small entrenching tools made it an interminable task. Several times in the darkness I thought I was removing a generous hunk of dirt only to realize by its weight that the shovel had practically nothing in it. That frustrating experience gave me an everlasting standard for measuring a truly helpless feeling—it is like trying to dig a foxhole with a very small shovel on a very dark night. Before we left we tried to disguise the exposed earth by covering it with snow.

When at dusk the next day we came back with the anti-tank gun to occupy the position, we received a rude jolt. German artillery had enlarged some of our fox holes by dropping shells in and around them. We abandoned the site in favor of a partially standing shed at the edge of the village. We knocked a hole in the wall to accommodate the barrel of the 57 and tried to disguise its presence. A small cellar beneath a ruined house in front of the shed offered some security as we took turns sleeping.

In giving up the area, the enemy had left behind some of their dead. One body lay in a ditch directly across the road from our position. The absence of odor reminded us of at least one good thing about very cold weather.

All houses in the village suffered some degree of damage. A camouflage net had been strung across one side of the roadway through the village. This afforded some semblance of cover as we moved about during daylight hours.

A 311th rifle company was in and near the village. I think it may have been Jim B.'s, but I never came across him. By this time an anti-aircraft battalion (552d AAA) had been attached to the division, and one of its batteries was positioned nearby.

German planes showed up here also. One came down the middle of the road firing his machine guns, and I fully expected him to put bullets into our inadequate shelter. The anti-aircraft boys hit him just before he reached us, however, and he limped away smoking. About this same time I saw my first dogfight. Although obviously deadly real, it was a thrilling sight with each plane diving and maneuvering around to come swooping down on the other with tracers spitting from their machine guns.

Beginning back in Belgium, there were nights when we heard British bombers on their way to targets in Germany. After we moved into Germany, again there were nights when we heard the heavy drone of bombers. But one December night we heard plane noises that sounded markedly different, both lower and closer to us. Strangely they appeared to be going in the opposite direction of the usual flow of the RAF.

The next day reports began to reach us that German paratroopers had been dropped behind us, that they were dressed in American uniforms, possessed American equipment, and spoke fluent English. This was most disconcerting news to a bunch of green troops. We soon were aware that all plans for an attack on the morning of the 17th had been placed on hold, and we shifted to a defensive mode. All of us were very jittery and not helped much when, at nightfall, our platoon sergeant cautioned us to be especially careful: "There's hellza lotsa German paratroopers in the immejit vicinity!"

In following the north and west route taken by earlier divisions, the 311th provided a diversion for the division's main plan. To 78th Division planners, the most tactically sound direction to the Roer dams was south from Aachen to Lammersdorf, just inside the border, and on to utilize the ridge line of the Monschau Corridor. But while this avoided the denser forests and deeper ravines of the northern approach, it presented some of the most formidable parts of the Siegfried Line.

Some three or four days after we got into the Hurtgen, the Division's other regiments (309 and 310) launched the main attack. They breached the first band of the Siegfried Line at Lammersdorf and with much hard fighting started moving south and east only to run into a German counter attack on the 16th of December.

Dates escape my recall, and most likely I was not always clear on them at the time, but sometime after the 17th our platoon was ordered south to relieve an anti-tank unit of the 309th in a place called Simmerath. In order to get south, we first had to back track north and west through the forest, retracing some of the route by which we had entered. Then somewhere below Aachen we turned south to Lammersdorf.

There I got my first good look at what was most often depicted in American press pictures as the Siegfried Line—the conspicuous line of concrete dragon's teeth marching off into the distance. Less noticeable, but much more deadly barriers, however, were the mutually supporting pillboxes. In some places along the lengthy West Wall, the more official German name for the line, there would be a second band of fortifications. This happened to be one of those places.

I got my first look at the "Dragon's Teeth" of the Siegfried Line near Lammersdorf, Germany. (From *Combat Journal*)

Situated about four miles south and east of Lammersdorf, the town of Simmerath would be our platoon's locale during what came to be known as the Battle of the Bulge. The other three platoons that made up our company were in and around some of the neighboring towns and villages. We went through some of these on the way to take up our position.

We arrived in Simmerath as darkness fell and proceeded several hundred yards down what appeared to be the main roadway through the town. At what looked to be one of the last buildings on the right side of the road, we stopped. It was a solidly built brick structure that had withstood the battering from exploding shells better than many of the town's buildings, some of which were completely destroyed and all damaged to some extent. Attached to the house, and also of brick, was a blacksmith's shop. Millsaps was glad to see that the shop had a door just barely wide enough to accommodate his small truck.

Returning to Lammersdorf over four decades later, the author found trees growing among some of the "teeth."

Almost thirty feet beyond the shop, a kind of fence row ran at right angles to the road. The fellows of the 309th had dug in their 57, along with a few foxholes, behind this hedge. This gave a good field of fire against both road traffic and anyone approaching through the small open field beyond the fence row. We made a quick exchange of guns, Millsaps hastily backed his truck through the shop's narrow doorway, and some of us jumped into the ready-made foxholes.

Understandably, the men we relieved were in a hurry to get away from the area. But they lingered long enough to fill us in on what to expect. None of what they had to say was at all reassuring. During daylight hours, they said, we would get a lot of artillery fire and some mortar fire. The Germans had some observation of the area and liked to drop mortar shells on anyone spotted in the open. Snipers, too, liked to take a shot at the unwary. Be on guard at night, they cautioned, against enemy patrols trying to penetrate the town. In addition to at least two men in the foxholes by the gun all the time, at night the 309th had placed a couple of men at a window on the second floor of the house. From that spot they could detect anyone coming up the snow covered road.

Aftermath in Lammersdorf, the jump-off town for the 78th attack, December 13, 1944.
(From *Combat Journal*)

Although we entered Germany with the normal anti-tank complement of 10 men, our squad had been reduced to eight by the time we took a position in Simmerath. Sgt. Jarzylo divided us into four pairs of combat buddy teams. He paired me with Richard Meade who at 33 was the old man of the squad. Short in stature and often stooped from the cold, he looked and acted his age which, at that point, seemed very advanced to me. The life we had been forced into was hard on us all, but I thought it especially hard on him.

From an urban background in Massachusetts and Catholic in religion, Meade would have seemed a mostly unlikely partner for a Protestant farm boy from Missouri. But the nature of the circumstances and the sharing of fear, danger, and discomfort quickly drew us together. We made a good team, I think, and could depend upon each other. But it did appear that in dangerous moments, luck was more on my side than his. Sadly, I came to think that fate was against him from the outset.

At night two men stayed with the gun, two took rifles and observed the road from a point on the second floor, and the other four took a turn at sleeping in the small cellar beneath the house. In the beginning we tried to rotate teams about every two hours. It was bitter cold in the foxholes and not a lot better upstairs where the wind blew through a shattered window. Fear and nerves made the cold feel even more intense. I never liked the dark and in boyhood could conjure up all kinds of imagined terrors. Darkness in Simmerath held real threats and the wind whistling through the trees and the damaged buildings nearby created an unsettling atmosphere. Only an occasional artillery shell fell during the darkness. Sporadic small arms fire could be heard coming from other parts of the town, but none of us spotted any attempt to penetrate our sector.

With daylight the artillery fire began. That was bad enough in itself; but both puzzling and frightening, it appeared to be coming at us from all sides. This did not make any sense, and we began to think that some of it had to be from our own artillery. As it continued through the day, we developed bitter feelings about this possibility, and wondered why such an obvious error in fire direction had not been corrected.

The following morning our squad learned from Lt. Janowitz what was really happening. The news was bad and likely to get worse. Already we were surrounded on three sides by enemy troops. The ferocious German attack on the 16th that had driven our forces from much of Kesternich, a mile or so east of Simmerath, was not an isolated attack upon the 78th Division, but part of a large scale counter-offensive. The main thrust had broken through a thinly held line a few miles south of us, and already the Germans had created a huge bulge in the American line by pushing into Belgium to the south and west of our position.

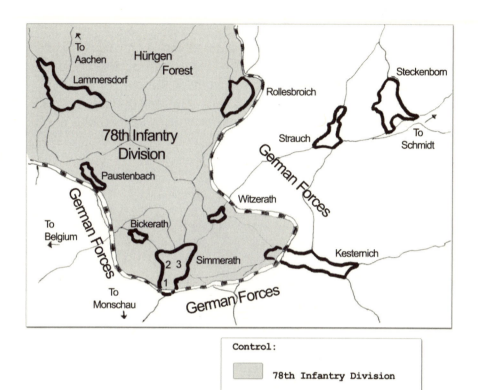

**The 78th Holds the North Shoulder
of the Battle of the Bulge**

1. 1st Squad, 3rd Platoon, AT Co., 311th Reg.
2. Headquarters, 3rd Platoon
3. "88 Corner"

Distances:
Simmerath is less than 2 miles from Kesternick,
approximately 4 miles from Lammersdorf,
and about 5 miles north of Monschau.

The 78th was left on the north shoulder of the bulge. As the division history would describe it later: "The Division stuck out like a sore thumb two miles into the German lines." (Chapter 3 of *Lightning*) Even though this was definitely an unenviable position to occupy, it could have been worse. If, when the division had been ordered into combat, we had been sent to Monschau (5 miles or so south of Simmerath), we would have been caught in front of the enemy advance rather than on its flank. Another new and inexperienced division (the 106th Infantry) had been sent to that area and the results were catastrophic.

During the Battle of the Bulge, the cold was bitter and penetrating. This unidentified 78th soldier has an inadequate field jacket, much like the one I wore. (From *Combat Journal*)

Later I understood why Kesternich and the surrounding area was so very important to the Germans. It was practically astride one of Field Marshal Von Runstedt's supply routes. According to the division history, the 78th was under orders to hold the road center just north of Konzen and the Paustenbach knoll "at all costs." (Chapter 3) Paustenbach was a small town about two miles northwest of Simmerath.

The division successfully held this defensive position from December 16th to the end of January when enemy troops were cleared from the Ardennes. Thus, our platoon spent the Battle of the Bulge in Simmerath. Another squad was dug in diagonally across the road from us. They had a large open field in front of them and were glad when our fourth platoon came one night and laid a protective belt of mines in front of them.

Lt. Janowitz, the sergeant, and the other members of platoon headquarters were located several hundred yards behind us in the basement of a church. The church was down a slope on one of the secondary streets running off the crossroads at the town's entrance. Though slightly damaged, this solidly built stone structure was one of the most secure spots in town. I do not recall, but I am sure our people must have shared the space with some of the other units in town. When 44 years later Christel and Dan took me back to a rebuilt and much larger Simmerath, the church was the only place in town that looked the least bit familiar. Company headquarters and the kitchen were located in one of the nearby towns, either Witzerath or Bickerath, I believe.

Beyond our position was one more building on the right side of the road. The 2nd Ranger Battalion had been attached to the 78th and some of its men were dug in near this house. It made our squad feel a little more secure to have these tough and experienced soldiers there with us.

In this narrative when I have located sites and positions by direction (north, south, etc.) I have done so by studying maps. At the time I was badly disoriented. Although our squad's position was at the edge of Simmerath on a road running south toward Monschau, it seemed north to me. We were two miles inside the frontier. If I had been turned loose on my own and told to make my way back to Belgium, I would have turned east (my inner compass telling me that was west) and gone deeper into Germany!

Simmerath's inhabitants had been evacuated earlier and, combined with the condition of its buildings, this absence of a civilian presence made it seem like a ghost town. Quite frankly we showed no respect for these people's property or things that undoubtedly were dear to them. If we found something we needed or simply wanted , we took it, or "liberated" it as one of the boys from New York was fond of saying.

This disregard for the possessions of others was another example of the dreadfully erosive effect of war upon our innocence and what most of us supposed were deeply ingrained and unshakable ethical principles. I found myself blaming these people for supporting, or anyway tolerating, a thoroughly evil political system that had disrupted my life and brought injury and death to my buddies. Consequently I could pick up a bunch of old coins (possibly valuable) and some multi-million mark notes issued in Germany's post-World War I inflationary era (worthless except as souvenirs) from their damaged homes without a twinge of conscience.

Not just my squad but other units in and around the town ransacked the houses in search of sheets and other white cloth. From these items we fashioned pieces to cover our helmets and uniforms and provide some camouflage as we moved about in the snow.

As we searched houses for cloth and anything else of use, we found evidence of Nazi influence (pins with Swastikas for example) and party membership (the lapel pins that members wore). But surprising to those of us still naive enough to believe our own propaganda, we came upon signs of deep religious feeling (such as Bibles, literature and various religious medals) in many homes. Somehow we had been led to believe that the Nazi assault upon religion had removed its influence. In a related vein it seemed perfectly clear to us that we were fighting for Right and that surely God was on our side. Therefore it was an eye-opening revelation to discover that some German soldiers wore large belt buckles boldly imprinted with the words "Gott mit uns." (God is with us)

The enemy soon figured out that we changed guard shifts every two hours. They were ready to drop a few mortar rounds on the open area between foxholes and the building when one group relieved another. To counter this, we varied shifts, anywhere up to six hours at a time, and did not always make the change on the clock hour.

My third Christmas with the army was the strangest ever. The morning of the 25th (in civilian life a time of warmth and eager anticipation) found me and Meade in a foxhole surrounded by snow. But while it did not seem at all like Christmas, quite literally there were bright spots. The sun made a rare appearance and the snow glistened as we looked out across the field. There was a marvelous and unusual hush in the air.

No shells passed over us, either incoming or outgoing. No mortars dropped around us if we moved about. We did not exchange small arms fire with the Germans. There was no chatter of machine gun fire, either the very rapid sound that identified the German or the slower staccato of our own heavy weapons company. I had read that such an unspoken cease fire existed on the Western Front in World War I. Indeed, it was a wonderful Christmas gift.

A few pieces of hard candy for each of us were sent with our food delivery. Since my father always had hard candy in the house for the Christmas season, this nostalgic reminder was as close as I could get to feeling at all like Christmas. The medic sneaked a little extra alcohol from the aid station, and someone got hold of a few tins of army issue grapefruit juice to concoct a Christmas punch.

Christmas night we nearly had a disaster of our own making. We had found an old lantern like the kind my father used in doing early morning chores; but lacking the kerosene normally used in it, we turned to gasoline to give some light to a windowless cellar. Early that evening the fuel burned out and we were plunged into darkness.

Thoughtlessly, Sgt. Jarzylo picked up a can of gas and began to pour. The moment the gas hit the hot metal it exploded in a flash of fire. The cellar was narrow and the burning lantern was between most of us and the stairs. In near panic we fled the cellar and streamed out into the street. Behind us we began to hear exploding shells as flames reached some ammunition and a carbine with a full clip that had been left behind. Then we began to fear that the noise would arouse the Germans and they would start dropping mortar shells upon us. But the Christmas spirit must have remained with them, for they passed up this opportunity to catch us exposed on a bright night.

Fortunately we came through this with no serious injuries. The chagrined sergeant emerged with only a good singeing and a few burn spots on his clothing. Later that night we were able to reenter the smoke filled cellar and discovered that most of our gear had not been reached by the fire. Christmas, 1944, could never be described as merry, but it certainly was memorable.

My last visit to a barber had been in Camp Pickett. By the end of the first month in Germany, my hair was a shaggy and unkempt mess. One day I sat on a gasoline can beside Millsap's truck and, using scissors from his sewing kit, he gave me a crudely fashioned haircut. We had few opportunities and little interest in shaving. Some of the youngsters (18 and 19) had little more than peach fuzz anyway, and I did not have much of a beard. On the other hand Gordon Gracey (from a town on Long Island) had a bushy beard and by mid January, we jokingly called him our "mad Russian" as he reminded some of us of the old caricature of Russian anarchists running around with hand bombs.

Cleanliness became a problem for us individually and had it not been for cold weather would have been so for those forced to be near us. Although I got frequent changes of socks, I had not had a complete change of clothes since leaving Belgium. Division leaders recognized this as a problem of both morale and health, and began to address it when matters stabilized in our sector.

The establishment of a rest center at Raeren, northwest of us in Belgium, gave a few fellows from my platoon an opportunity for a shower, fresh clothing, and a chance to sleep on a cot. Carl Hill was the first from our squad to get an overnight pass. He came back grateful for the shower and clean clothing, but otherwise disgruntled. It seems a German plane had strafed the building the one night he had been promised a decent night's sleep! Richard Meade had a happier time, either there or at another rest center, and looking back I expect it was the last good experience he would ever have.

In my case I caught a one day trip to some spot over the border in the Netherlands. Big shower tents had been set up and what a delicious feeling it was to stand beneath a stream of hot water! My pleasure was only slightly disrupted by the mischief of two small Dutch boys who opened the tent flap and tossed a snowball at my backside. Of course by the time I had dressed and moved outside they had vanished. Never has fresh underclothing felt so good to my skin, and I was very happy to exchange a badly soiled woolen uniform for a clean one.

Along with our food, we were sometimes brought five gallon cans of water, but this could be for drinking purposes only. Finding a child's sled and a large kettle, a couple of squad members were determined to get water for shaving and face washing from a well at the church. They started from there with a kettle full of water and managed to work their way back down the road without drawing enemy fire. But to their disgust, much of the water had sloshed out on the way. They were skeptical when I told them that my grandpa had taught me a trick they could use. During a very dry season in the 30's, he hauled many barrels of water for his cattle. Float a small board in the open kettle, I told them, and it will slosh back and forth with the water, and prevent it from spilling over the top. Far from convinced but willing to give it a try, the city boys went with me for another load of water. To their obvious astonishment, but pleased with their success, they discovered that the farm boy had been right.

After we had been at the front for the requisite 30 days, the 311th began awarding the Combat Infantryman Badge. Mine was issued January 10, 1945 and brought to me by Lt. Janowitz. This beautiful badge is very special and I always have been proud to receive it. (In 1999, my 77th birthday present from my wife was a Missouri license tag for our car, with the Combat Infantry Badge logo on it. It is one of the few "vanity" plates that ever caught my interest.)

Some time after mid-January my combat buddy was wounded. Meade and I had just completed a guard shift and were making our way back to the cellar when we heard the identifying "plop" of a mortar being fired. We were side by side, no more than two feet separating us, but he was between me and the exploding shell and caught all the shrapnel. A wound to the side of his face appeared to be the most severe injury. When he left for the aid station with our medic, I never expected to see him again. I assumed (erroneously) that after a period of hospitalization somewhere on the Continent or in England he would be returned to the States.

One other close encounter with mortars remains fixed in my memory and seems worth relating. The origins of the story remain obscure but for some reason Terry Millsaps drove the truck back to platoon headquarters. Sgt. Jarzylo, Louis Kolman and I rode with him. While there, we helped Terry put chains on the rear wheels for better traction in the snow. For some inexplicable reason Millsaps was then required to go on somewhere else and, concerned about the truck, he asked me to drive it back and get it under protective cover.

The dreaded "88 corner" at Simmerath, Germany.
(From *Combat Journal*)

From the church we would have to drive up to the crossroads, a spot known as "88 corner" because the Germans had zeroed in on it and liked to drop the dreaded 88 mm. shells on passing traffic. Millsaps urged that, once on our road at the corner, I "drive like hell." With the sergeant beside me and Kolman hanging on in back, I did just that, pushing it to the limit once we established traction.

The chains made a dreadful clatter and heralded our approach to the Germans down the road in front of us. It seemed an interminable distance to our destination, the blacksmith shop. About 200 yards short of our goal, the first mortars fell. With the first explosion, I became aware that the little redhead had dropped off the back of the truck and rolled into a ditch. Then the sergeant dropped off and hit the ditch. As he jumped he shouted something only partially intelligible: "-----------get off this damn thing." Whether the first part was an order for me to jump, or simply an announcement that he was leaving, I did not know. It did not matter anyway, for my subconscious took over and told me the truck had to be saved.

In a more rational moment I would have headed the truck directly into the shop's narrow opening. But my subconscious said that Millsaps always wanted the truck backed in, so applying a heavy foot to the brake, turning sharply to the left, and smoothly shifting into reverse, I shot the truck backwards through the doorway without touching either side, just as another mortar fell where I had been a fraction of a second earlier. The truck was saved, I did not have a scratch on me, and only one thing could have made it better—to have had a certain first sergeant from field artillery (back at Camp Pickett) seated beside me, and dare him to stay there until the truck had been parked precisely where Millsaps wanted it. He would have been dumbfounded by my sudden flair for driving.

One of the youngest members of our squad was from Brooklyn, N.Y. Arthur Warshak must have been just out of infantry basic when he joined us as we prepared to go overseas. I never became well acquainted with him. Unlike a few extroverts I knew from Brooklyn, Warshak appeared more reserved and at times almost detached from things going on around him. He moved about at his own slow and unhurried pace, that is until the day he had a close encounter with a German bullet. Happening to be in a position to observe him as he completed a foxhole shift, I watched him begin his usual stroll toward our building. A small shed was located not far from the gun. Just as Warshaw was about to clear the corner of the shed, I heard the crack of a rifle and a splintered hole appeared on the corner board of the shed exactly where his backside had been a millisecond earlier. We all noticed an alertness to his movements thereafter. Luck did not remain with him, however, for not long afterward he was wounded and never returned to us.

One cold January night a special unit came to Simmerath and set up loud speakers in our area. Promising cold "Deutschen soldaten" a warm shelter and hot food, the broadcast urged them to come over to our lines and surrender. I am not aware of any success with the enemy but we found it interesting. Shivering in foxholes and recalling a meal of cold C-rations, some fellows in my squad found the message (they understood the meaning if not the language) amusing in an ironic sort of way. It was probably Gracey who asked: "Where do we sign up to get in on that?"

It was probably near the end of December when the first replacements came to our company. The Bulge created a sudden and enormous demand for fresh manpower, especially in infantry regiments. The limited number of available men with infantry training led to a mixed bag of replacements. Along with men from infantry replacement training centers and some stripped from divisions recently arrived in England, there were men from a variety of rear echelon outfits. Most interesting of all were the non-coms among the latter. As I understood it, some actually had volunteered for this reassignment. We got at least one staff sergeant, possibly two, and a buck sergeant in our third platoon. They served their new units capably enough, but without experience and proper training their role in the platoon was little different from that of any private. Because the army's Table of Organization called for a certain number of ranks in a unit, I suspect the presence of these men who possessed rank but no leadership responsibilities blocked corporals and privates first class (thrust by circumstances into responsible roles) from ever gaining higher rank.

My letters home are of little use in trying to recall the winter of 1944-45. Looking back I find it appalling that I dared take a chance on not even telling my parents I was on the Continent, let alone in Germany. Of course I realized there was some risk that they might learn of this in a more devastating way, but I had a really profound conviction that nothing bad would happen to me. Some of my less fortunate friends, I should add, did not think it would happen to them either. Yet it did.

A few lines from a short V-Mail note hurriedly written four days after I entered the Hurtgen Forest set the tone for all my letters. "Just a few lines this afternoon to let you know I'm in good health, feeling fine, and getting along swell. . . . I hope you are both well. Please don't worry about me." (12/13/44) And four days after Christmas, a short V-Mail ended with: "I'm o.k. and hope you are the same." (12/29/44)

By the beginning of the new year, however, I had grown concerned enough to believe that someone in the family better know the truth of my location. Still, in my foolish thinking, I held back from laying a heavy burden of worry upon my mother. Instead, on January 4, 1945, 1 wrote to Aunt Georgia Breeze and put "Somewhere in Germany" at the top of the letter. "Does either the folks or Grandma know or suspect that I'm up here in combat?" I asked. "I didn't tell them that I'd even left England because knowing Mother I was afraid she would worry a lot without good cause. [As if there could be a much better cause!] As long as I can remain all right I don't think that I should tell them, do you? I've been up here quite a while and so far with the help of the Lord I've made out all right." (Aunt Georgia saved the letter and returned it to me many years later.) I do not recall her reply, but I continued to try to shield my parents from the truth and ran a frightful risk in so doing.

With one significant exception, all my letters to my parents from early February to early May have been lost. The lone surviving letter was written a few days after I had crossed the Rhine at Remagen and at an extremely bad time in my life. Obviously in a letter to me, Mother had revealed great worry about me and about something I must have written about my good friend from UNH, Frank Galloway.

"Mother," I replied to her letter:

> I'm afraid you are borrowing a little trouble for yourself and imagining things that you shouldn't. I didn't see Frank as I've never been over where I said he was. [probably France] I only had a letter from him. I haven't heard from him for a while so he might be over in Germany now. I'm sure he will be all right if he is there. (3/12/45)

This attempt at misdirection regarding my own location appears unbelievably reckless to me now. The fact that I continued to remain outwardly unscathed suggests that a higher power must sometimes look out for the young and foolish. Near the end of March I finally had to acknowledge to my parents that I was in combat. My March 30 V-mail to Aunt Georgia (this one also saved and returned to me years later) explained that Mother had read something about the 78th Division (probably related to Remagen.) Growing "pretty suspicious," she had asked directly if I was "still with" the division.

During our first two weeks or so in Germany, we saw our platoon sergeant two or three times each day. The company mess sergeant tried to send us two meals each day. Whenever possible, the platoon jeep driver, often accompanied by the sergeant, brought us big containers of food which on a good day might still have a little warmth when it reached me.

A side note on the food carried with us—usually we each had a box of K-rations or we might have access to a can of C-rations and hope we could build a fire to heat it. Actually I preferred the K-rations to anything else. It contained a small tin of either potted meat or cheese with bacon bits, a package of crackers, and either a bar of chocolate or fruit, plus a packet of Nescafe. A five gallon container of water would be supplied from which we filled our canteens.

When our platoon took up a defensive position in Simmerath, the kitchen was somewhere to our rear. But given the circumstances of the Bulge and our regiment's vulnerable position, our kitchen was still within enemy artillery range. I learned of at least one hit on it, and there may have been others. Even so, the mess staff still got food to us whenever they could. But if delivered to or near our position, it was usually done so by the jeep driver accompanied by either Lt. Janowitz or the platoon messenger.

We saw less and less of the platoon sergeant during our days in Simmerath, unless we went back to platoon headquarters. The lieutenant came around to our squad frequently but I do not recall seeing much of the sergeant. It struck me and others in my squad that he was developing a very bad case of nerves. For a while we were glad that he just stayed low in the church basement. It seemed best for all concerned when he stayed out of the way. But to our jeopardy as we saw less of him, we began to hear more from him.

The messenger, Wilbur Wishart, had strung several hundred yards of wire between platoon headquarters and each squad. We had a field telephone in a foxhole near the gun. We whistled into it whenever we wanted to raise someone at another phone. The whistle signal seemed loud and clear in the cold winter air, especially at night, and obviously it was meant to be used only for emergencies and to pass on vital information. The platoon sergeant, unfortunately, seemed incapable of distinguishing between a genuine emergency and his own worries and fears. On too many occasions someone in a foxhole responded to a whistle only to hear his excited voice say: "I hear there's hellza lotsa Germans out there tonight." "Hellza lotsa" was the sergeant's favorite quantitative measurement.

One dark night I was straining eyes and ears to determine if there was any movement around, when a piercing whistle suddenly broke the quiet. To me it sounded loud enough to be heard by anyone within a hundred yards. To stop it I quickly grabbed the receiver and from the other end of the line the sergeant asked: "See any Germans out there tonight?" I regret not having the audacity to say, "No, you damn fool, but with you calling attention to us we can expect them to drop in any minute now." My goal at the moment, however, was to get him off the line as quickly as possible.

Given the man's rank and his status in the company, especially with our commanding officer, there was nothing we could do about him. Even worse, I am afraid the lieutenant had little control over him. The phone could have been disconnected, but undoubtedly that would have led to

panic and forced poor Wishart out into the dark to track down the problem.

Exactly when and under what circumstances the platoon sergeant left us is not completely clear to me. It must have been either just before or soon after we went on the offensive from Simmerath. I recall Sgt. Jarzylo returning from reporting to platoon headquarters and telling the squad that the platoon sergeant had been sent somewhere, presumably for a needed rest. I also recall thinking that if anyone could get an extended rest, it surely would be the sergeant. At the same time I had to admit that if anyone needed a rest, in this case a rather euphemistic term for dealing with frayed nerves, it was the sergeant. But I was not alone in thinking that we were a lot better off without him, especially as he had been replaced with a staff sergeant who led another squad. Soon we began to hear stories that the old platoon sergeant had been sent to England.

Talking to his successor in the summer of 1999, I learned that while he was not clear as to the date he became platoon sergeant, he thinks it had to be in late January or early February. As to circumstances, all he remembers is that his predecessor needed a rest, was sent to England, and somehow never managed to get back to our outfit.

What remains mysterious is the fact that our former platoon sergeant's name is listed in the division history as a recipient of the Purple Heart. If so, this means that unknown to at least two of his squad leaders, he must have received some type of wound that led to his evacuation.

In the spring of 2001, I established contact with the driver who towed the gun for another squad. His assessment of our old platoon sergeant coincided exactly with my own: "He [the sergeant] couldn't hack it on the line." Also he recalled something that brought back a vague memory of what I had heard myself—a preposterous sounding rumor that the sergeant was back in the states to help raise money at war bond rallies!

In any case S/Sgt. Emerson Fett from Iowa became our

new platoon sergeant. We had come to the 78th at about the same time. He came from the Air Corps, however, not the ASTP, and there he had been allowed to retain the rank earned as part of a training cadre with the armored force. Immediately upon joining the anti-tank company he became a squad leader in the third platoon. Thus when he took over our platoon, all the old hands knew him, liked and admired him, trusted him and recognized him as a proven and courageous leader.

In my limited experience with games of chance or drawing for prizes and the like, I had never been lucky. But near the end of January, 1945, it appeared my luck had changed in a big way. With the ending of the Bulge, authorities at some higher level, whether regimental or even divisional I do not recall, decided that a few lucky men should be rewarded with a three day pass to Paris.

One such pass was allotted to my company. By some process it got to the third platoon and then to the first squad. Lt. Janowitz got us all together, shuffled a pack of cards, and announced that the holder of the highest card could go to Paris for three days. To my amazement, I won! I was going to Paris! Too good to be true—which of course it was, but neither I nor my somewhat envious buddies could know that at the moment.

Arrangements were made for me to get to Paris. I went back to the headquarters of some outfit (long since forgotten) from which I was to catch a truck the next morning and begin my journey. Unrolling my sleeping bag in a corner of a crowded room, I settled down to thoughts of a great adventure. Sometime after midnight I was rudely awakened by a noncom who told me that I had been ordered back to my outfit. We were, he informed me, jumping off on the attack at an early hour in the morning.

So, back I went to join in a totally different adventure from what I had anticipated. It would be 39 years before I got to Paris, and then at my own expense. I have always felt that someone (the army or perhaps the government) owed me a trip to Paris. When I met my old company commander 49 years later, he had completely forgotten the incident but saw no way I could ever collect.

The experience of appearing to win something that big only to have it snatched away in such brutal fashion convinced me that I truly have no luck at chance. Therefore casinos and lotteries, anything else that promises something for nothing, have never tempted me. I know better!

In the offensive push out from Simmerath I had my first contact with British troops. An armored squadron from the Fife and Forfar Yeomanry was attached to the 78th from late January to very early in February. They had a deadly flame-thrower mounted on a tank (Churchill type, I think). As we waited that first morning for our artillery to complete a pre-assault barrage, a Brit leaned out of his turret and I heard him promise: "We are going to give Jerry a hot time today." And they did. Their work against some of the more strongly fortified positions had a very convincing effect.

There was enemy resistance nearly everywhere in the area, but our second platoon probably got into the heaviest of it. As part of the 2d Battalion of the 311th, they were involved in the battle to take Kesternich, the place that had already cost so much. The Germans were still reluctant to give up this town that *The Stars and Stripes* called "Little Aachen." It took a lot of fierce fighting and a lot of casualties on both sides before it fell. For its action here and in surrounding areas the 2d Battalion (which included the AT's second platoon) was awarded a Presidential Unit Citation. Kesternich also produced the division's only Medal of Honor, awarded posthumously to a squad leader in a 311th rifle company, S/Sgt. Jonah E. Kelley of Company E.

In early February, 1945, the division was finally in a position to resume the long delayed attack upon Schmidt and seize the dams on the Roer. The weather changed enough that now we had cold rain instead of snow. Rain together with the snow melt led to mud problems.

Many of the details of this period elude me, but I remember that the company took many casualties. As we advanced on Schmidt I was temporarily assigned to another squad in the platoon. To the best of my knowledge this is the only time during that winter of 1944-45 that I was not with the first squad. Whose decision this was and for what purpose is beyond my recall, and I can think of no logical reason for it. For whatever reason it may have been a fateful decision for me, for by the time I returned to the first squad, somewhere on the other side of Schmidt, the squad had been decimated, suffering the highest percentage of casualties in the entire company.

The Roer and its tributaries flowed through treacherous terrain. (From *Combat Journal*)

In approaching Schmidt, our anti-tank guns had to be taken up a road that the enemy covered with rolling fire from 88's. To get off the road was to run the risk of getting into mine fields. From time to time, however, both foot troops and drivers of vehicles tried to avoid the obvious dangers of the roadway only to get caught amidst the mines. Sadly, this happened to the first squad as the company moved toward Schmidt in the dark.

Except for an image of devastating ruin and destruction all around (perhaps partly due to photographs seen later) and a memory of apprehension and fear (a normal recollection under the circumstances), my mind is blank on what happened as we moved into and through Schmidt. Emerson Fett, my platoon sergeant at the time, recalls getting into town, a confrontation with German soldiers and "all hell breaking loose." (telephone conversation, summer, 1999)

Schmidt, key to the control of the Schwammenauel Dam. (From *Lightning*)

A letter (Sept. 30, 1999) from Harold E. Tiedeman (a 1st lieutenant in our company) gave me the benefit of a platoon leader's recollection of Schmidt. Also, he enclosed a copy of a short piece he had written about the experience. In taking the guns of his platoon (the first, I believe) into Schmidt, he passed burning and destroyed American tanks. As he and Capt. Gapen checked out a road intersection, they came under rifle fire. The lieutenant found shelter in a basement of a badly damaged brick building. Some soldiers from another unit also found refuge there. Fire from 88's continued through the night and at daybreak a mortar shell set fire to the truck carrying ammunition for the anti-tank platoon. At some point the lieutenant received what he described as a "minor" wound.

By February 8th, the 310th and the 311th had taken Schmidt, the fortress town that guarded the Roer dams, and a sign was erected at its western approach road: "You are now entering the town of Schmidt through the courtesy of the 78th Division." By February 10th the 309th had control of the Schwammenauel Dam and the 78th had completed the major mission assigned it when we left Belgium two months earlier. A special team from the 303d Engineer Battalion found that the Germans had blown enough of the dam's controls and the penstock to cause some flooding of the Roer. But the major part of the dam with its impounded water remained intact and Gen. Eisenhower's plan for the invasion of northern Germany could no longer be threatened by the Roer River.

The 78th captured the Schwammenauel Dam and found the penstock gates blown causing a minor flood on the Roer. (From *Combat Journal*)

Beginning around the first of February, the 78th once again became a part of the First Army of Lt. Gen. Courtney Hodges. During the Battle of the Bulge we had been cut off from the main part of the First and had come under control of the northern most American army, the Ninth. In the battle for Schmidt and the dams, two other divisions were in the area; the 82d Airborne to our left and the 9th Infantry on our right.

Imagine both my astonishment and my unhappiness in 1979 when I read an article in the *American Heritage* by Gen. James M. Gavin in which he gave his division, the 82d, credit for capturing Schmidt. The 82d had been operating in that part of the Hurtgen Forest where the 311th had been at the onset of the German counter-offensive in December.

The 82d did get to Schmidt from this difficult direction but only after the 78th had already been there. My efforts to get the *American Heritage* to correct this error in the historical record were futile. I received a rather patronizing letter from the general in which he downplayed Schmidt as not meaning "a thing" to the 82d anyway, "just one more of many towns" on the way to the end of the war. But he did acknowledge the 78th capture of the dam as "one of the great feats of the war." (Letter from Gavin, Cambridge, MA., 1/18/90)

78th Engineers (303 BN) span a cratered part of Schwammenauel Dam (From *Combat Journal*)

After Schmidt there were only three of us left in the old first squad. Cpl. Carl Hill, Louis Kolman, and I were still together, although both of them had been evacuated for a few days: Hill, with a slight wound and Kolman from shock. Hill, I am proud to say, was awarded a Silver Star for "gallantry in action" at Schmidt.

Walter Jarzylo had been severely wounded, losing a leg I believe, and a buck sergeant from one of the other platoons became our new squad leader. Like Fett, Sgt. Everett Parsons was from Iowa. At the same time we got some replacements fresh from the States. Among them I recall Charles Stuart from California, who became our new driver, and Guy Walker from Pennsylvania. Walker was extremely likeable and so very young that as much as we needed him, I hated to see him thrust into such a situation. Drafted soon after reaching 18, he had married his high school sweetheart (he proudly showed me their picture together.) After basic, the army apparently wasted little time in shipping him overseas and hurrying him to the front. We got other replacements from time to time, but I do not recall the others who must have joined at this particular time to fill out a squad of ten.

These 78th Aid Men (303 Medical Battalion) evacuated the wounded using a litter mounted on skis. (From *Combat Journal*)

Having successfully broken through the Siegfried Line and achieved our first major objective we could look to advancing to the next formidable barrier—the Rhine River. It was a barrier that I dreaded to face.

Before proceeding with my account of our push across the Roer and on to the Rhine, it is important to place the action of the 78th Division within the overall context of the Battle of the Bulge. It will be noted in the chapter on occupation that, following VE Day, my outfit spent a few weeks in Hersfeld. A member of the staff of the 311th regimental newspaper, *The Timberwolf,* was allowed to interview some of the German generals in the Hersfeld P W camp. The results were published in a feature article on November 17, 1945. I mailed a copy to my parents who saved it for me.

These 78th Medics (303 BN) use a weasel to evacuate the wounded. (From *Combat Journal*)

Among those interviewed was the commanding general of the Wehrmacht's 326th Volksgrenadier Division, Erwin Kaschner. According to him, part of the plans for the Ardennes offensive (the Bulge to us) called for the 272nd Volksgrenadier Division to use Simmerath, just inside the border from Belgium, as a pivot point for a drive to Liege and on to the coast, thus cutting off and pocketing the U. S. Ninth Army.

But these plans suffered a severe setback on December 13 (three days before the German offensive began) when a newly committed American infantry division (the 78th) attacked and drove forward in the Simmerath-Kesternich area. Pushed out of both towns with heavy losses, the German 272nd had to call upon the 326th, positioned south of Simmerath toward Monschau, for assistance. After hard fighting and many casualties on both sides, the Germans regained a major part of Kesternich. But, said the general, the 272nd was unable to fulfill its assigned mission in the counter-offensive. More than that, with the 78th presence in Simmerath (see map) the Germans were forced to add many extra miles to their supply route.

Although the role of the 78th in affecting the German offensive of December 16 seemed clear enough to some German leaders at the time, it long escaped the attention of American writers on Bulge history. Positioned as it was on the far northeastern shoulder of the Bulge, and far removed from the crucial action at Bastogne, perhaps it was easy enough to overlook its significance for the flow of the action.

Exactly a half century later Trevor N. Dupuy, David L. Bongard, and Richard C. Anderson, Jr., offered some correction to that omission in *Hitlers' Last Gamble, The Battle of the Bulge, December 1944-January 1945.* (Harper Perennial, 1994). They explain how SS Gen. Sepp Dietrich's Sixth Panzer Army (chosen by Hitler to lead the offensive) was deprived of some of its major resources by the action of the 78th. (pp. 28-29, 49 and 505-506).

The 272nd VGD was one of three assault divisions in the offensive plan of Dietrich's Sixth Army. The 326th VGD was also a part of that army. Thus the 78th at Simmerath-Kesternich had deprived Dietrich's panzers of a significant portion of their infantry support.

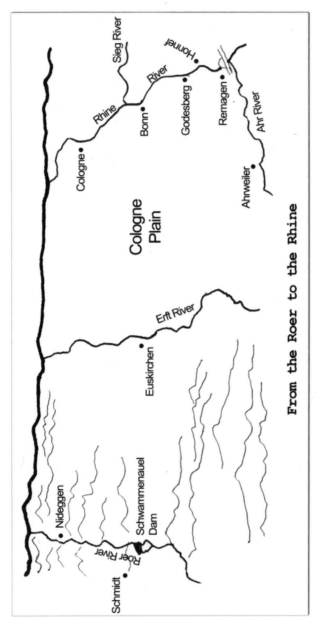

From the Roer to the Rhine

The 311th AT Co. crossed the Roer at Nideggen and was on the Ahr River between Ahrweiler and the Rhine when ordered to the bridge at Remagen, March 1945.

Chapter Eleven

The Rhineland and Central Europe

Following the fall of Schmidt, the 78th enjoyed a short period of relative inactivity. The division settled down to consolidate its position west of the Roer and to prepare for the push beyond the river and across the Cologne Plain to the Rhine.

This was a time for many men to receive showers and clean clothing. Some of us received short passes to rest centers. Three of us from the platoon, along with Lt. Janowitz, got to Liege, Belgium for a couple of nights. Accommodations that included a bed with sheets and an opportunity for uninterrupted sleep sounded absolutely luxurious to me. It had been so long since I had experienced anything like this, however, that I believe this could have been the time I was given a sleeping pill. Strange as it might sound, I recall that at one rest center we were told that after being at the front for awhile, some men had difficulty adjusting to comfortable sleeping arrangements, so a sleeping pill was provided. In any case, I left Liege feeling that I really had rested for the first time in two or three months.

Liege, a city of probably 175,000 people, looked like it had returned to the hustle and business of normalcy. As with the small towns and villages around Tongeren earlier, the city showed a friendly face to Americans. Some lucky (in our judgment) rear echelon troops were positioned there, and it served as a good rest center for front line troops. Lt. Janowitz found a place that served ice cream and took us there for a delicious and greatly appreciated treat. As far as the three of us were concerned the lieutenant really knew how to treat his men well, for at another place on this pass he found wine for us.

At the end of February we crossed the Roer. Terrain on both sides of the river was rough and hilly. Movement would have been difficult even without an enemy that wanted to hold us at the Roer. My company crossed the river on a Bailey Bridge at Nideggen a few miles northeast of Schmidt and in the zone of the 9th Infantry Division. Since the bridge was sometimes under fire, smoke pots were used to give us some protective cover.

My company crossed the Roer River on this bridge at Nideggen. (From *Combat Journal*)

Once across the river the 311th turned south and eventually southeast. The enemy had created a strong line of defense east of the Roer that in some places included a line of trenches reminiscent of pictures I had seen of the First World War. By the early days of March we were through these. Beyond the last hills we came out upon a great level area which had been described to us as the Cologne Plain.

At last I could begin to see that Germany was more than a collection of small towns set in rugged hills and never-ending forests. There were still many little towns to be taken, but those before us were set in an agricultural plain. To a farm boy it soon became evident why the Germans were trying so desperately to deny us control of such an important source of food supply.

Units of the 78th Division moving across the Cologne Plain, March 1945. (From *Combat Journal*)

The names of the many small towns across the Cologne Plain did not register in my memory. Only one name is the least bit familiar, Euskirchen, and that because it was the area's one large town and not because my platoon played any part in its capture.

Euskirchen, largest city between the Roer and the Rhine. The author first encountered slave laborers in this city. (From *Combat Journal*)

Beyond the Roer we began to encounter civilians. They had not been evacuated from any of the towns on the Cologne Plain. In some of these towns people had hung white sheets signalling surrender from their windows. Whenever possible a team from Military Government followed the infantry and took control of the civilian population.

In crossing the Plain, we ran into something else new and in this case totally alien to us—slave laborers. True, I had heard something of this horrible phenomenon, but my innocence was still sufficient to find it incredible that such inhumanity really existed in the 20th century. But there they were in terrible reality, hundreds of people forced into servitude when their nations fell to the German war machine. And the numbers would greatly multiply when we got into the great industrial area east of the Rhine. Many nationalities were represented: Polish, Belgian, Dutch, French, Russian, and most surprising to me, Italian. The latter, I thought, were supposed to be German allies; so how come I ran into some of them that had been enslaved?

Some of these poor people were liberated, but many others freed themselves and hid out to wait for the approach of American troops. The division had a special detachment plus an attached unit to deal with these people. Quite frankly, my view of the German civilian population was prejudiced by the presence of these unfortunate people. And they more deeply confirmed my conviction that fascism is a monstrously evil force.

In an earlier age armies were noted for living off the land. To an extent some of us followed this example after we got into a good agricultural area. The good food we found was a welcome respite from a diet of army chow. My squad raided cellars and pantries for such goodies as canned fruit and the great sausages and salamis that the Germans made. We raided hen houses for real eggs, so welcome after all the powdered stuff sent up to us on the chow trucks. When some of the fellows, tired of powdered milk, found a dairy cow and saw an opportunity for some of the fresh stuff, they called upon me to do the milking. We came upon one of the rifle companies in the act of butchering a hog. And I heard that other units butchered beef cattle. Perhaps if our whole company had been kept together, we would have done something that ambitious.

A private's perspective of an action in combat differs dramatically from that of a general. If the latter notices it at all, he views it as a very small part of a larger whole. And if he is at corps or army level, that whole can be very large indeed. But something that can be reduced to microscopic insignificance to a general looking at the big picture can reach overwhelming proportions for the private, his sergeant and his platoon leader (usually a second lieutenant). To him it can seem that the whole war has narrowly focused upon him and his buddies and the outcome is a matter of life and death. At the moment there can be no larger picture than the hellish situation encompassing them.

To a journalist, unless he is an Ernie Pyle, the perspective is more likely to resemble that of the general than the private. This was brought home to me following one particularly bad time for our platoon that winter. Two or three days later a newspaper was brought up and I read the war news for that particular date. Action in the 78th sector (which would have included our incident) was dismissed as "light". Admittedly this had to be true for the larger picture, for what happened to us had no bearing on the outcome of the war. But for those of us personally and intimately involved it was unquestionably "heavy" action. A frightening experience that resulted in the death of a fellow soldier and serious injuries to others could be "light" only when viewed by a distant and detached observer.

It must have been soon after we entered the Cologne Plain that another Missourian joined the squad. From Joplin and looking even older than Meade, Cline Gibbs had been in the Aleutians helping keep the Japanese out of that area when suddenly he found himself shipped several thousand miles to face a different enemy. By this time we also had, in addition to Stuart, two more southern Californians, Fred LaGrande and James Quinn. Both appeared to be in their mid-twenties.

A couple of days before we crossed the Rhine, I got a tremendous surprise, even shock. Accompanying the jeep driver as he delivered afternoon chow was none other than Richard Meade, returning to duty. I had never expected to see him again and sincerely hoped that he had been returned to the states. Of course I was glad to see him, but I was very distressed at his physical condition. Outwardly his wounds had healed leaving only a very noticeable facial scar. With my strong feelings of right and wrong, however, I was outraged to learn that doctors had left a piece of metal in the side of his face that practically locked his jaws. He could open them no farther than to get the end of his forefinger between his teeth. Trying to eat was a dreadful chore.

I had heard that every effort was made to return an infantryman to duty as quickly as possible, but I found Meade's case absolutely appalling. Understandably he was bitter at his shabby treatment. Military authority was under no obligation to explain to a private first class why it behaved either unfairly or stupidly. Apparently all they told him was to report to a military hospital after the fighting ended and the metal would be removed and his jaw repaired. My indignation rises once again as I think about him and write this.

These 78th riflemen hitched a ride to Remagen with the division's attached tank battalion, the 774th. (From *Combat Journal*)

Near the end of the first week in March we were close to the Ahr River, a tributary that enters the Rhine a short distance below Remagen. Some units of the division may already have crossed the Ahr by March 7. The 311th was under orders to cross and drive south to effect a juncture with a division of Patton's Third Army. But our orders changed dramatically on the night of March 7 when it was learned that a unit of the 9th Armored had captured a Rhine River bridge. We were to hold our position on the Ahr until relieved by the 2d Infantry Division and then to proceed rapidly to a place called Remagen.

Remagen, a small town fifteen miles south of Bonn, was unknown to us and probably to most other people outside that small Rhineland area of Germany. But events of March 7 and the days immediately following would give it a permanent and prominent place in the history of the Second World War.

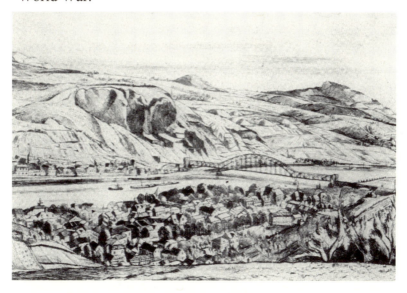

Artist's conception of Remagen and the Ludendorf Bridge (From *Combat Journal*)

In an ironic twist of history a railroad bridge, built at the insistence of the army in the First World War in order to move troops against Germany's western neighbors, became the means by which the U. S. First Army got across the Rhine in the Second World War. Named after General Erich

Ludendorff, the double tracked bridge was completed in 1918, the last year of the First World War. Twin stone towers with gun ports were built at both ends of the bridge. Today these are all that remain of the Ludendorff Bridge.

Although damaged a few times by Allied aircraft during the winter of 1944-45, the bridge had been kept repaired sufficiently for continued use. Planks had been laid over the girders to accommodate the vehicles of an army retreating across the river in early March. Plans to blow it up before advancing Americans could seize it resulted in some damage but left the bridge basically intact. In the late afternoon of March 7, 1945, an armored infantry company crossed to the east side. Other elements of the 9th Armored crossed and early the next day, March 8th, a battalion of the 310th Infantry Regiment of the 78th division crossed. Later, the 311th of the 78th Division would become the first complete regiment to cross to the east side of the Rhine.

There were long lines of men and vehicles waiting to cross the bridge at Remagen.
(From *Combat Journal*)

The loss of the bridge dealt the Germans a tremendous military blow, for in less than two weeks one armored division (the 9th) and three infantry divisions (9th, 78th, and 99th) had secured and expanded a bridgehead east of the

Rhine. It was also a devastating psychological blow to the Germans and most especially to their unstable leader, Adolf Hitler. He appeared to take it as a personal affront and reacted brutally toward everyone that he held responsible for its loss. He seemed fanatically determined to go to any lengths to destroy the bridge.

Damage to the bridge at Remagen.
(From *Combat Journal*)

The rainy weather and overcast skies kept American fighter-bombers grounded that first day, the 8th, but at least ten German raids on the bridge, mostly by Stukas, were recorded. Despite a heavy buildup of anti-aircraft defenses on both sides of the river, German planes continued to attack the bridge. According to *After the Battle*, 367 German aircraft attacked the bridge from March 8 to 17, of which 106 were destroyed.[1] *(, a* quarterly publication from London, 1977, p. 9) Along about the 12th of March we got our first look at the amazing new jet plane.

Hitler even ordered the V-2 to be fired from a base in the Netherlands. One of the rockets landed nearer to Cologne (25 miles away) than Remagen and the closest hit about 300 yards from the bridge. He also failed in his efforts to send

---

[1] "After The Battle: Crossing the Rhine: Patton's Hat-Trick", *After The Battle* (no. 16): 9, 1977

frogmen to destroy the bridge.

The bridge area remained under almost continuous artillery fire, but the Germans never got the kind of hits they needed to destroy it permanently. Throughout it all the combat engineers worked to repair and strengthen the structure. I cannot say enough about the fortitude and bravery of these men. Just crossing the bridge was a frightening experience to me. When the weakened bridge suddenly collapsed into the river on March 17, over two dozen of these men were trapped and killed. For several days pontoon bridges (built under fire and also subject to attack) had carried traffic across the river.

Engineers laid this pontoon bridge near the bridge at Remagen. (From *Combat Journal*)

Our company crossed the bridge on the afternoon of either the 9th or 10th of March. As we neared Remagen we joined a long line of slow moving traffic. We came out on a bluff above the town on the northwest. As we turned a corner, there far below on our left was the mighty Rhine. Under better circumstances my first view of this river, that in my mind represented so much history and romance, would have been truly sensational. But any romance was removed by the reality of seeing a bridge upriver that I would have to cross. Amid puffs of smoke and flashes from explosions a lot of movement could be seen on and around the bridge.

Troops of the 78th Inf. Div. and the attached 774th Tank Bn. Cross the Bridge at Remagen. View on the east side. (From *Combat Journal*)

Our column slowly made its way down the hill and into the town. At one point we stopped while a Stuka came diving on a bombing run. Anti-aircraft fire failed to bring him down, but it may have caused him to miss his target.

The narrow streets of the town were crowded with men and vehicles. As we drew closer to the bridge I believe we waited for another German pilot to make a futile pass at it. The approach to the bridge looked forbidding, the massive stone towers looming up like sentinels ready to deny passage. An enormous crater in the roadway at the entrance appeared ready to swallow truck, gun and all of us. Enough debris and dirt had been pushed into one side of it for Charles Stuart to negotiate passage and pull up onto the bridge.

In recent years I have traveled across some very long bridges, but none have seemed any longer than the Ludendorff that afternoon. The horrible condition of the bridge made it look like nothing one would ever cross willingly. There were wide gaps in the planking and holes where explosions had ripped away parts of the structure. It was frightening enough to cross it and be aware of that water below, but the thought of working on it, as some men were doing, was enough to give me sweaty palms. We managed to cross between bombing runs and no artillery shells landed near our platoon. As far as I know, the whole company got across without damage to vehicles or injury to men.

These captured defenders of the bridge are being led away. (From *Combat Journal*)

Beyond the eastern end of the bridge the railroad entered a tunnel in a 600 foot cliff. I remember seeing several men who had taken shelter there. Just short of the tunnel entrance, we turned off and got down to the roadway beneath the bridge. Signs of damage and destruction were all around. Some of the hits were so recent that destroyed vehicles were burning still, and a burned body remained seated in a jeep.

We turned north on the road under the bridge. Beginning with Erpel, opposite Remagen, we encountered one town or village after another along the east bank. We had moved only a few hundred yards beyond the bridge when another German plane appeared. All vehicles pulled off the road and a corporal in our second squad began firing the platoon's 50 caliber machine gun at the plane. Although this plane got through all the fire thrown at it, at dusk I saw another one as it was hit and exploded in a ball of flame.

These troops of the 78th on the east bank of the Rhine at Remagen are heading south. My group was sent north. (From *Combat Journal*)

The different platoons of the company split off to take up assigned areas. Exactly where our third platoon went I do not recall, but it must have been between Unkel and Honnef. Developments between this time, late afternoon of either the 9th or 10th, and the late afternoon of the 11th are very hazy in my mind. This would have been the period that, according to the regimental history, the AT Company "moved up in time to help [the rifle and heavy weapons companies] in the breaking up of numerous enemy armored attacks." *(Combat Journal, The Story of the Timberwolf Regiment of the 78th Lightning Division, 1945, p. 46)* This must have been the time when one of the other platoons knocked out a German tank, and probably when a friend, Lowry Rifenberrick, was wounded.

In the late afternoon of March 11th, Sgt. Parsons took a man and scouted out the position we were to move into once darkness fell. They found the position at the edge of Honnef and planned to place the anti-tank gun in a fence row several yards from the roadway. The position was about 25 yards from the corner of a large house that, they learned, was the home of a former consul for one of the Latin American countries.

Sometime after dark, and with Stuart driving with the aid of blackout lights, the sergeant directed us to our new location. Then leaving Cpl. Hill in charge of placing the gun and preparing foxholes, the sergeant and driver drove back somewhere. At the time I probably knew their purpose, but I cannot figure it out now.

We had turned only a few shovels full of dirt when we heard the frightening sound of artillery exploding right on top of us. It was big and heavy, and we had no holes or cover of any kind. The sergeant had told us the house had a big basement, not the usual small German cellar. Hill decided to lead us to that, hopefully between bursts, and I was to bring up the rear.

Somewhere ahead of me I heard some terrible moaning. At about the same time I was certain that I heard the faint and distant voice of Meade calling to me: "Breeze, Breeze." The direction from which his voice came from seemed to be ahead on the right, not left toward the house. The moaning sounds came from young Walker. Kneeling beside him in the dark, I knew immediately that he was severely wounded. He appeared to be bleeding heavily from a wound to his left leg. Where else he had been hit, I could not tell; but my subconscious told me that the bleeding had to be stopped. Pulling off the web belt that held up my trousers, I tried to use it as a tourniquet. (Of total insignificance, I remained beltless for the next two months or more). I still remember that I spoke aloud, asking God to help us. I remember that Gibbs, dazed but apparently not hit, was nearby. I told him to see if Quinn and LaGrande were up ahead and if they were able to carry Walker (who was a big fellow) to the basement. They did so, and I then began searching for Meade.

Fearing that he might be down somewhere, wounded and in need of help, I frantically searched the ground in the direction from which he had seemed to call. I assumed that he had been disoriented and gone that way. Several times during the night, I repeated and expanded my search. After my first futile search, I went to the basement. To my sorrow Walker was dead, and in retrospect I realized that he had been dying while I worked on him. All deaths hurt me deeply, but many times over the years I have felt very sad about the waste of this young life and the effect it must have had upon a young bride back in Pennsylvania.

Both Hill and Kolman were wounded and had to be made ready for evacuation. Even his own wound had not kept the gritty Hill from trying to help Walker when they brought him to the basement. Kolman was no longer the youngster of just a few weeks ago. Stoically he endured the pain of a wounded arm and calmly waited to be evacuated. Gibbs, LaGrande, and Quinn were all badly shaken but showed no visible signs of physical harm.

Sgt. Parsons was shocked to return and discover what had happened to his squad. The two of us set about to complete the emplacement of the gun and the digging of foxholes. But before we could complete it, the Germans sent in still more rounds of shells, wounding the sergeant and leaving me to finish the task.

In the first touch of daylight I found Meade's body. To my bewilderment he lay only a few feet from the gun. The sergeant and I had missed finding him. My searching during the night had carried me much farther away from the gun. It is still rather eerie to realize that I was so certain I heard him call to me for help. There is no way that could have been true in any physical sense. He would have been dead by that time, killed by one of the very early rounds. From the horrible nature of what hot shrapnel had done to his face, I knew that death had been instantaneous giving him no chance to say anything. It was a sight that I can never forget and an everlasting reminder that had he been treated fairly, he never would have been in Honnef that night.

Before the remnants of my squad moved on from Honnef, we got a new squad leader, my third since entering Germany. Like Parsons whom he replaced and Fett our platoon sergeant, S/Sgt Doyce Hildebrand was from Iowa. Unlike most of the other men with non-commissioned rank who joined the company during or at the end of the Bulge, he had infantry training. Back in the states he had been with an anti-tank company in an infantry division and had spent some time at Ft. Benning, well-known for its infantry training. Immediately upon Hildebrand's arrival, Capt. Gapen had placed him in charge of another squad that had lost its leader. Now, the captain moved him to our squad. He proved to be a good leader and became a good friend. We have been in contact at various times over the years and had a good visit at the division reunion in St. Louis, 1994.

Evidently we also got the first of much needed replacements while still in Honnef. Roy Pooley, a tall, slim Floridian, remembers crossing the bridge, spending the night in a schoolhouse, and then being brought by jeep to the company.

For days after that night of March 11th, I could not hear anything with my left ear. And for years after the war certain kinds of sound (some church singing, for example) would produce an annoying vibration in it. The loss of hearing increased with age and today I can accurately describe it as "my deaf ear."

Undoubtedly the trauma of that night also aggravated the stomach problems that became noticeable sometime after leaving Schmidt. Hard to come by anyway, sleep was often interrupted by a ferocious pain that felt like a giant hand was squeezing my stomach. Eventually I learned that a self-imposed diet (avoiding Spam and some C-rations, and anything prepared by one particular cook with a fondness for hot and spicy food) brought some relief. When the same symptoms recurred at a time of stress after the war, a doctor treated me for an ulcer. Both ear and stomach problems seemed so relatively trivial within the context of more serious matters in 1945, that it never occurred to me to seek medical assistance. Consequently none of my records would show that anything had ever been wrong with me during my army career.

In the period following March 11th, there were times when I thought my mental state of more consequence than my hearing loss, heartburn and stomach ache. After that date I was the only man left from the old squad. Meade's death and the departure of the wounded Hill and Kolman created within me an odd mixture of feelings of loneliness, apprehension, anxiety, and sadness. The feeling is truly beyond my capability to be precise.

Many decades removed from the causal events of 1944-45, I now realize that the numbing shock of finding the nearly faceless body of my combat buddy completed a traumatizing process that had begun with the first loss from that close knit group who entered Germany together. Blessed with a strong will and great determination, I was able to carry on in 1945. My mind, however, remains forever vulnerable to entrapment in a dark morass akin to my mental state in March-April, 1945. Even in old age my mind has fallen, thankfully infrequently, into a chasm of depression reminiscent of 1945. It can take days, even weeks, for the dreadful fog to clear and free my mind. These episodes often begin in the darkness of night in the confining season of winter rather than, but not always, the openness of summer.

Although the explosion of incoming shells, even beyond the zone of most immediate danger, made me cringe and look for cover, I retained the earlier feeling that no serious injury would befall me. In fact it struck me quite strongly that fate dictated that buddies would come and go while I remained behind as almost a detached observer of the grim scene. At times my mind seemed overwhelmed with depressing thoughts that this would go on and on indefinitely, especially as we began to hear stories of a formidable redoubt manned by die-hard troops in Germany's southern mountains.

The 311th fought northward from Honnef and into the Konigswinter area (largest town in the bridgehead). Under better circumstances I could have seen this as a place of great scenic beauty. A string of seven mountains (Siebengebirge) rises up abruptly to a height of a thousand feet or more just a short distance away from the river bank. They form the setting for the exploits of the legendary Teutonic knight, Siegfried; the scene of much ancient and medieval history; and the site of a notorious contemporary (i.e. 1945) event. An English-speaking German civilian called the latter to my attention by pointing to one of the mountains, Petersburg, as the site of a hotel where British Prime Minister Neville Chamberlain stayed in September, 1938, and then crossed by ferry to meet with Adolf Hitler at Godesberg on the west bank of the Rhine. At this meeting Chamberlain agreed to the shameful transfer of the Sudetenland to Germany, only to discover that not even this was enough to satisfy Hitler. It took a later meeting at Munich before the prime minister could make his dubious claim to a "peace with honor."

In taking another of the mountains, Drachenfels, some 311th rifle companies found the cave where Siegfried supposedly slew the dragon. Instead of a dragon they found a large underground factory manufacturing airplane parts using several hundred slave laborers. In taking control of Drachenfels, the regiment learned why the Germans fought so hard to hold the Honnef-Konigswinter area, and why its capture had cost us all so much, especially the rifle squads who always had it much worse than the anti-tank squads. The top of the mountain gave a view up and down the river for miles and had served as the principal observation post for the direction of fire upon the bridge, upon key spots in the bridgehead and upon American forces and positions across on the west side of the Rhine. With the capture of Drachenfels, the 311th insured the ultimate success of the Remagen Bridgehead.

Drachenfels, highest point in the area, was used by the enemy artillery to direct fire upon the bridge at Remagen. (Image from a postcard)

It was during the Remagen operation that the Germans tried some clumsy propaganda on us. In some of the river towns they left leaflets that were supposed to discourage us. Some fellows in the platoon, finding the leaflets more amusing than alarming, pocketed them as souvenirs. The Germans knew that each soldier had life insurance in the amount of $10,000. Somewhere east of the Rhine I witnessed their attempt to exploit this knowledge. To my intense relief one morning, I found that some falling German shells were scattering harmless paper and not dreaded shrapnel upon us.

The pieces of paper were green in color and made to look like a check drawn upon the "Philadelphia National Bank," dated "25 February 1945," number "13," and payable to "your widow," in the amount of "Ten Thousand dollars," and purportedly signed by "The Adj. Gen. U.S. War Dept." Written on the back was the German propagandist's idea of a troubling question for us:

> This will give your widow a chance to buy a new husband. Her dowry will be your suits and things. Are you going to let this check be cashed?

Putting one of these "checks" in my wallet, I brought it home as a souvenir.

It was probably in this vicinity also that we held a position near an impressive looking house, surely the home of someone of influence and or wealth. We learned that it was the home of a manager for a branch of an American company that had done business in Germany. Important to us was the discovery of a well-stocked wine cellar which we sampled with considerable appreciation. It was my first experience with champagne, and somehow it was better than any since tasted. Some of the wine, I recall, had been produced in the Mosel River area across the Rhine to the southwest.

A week or so after leaving the Honnef-Konigswinter area we added two more replacements to the squad. One, Harold Lewis, was from the state of Washington. As I was acting as the assistant squad leader, it fell my duty to collect the other and try to fit him into the squad. His rather strange bearing and broken English made it a difficult task. With my hearing impairment and natural trouble with sounds, I had a terrible time figuring out his name. In fact, I had to see it in print (Unto Raitio) before I could begin to understand what he was trying to say. His home address was given as New York City, but it turned out he was a native of Finland. Possibly enlisting in the army was his road to citizenship, but I was never clear on what he meant by that. From some of his features, I would guess that he was at least related to the Mongolian people of northern Finland. Whether or not he had infantry training was difficult to determine, but I did understand that he had been in some Texas camp. Although I do not think he ever fit easily into the squad, he proved to be a tough soldier and well able to endure the kind of life we led.

Expanding upon a public works project initiated by his immediate predecessors, by the outbreak of war in 1939 Hitler had built several hundred miles of a super highway system *(autobahn).* Like some railroads earlier, the Ludendorff Bridge as an example, many of these highways were built with military needs in mind. The division's first contact with an *autobahn* came a few miles east of the Rhine. Paralleling the river a super-highway ran from the industrial Ruhr south to Frankfurt. While the 311th was engaged in the seven mountain area, another regiment (309th) pushed outward and eastward to cut the *autobahn* and seize control of a large stretch of it.

Viewing the *autobahn* for the first time, I was tremendously impressed with the engineering behind it. Its size, scope, the tremendous sweep of its curves, and the cuts through hills made any U. S. highway I had seen look primitive by comparison. Another decade would pass before I began to see anything approaching it in this country. Many of its overpasses had been destroyed, but we were still able to made good use of large portions of it.

Flowing from east to west, the Sieg River enters the Rhine near Bonn, and by the 21st of March the 311th had reached the river. At that point the regiment was relieved by another outfit and given a few days rest and recuperation time. No doubt it was during this period that I got to a rest center in Verviers, Belgium. By this time there were several pontoon bridges across the Rhine, but I do not recall where I crossed.

The Ruhr-Frankfurt autobahn east of Honnef.
(From *Lightning*)

When the regiment went back on line, it relieved the 1st Division in territory it had acquired east of Bonn on the Sieg. The 311th occupied a front of about six miles along this river and one night my platoon dug in along the river bank. We were in a small town and directly across from us another small town was occupied by some German soldiers. I cannot recall the name of either place, but only about 200 yards separated the opposing forces.

It was an easy distance for the exchange of rifle fire, but much of the time things were relatively calm. Two incidents I recall very vividly, one on each side of the river, that surprised me and left me with considerable respect for the civilians involved. A unit of the 78th field artillery was located somewhere in the hills behind our position. One afternoon someone must have called for fire on a position inside the enemy-held town. Some of the shells were phosphorous and flying sparks ignited some nearby roof tops. The moment the firing ceased, I watched in amazed admiration as civilians scrambled out of hiding, placed ladders against their houses, and began carrying buckets of water to the roof.

The other incident took place along the roadway running beside the river and in the streets behind us. It was Easter Sunday, April 1. Appropriately the day was sunny and the temperature pleasant. But a war was still on, and I was astounded to see women and children on their way to a church down the road. Encouragingly, neither side fired a shot that morning. It would have seemed a sacrilege to have done so.

Near the Sieg River, the 78th captured this airfield littered with smashed planes. (From Combat Journal)

At another point on the Sieg one of the regiment's rifle companies moved across the river and seized some important ground. We expected to be ordered to cross and take the town opposite, but significant developments elsewhere changed the division's mission. Consequently, on the night of either April 4 or 5, we were relieved by an anti-tank unit from a division (97th Infantry) newly committed to combat and awaiting its first action.

In sharp contrast to our crumpled, dirty, and well-used look, the men and equipment of the 97th looked fresh and new. They had been in Europe approximately a month and in Germany only a few days. Much later I learned that the 97th, training in California for amphibious landings, had been slated to go to the Far East in December, 1944. The enormous casualty toll of the Battle of the Bulge, however, brought an abrupt change in plans and sent the 97th to Europe instead.

These men from another unit in the 78th are loading a 57mm. gun like that used by my company. (From *Combat Journal*)

The development that affected us in early April was the spectacular encirclement of the entire Ruhr by two American armored divisions. On March 23, Montgomery's forces, which included the American Ninth Army, had crossed the Rhine north of the Ruhr. The Ninth Army's 2d Armored Division hurried eastward and the First Army's 3d Armored Division sped northeastward. Encircling the Ruhr and cutting off Germany's greatest industrial area from the rest of the country, the two divisions met at Lippstadt, about 223 miles from Berlin.

Trapped inside this large pocket were all of Field Marshal Model's forces, thought at the time to number a little over 100,000 men, but which in the final analysis was discovered to be well over 300,000. The area was heavily defended, but American divisions quickly began reducing the pocket from three directions north, east, and south. General Omar Bradley wrote later that 18 divisions were assigned to it.

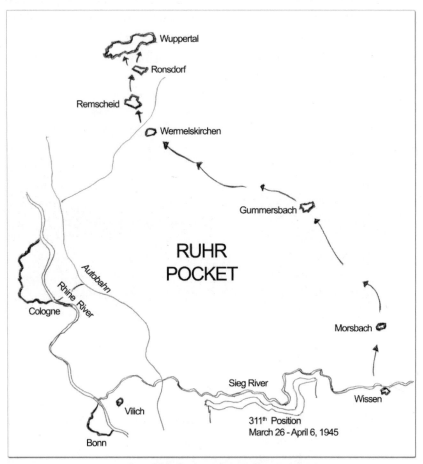

**The 311th in the Ruhr Pocket
April 7-17, 1945**

The 78th was sent farther east to attack across the Sieg at Wissen. From there we advanced into the Ruhr pocket in a northwesterly direction. Our ultimate objective was 50 miles away, the large industrial city of Wuppertal. The area we entered was heavily populated and we captured several towns. Except for one or two of the larger ones, I do not recall the names of any of them.

Our platoon was used in different ways during the advance. Sometimes we were used for defensive purposes, that is, we would set up a roadblock at important road junctions in some of the captured towns. On occasion we were used as a rifle squad. Approaching a town, we left the anti-tank gun behind with the driver and the rest of us took our rifles and carbines, and helped clean out the area.

Wuppertal, industrial city in the Ruhr. The 311th saw its last action in this area.
(From *Lightning*)

The rapid advance on a broad front and the many units involved created some communication problems. On one occasion our whole company had been brought together and was moving through territory supposedly already taken by another unit. The captain was leading a long line of us through the main street of a small town, when suddenly we spotted enemy troops in some of the buildings and realized the place had not yet been taken. Luckily for us, these particular German soldiers did not care to take on a whole company even with surprise on their side.

Another time our platoon helped take a town and that night we dug defensive positions on its outskirts. At first light we found ourselves about to be attacked by another company in the regiment! They thought, rightly or wrongly, that the town had been designated as their responsibility to capture. At any rate we were able to identify each other before any real harm had been done.

Many prisoners of war were liberated as we advanced through the pocket. One of the other regiments (309th) evacuated a considerable number of hospitalized American prisoners. At another place, the same regiment freed a number of French, Russian and Polish prisoners from their cages. A battalion of the 311th liberated around 9,000 French and Polish prisoners from another camp.

To my knowledge no part of the 78th came upon a concentration camp. The most notorious of these were to be found elsewhere anyway. As to be expected in a highly industrialized area, however, a vast number of slave laborers were in the pocket. Our regiment liberated thousands of them, and then found it necessary to leave guards behind to protect supplies and food stocks from them. The special units responsible for handling these people must have been overwhelmed by the enormity of the problem.

Some of the newly liberated could be a nuisance. My platoon spent a night in one large place, possibly Remsheid, where newly freed Frenchmen were soon wandering around. A group of them had found a few bottles of wine and, to our disgust, these happy fellows wanted to show their gratitude by trying to kiss us.

The 78th experienced some incidents of hard fighting in the pocket. But with the exception of SS troops and those they were in a position to intimidate, many German soldiers knew they had already lost the war and were ready to acknowledge it. After a few rounds of fire, many were ready to give up. Some did not even bother with a token shot before surrendering. And some, if we were to take them seriously, believed that, after they surrendered, American, British, and German troops would join together to defeat the hated Russians (or "Rooskies," as it sounded to me they were saying.)

A long line of prisoners, usually under the charge of one or two guards, on their way back to a POW camp became a common sight as the pocket shrank in size. Included in the bag of prisoners were youngsters, some of them the fanatic products of Hitler Youth *(Jugend),* and overage men pressed into the defense of the homeland. In between were soldiers good to the end, but Hitler had wasted too many of these good troops in his futile December gamble for the German nation to make a successful stand on its own soil.

Of the 325,000 (General Bradley's figure) prisoners of war taken from the Ruhr pocket by April 18, 47,581 had been captured by the 78th Division, and of these the 311th had taken over 15,000. Indicative of the enormity of the defeat for Germany was the fact that the 78th alone had bagged seven officers of the rank of general. Field Marshal Model had committed suicide by shooting himself.

The highest rank our platoon picked up was the equivalent of a colonel in our army. The entire platoon was following our leader's jeep down the road in open countryside one day. Waving a white cloth, a German soldier came running out from the woods about a hundred yards to our left. He wanted to arrange for the surrender of a high ranking officer. There seemed to be a long discussion and a difference of opinion. The officer, as I understood it, really wanted to surrender to someone of equal rank, but our leader was not about to arrange a surrender to the colonel of our regiment or even the captain of our company, for that matter. All had far more important things to do than accommodate the vanity (perhaps it was a matter of protocol to him) of a German officer. So this haughty officer in the sharp looking uniform. (a striking contrast to the looks of most *Wehrmacht* surrenders we took), and with his small dog, was brought out of the woods. Forced to be content to surrender to a second lieutenant, he was placed unceremoniously, along with his dog, in the back of the platoon jeep. As far as I know both he and the dog were turned over to the prisoners of war team attached to the division.

Civilians in the Ruhr also showed a readiness to see the end of the war. The area had been subjected to heavy bombing, and in some places it appeared to me that more houses than factories had been destroyed. Interestingly, I encountered any number of civilians who wanted to disassociate themselves from Adolf and his nasty regime. Not that my opinion could affect their future one way or another anyway, but I had lost too much of my innocence to be moved by protests of "nicht Nazi."

To those of us on the ground the lessons of air power were obvious. The much publicized bombing raids had wrought frightful destruction, but they had not stopped war production. We saw examples of factories working underground and instances where aboveground facilities were still operating. Despite all the damage done in the city of Wuppertal, some of its industrial structures were still standing. In another place a steel mill remained untouched and in production. As we came upon this kind of scene in one place, it made such a profound impression upon me that I recall remarking to a squadmate something to this effect: "It looks like Herman's house has been turned upside down into his cellar, but his work place is still there."

Nor did heavy bombing appear to have diminished the nation's will to fight. When the artillery began firing and the infantry and tanks showed up, and German forces were beaten on the ground, only then did civilian will crumble and capitulate. In retrospect the truly amazing thing about bombing was the way Winston Churchill (to me the great towering figure of the war) ignored the heroic lesson presented to the world by his own nation. Hitler had expected the horrors of the Blitz to crush the will of the British people, but it had the opposite effect. Yet Churchill channeled an inordinate amount of Britain's limited resources into bombing campaigns, aimed at destroying the German nation's ability to fight, but also expecting to crush its will to continue.

None of this is to say that air power was of little importance in winning the war. When properly used, and it was often enough to count, it made a significant difference in the crucial battle on the ground. As I saw it, the single most important result of the bombing by the RAF and the USAAC was the destruction of communication and transportation resources. It did little good to produce war goods and find fuel if these materials could not be put into the hands of German soldiers in the field.

Weather permitting, the air corps came to control the skies so completely that it was hard for the *Wehrmacht* to move in the closing weeks of the war. Getting supplies to their soldiers had to be a daunting task at best, and, thanks to our air corps, in many cases proved completely impossible. We came upon numerous trucks and armored vehicles stalled by empty fuel tanks. Some aircraft were caught on the ground by lack of fuel. Near the railroads, a common sight was a long line of freight cars burned to skeletons by attacking planes. I witnessed many such sights in the pocket.

A unit of the 311th found these slave workers in an underground airplane parts factory in the mountains near Drachenfels.
(From *Combat Journal*)

Significantly, the incessant bombing, hitting as it did in so many different places and on such a continual basis, had the important by-product of forcing the *Luftewaffe to* concentrate on home defense and in the process lose planes in unbearable numbers. Still, enough German planes appeared over and around me at various times for me to realize how fortunate we were that the *Luftewaffe* of the earlier war years was no more. When our own fighter planes appeared on the scene, they were a great help and a comforting cover. The need for a more coordinated use of planes with ground troops was surely a lesson to be drawn from this experience.

Just at a time when the war seemed to be going so well for us, we got the shocking news that President Roosevelt had died on April 12. He had been president so long and appeared such a strong and invincible leader that initially we found his death difficult to believe. Someone in the platoon even suggested that the announcement probably came from another German propaganda attempt to shake our morale. When the truth finally sank in, the general mood of the platoon was a mixture of sadness and loss with a sense of uneasiness about the future.

On April 13th the 311th was ordered to hold up and wait to link up with an armored division approaching from the southwest. The division, I learned later from the regimental history, was my old outfit the 13th Armored. Looking around during this pause, some of us in the platoon found a few civilian automobiles. Nearly all of these lacked fuel or were otherwise inoperable.

A couple of buddies and I found a small car that still contained some fuel. It was about the size of the Volkswagon popular in America in the postwar years. Finally getting it started, we realized that someone had to keep the battery connected. Driving it around on a fairly level surface we discovered it had very little power.

Just off the road was a pasture with a long gentle slope. But where the terrain leveled off, a light looking wire fence ran across the pasture. One of the fellows wondered what would happen if the car hit the fence coming off the hill at maximum speed. Putting his question to the test, he drove while I used something to hold the battery connections. (The battery was located behind the front seat.) The fence did not look very sturdy, but it stopped the little car abruptly in its tracks. Later, one of the fellows took a picture, which I still have, of the abandoned car with horses grazing unconcernedly around it. More to my liking, I found a farm tractor which I started up and drove around. Unfortunately I could not ship it home as a war souvenir!

Sometime during this period we got another replacement, Floyd Garret from North Carolina, as well as a change in platoon leadership. For reasons never made known to me, Capt. Gapen switched the leaders of two platoons, 2nd Lt. Gerard O'Conner came to us and 2nd Lt. Julius Janowitz went to the fourth. Although I had known O'Conner since

Pickett and felt satisfied with him, I hated to lose contact with Janowitz. In my judgement he was a good officer and a fine person.

I believe it also bothered me that his departure severed my last feeling of contact with that close-bound group from the Hurtgen and the Bulge. Today I feel a special affinity for all my acquaintances in the old company who went through the war with me. That experience forges a bond that probably does not come in any other way. But in my memory, and perhaps especially in the nostalgia of old age, there is a unique kind of closeness with that small squad of comrades in the forest and in Simmerath.

When the expected linkup with the armored division did not occur, we were ordered to move on. On April 15th the 311th began moving toward Wuppertal and the 309th and 310th advanced on the city from other directions. Without another unit to our left, that flank remained exposed and enemy soldiers frequently infiltrated behind us inflicting casualties. This turned out to be the last day the 311th had men killed in action. Shortly after V-E Day, I learned that a good friend from UNH, Christian J. Gabriel, had been killed on the 15th. My new platoon leader was shot and killed that day, too.

The exact circumstances of Lt. O'Conner's death were never clear to me. The story that drifted into my squad late that afternoon was that the lieutenant and a private first class from another squad (the name escapes me) with him were surrounded, the officer with the gold bar painted on his helmet was shot, and the enlisted man taken prisoner. Within a day or two American soldiers freed the private.

All three regiments closed in on our objective and on the 16th the German army in that part of the pocket collapsed. The city was taken, civilians hung out the white flags of surrender, and forced laborers and other displaced people roamed about. Only mopping up operations in by-passed areas remained.

Although I could not know it at the time, combat action for the 78th came to an end with the capture of Wuppertal. The division came off the line, moving southward and eastward to guard important installations and protect lines of communication and supply as other elements of the First Army advanced eastward to link with the Russians. First Army patrols met Russian patrols at Torgau on the Elbe River on April 25.

Meantime the 311th Regiment occupied an area extending from the Rhine near Koblenz northeastward to Herborn. Our company spent some time in a relatively undamaged town somewhere in this area. Its name and exact location are beyond my recall, and my old platoon sergeant, Fett, cannot remember either. It was the site of a German military hospital, I know, and my platoon was assigned to guard it.

With a partner I would spend a two hour shift on some kind of guard duty. Sometimes this involved patrolling the perimeter of the hospital's extensive grounds. On other occasions it meant duty near the main entrance to the hospital. On patrol we passed by a small building and through its large open doorway stacks of simple wooden coffins could be seen. Many of the hospital's patients were severely wounded, and this often ended in a coffin being taken out and put to use. Amputations of arms and legs resulted in some platoon members being called to escort hospital personnel and their gruesome parcels down the road to the incinerator.

Being around enemy soldiers this way gave us an opportunity to converse with some of them. One interesting fellow remains in my memory. Before the war his family operated a hotel that served many English speaking guests. He spoke English quite well and seemed appreciative of an opportunity to do so. The poor fellow was a physical wreck with such an emaciated look that his age was difficult to determine. He had been in and out of various campaigns since the outbreak of the war in 1939. He had been in North Africa and then Russia before wounds sent him back to the West. The *Wehrmacht* awarded medals indicative of multiple wounds, and his was for the unusually high number (especially in a survivor!) of seven. All of the war had been tough enough for him, but the horrendous campaign in Russia possessed a nightmarish quality. Understandably he was grateful to place his fate in the hands of the Americans rather than the Russians whom he loathed.

Meeting him helped me see enemy soldiers in a new and more understanding light. Perhaps it should be emphasized that I am speaking of members of the *Wehrmarcht* and not the SS who in my mind always will remain a despicable lot.

Some of the many captured German Soldiers taken by the 78th Division. (From *Lightning*)

Sometime near the end of April, I believe, we moved somewhere to the southeast. I had heard that Hitler had a plan for die-hard Nazis, especially the SS, to hold out indefinitely in a National Redoubt in the mountains of southern Bavaria, and on into western Austria and northern Italy. I figured that we were being positioned for the 78th to participate in action against the Redoubt, a most unappealing prospect. I had also heard rumors of an underground army, composed of dedicated fanatics, appropriately called "Werewolves," that aimed to make occupation nearly impossible by the use of murder and terrorism.

After the publication in 1948 of General Eisenhower's *Crusade in Europe,* I learned that Allied intelligence had seen enough evidence of the existence of these Nazi plans for the general to make important moves to thwart them (p. 397). But as the truth came out later, it became evident that although a commander had been named for the Redoubt, it was never formed. Moreover, the "Werewolves" never amounted to more than a few fanatics murdering a city official who had cooperated with the Allies. Mindful as I am of ongoing Russian imperialism, initiated by the tsars and continued by communist dictators, I was not surprised to learn that the Russians had used disinformation to exaggerate the threat and divert the western Allies away from coveted parts of Germany and Central Europe. (Oxford, *World War II, p.* 1268)

During the first week of May, 1945, I began to hear encouraging news—perhaps there would be no Redoubt after all. A fellow in the platoon had picked up a radio and we listened eagerly and often to the English language broadcasts of Radio Luxembourg. Mussolini had been killed by Italian partisans. Then, the best news of all, we heard that German radio had announced the death of Hitler, fighting at the head of his troops. (Nazism maintained the big lie to the last, for Hitler had committed suicide as the Russians closed on his Berlin bunker.)

Then came reports of the capitulation of German armed forces on the various fronts, beginning in Italy. Finally, Admiral Doenitz (Hitler's chosen successor as head of state and the armed forces) was ready to accept unconditional surrender. On May 7 we heard the welcome news that in the early morning hours Field Marshal Jodl, chief of the Operations Staff of the German High Command, had signed the unconditional surrender document at Allied Headquarters in Rheims. At midnight the next day, May 8, the long war in Europe officially ended.

V-E Day brought no boisterous celebration for us, just a great feeling of relief seemed all around me. My adjustment to a less-threatening environment was not immediate. We were staying in a house at the time, and it took several nights to feel comfortable with lights on and occupants exposed to view from the outside. To be outside and see a cigarette glowing in the dark was enough for me to want to duck. Most startling of all was the night I first saw a military vehicle pass by with headlights blazing.

My letters home from this period have been lost. As a result, I do not have or remember what I wrote to my parents about the end of the war in Europe.

Chapter Twelve

Occupation

A few days after the end of the war in Europe the division moved deeper into Germany for occupation duty in an eastern section of the zone assigned to American forces. Division responsibility ran from Hofgeismar, a dozen or so miles above Kassel in the north, to approximately ten miles below Fulda in the south. The 311th became responsible for security and control of the southeastern part of this area. I believe that my company spent two or three days in Fulda, for I have some recollection of religious structures that dated from medieval times, and then we settled in Hersfeld for nearly two months.

Occupation involved a lot of guard duty and checking people for proper credentials. Civilians were restricted in their movement, and some German soldiers had tried to avoid capture by shedding uniforms and merging into the civilian population. It was necessary to cull these fellows out and also to be on the alert for high ranking members of the Nazi party.

For a while dealing with prisoners of war and displaced persons took up a lot of time. At Hersfeld the 78th became responsible for a First Army stockade that held around 26,000 prisoners under less than satisfactory conditions. I was more than glad when other companies were called upon to transport many of them to other areas and begin the tedious process of screening and discharging.

My company got involved in handling some of the thousands of displaced persons found in the regimental area. I recall what must have been a large work camp at Hersfeld comprised of many of the single-story wood structures associated with the camps of Nazi Germany. The place was crowded with displaced persons. Many of them were pitiful creatures who often reminded me more of a pack of animals than civilized human beings. But I suppose they had been treated as sub-human for so long that the descent to a more barbarous state was natural.

Hersfeld was on an east-west rail line, and it served as a collecting and shipping point for people of Slavic origin. My company, along with others from the regiment, brought in truck loads of displaced persons for, as we thought in our ignorance and innocence, shipment home. At the time it puzzled me that people supposedly going home to places in Poland and the Soviet Union looked more wretched than happy when loaded onto trains heading east to the Russian zone. I recall one occasion when a Russian officer was at a train being loaded. At the time I found it surprising that he seemed more irritated than pleased to see his fellow Slavs.

One of the men in our company was of East European background and could speak a Slavic language. Frequently called upon as an interpreter, on a least one occasion he accompanied a trainload of these people to some point in the Russian zone. Upon his return to Hersfeld, he reported that the Russians had treated the displaced persons badly as they unloaded them. Officers berated them as collaborators and charged them with going to Germany of their own free will. Apparently there was to be no haven anywhere for these unfortunate people. Astonishing as Russian behavior was to me in 1945, later in graduate study I realized that it fit readily into the context of Russian history.

In retrospect I deeply regret that my regiment had anything to do with the return of slave laborers to Eastern Europe. On the other hand I have no idea what could have been done about them. Together, Adolf Hitler and Joseph Stalin were not only responsible for the deaths of millions of people but for the displacement of millions more. More than half a century later, and with millions of people displaced by tyrannies all around the globe, there is still no good answer to the question. When I left Germany in 1946, vast numbers of uprooted and displaced people remained in the Western zones of occupation. Complicating the situation, especially in the British zone where food resources were scarce, was the presence of a growing number of German refugees expelled by the Russians as they annexed German and Polish lands and compensated the Poles for this theft of their land by encouraging them to push their frontier westward into Germany.

Soon after getting settled in Hersfeld we were marched to the town theater to see a War Department film made especially for soldiers in Europe. At the time I called it another propaganda film, perhaps the best of the lot put out by the War Department. Obviously it had been carefully made and unlike previous films it was in color. Admittedly it was a quality production with a theme that rested upon solid history. (I might note that in this respect it was superior to some of the "Why We Fight" series that had been required viewing, especially the one on our Russian ally which I learned later was based upon a faulty premise.) The United States entry into the First World War had determined the outcome of that conflict. At the peace conference the American president did much to shape postwar Europe. Unfortunately partisan politics led to our rejection of the treaty and, in an isolationist mood, the abdication of any responsibility for the Europe that we had helped shape.

Long before the Second World War ended, American political and military leadership understood that our postwar responsibility would be even greater this time. Concerned that once the war ended there would be great pressure to "bring the boys home," the War Department had a film ready to convince us of the need for a continuing presence in Europe. How influential this film may have been would be hard to say. I believe many of us and our families knew that we had to accept great responsibility. We further believed that we had fulfilled our particular mission, and it was up to others to follow into the next phase. Generally that is what happened, but surely everyone of us would have been absolutely astounded could we have looked into the future to see American troops still there at the end of the century.

At least two other companies joined us to view this film. One was Jim Burkhardt's company, and I was pleased to find him alive and well. It was our first opportunity to be together since our arrival in Europe. It was from him that I learned the sad news of Gabriel's death. Neither of us had seen or heard anything concerning Jim Fankle, and we had both lost contact with Frank Galloway. This was the last time I ever saw Burkhardt. In recent years I have tried unsuccessfully to find him through the 78th Infantry Veterans Association.

Sometime in May I had an unforgettable dental encounter, the kind that makes me truly appreciate the present day equipment in my dentist's office. Having lost a filling, I went to an army dentist to get it replaced. Some drilling was necessary, but a look at the dentist's source for power nearly caused me to flee his chair. The contraption reminded me of my mother's old treadle sewing machine. In this case a T/4 furiously pumped the treadle to power the drill. Effective it may have been, but painless it was not.

Following Germany's unconditional surrender, censorship at the unit level was dropped. Now we were free to identify our specific location, and it became permissible to discuss past activities and locations. For the first time since my arrival in Europe my parents began to receive letters of some substance. For example, it is from one of these that I can identify the Belgian village of Jesseren. (5/23/45)

Sometime during the early summer I received a short pass to a rest center in either Belgium or the Netherlands. The only memorable thing about it was my opportunity to travel through Cologne. This city had been bombed many times and appeared a solid mass of ruins from one end to the other. A bridge that once spanned the Rhine near the cathedral lay broken and fallen into the river. Army engineers had erected a temporary crossing near it. The famous Gothic cathedral had endured several bomb explosions but, though badly damaged, its lofty twin towers and enormous bulk still stood amidst all the flattened ruins around it. Twice in the 1980's it was my good fortune to visit the revitalized city and see the magnificent cathedral restored to its former, rightful beauty.

At various times during late spring-early summer some men were transferred out of our company while others came in from units elsewhere in the 311th. Among the latter was Bill Parsons, who had gone through the war with D Company. We became good friends and after the war maintained contact through yearly Christmas cards and letters. Through him I eventually joined the 78th Infantry Division Veterans Association. For several years he has been the very capable editor of the association's quarterly magazine, *The Flash*.

Me, 1945, in Belgium.

In June I heard a very demoralizing announcement. The army high command designated the 78th as Category II, meaning that after possibly a 30 day layover in the States, we would go to fight the Japanese. Divisions were to be sent to the Pacific in reverse order of their commitment to battle in Europe. While the 78th would not be at the top of the list, it seemed sure to go. Long afterward, I learned that the 97th, which replaced us on the Sieg, was very near the top, shipped out of Le Havre in mid-June, received 30 day furloughs, then sailed to the Pacific. The war was over by the time they got to Japan, so they served in the occupation force there.

From a military perspective it made good sense for the army to send experienced soldiers into the Pacific fight, but from a personal standpoint it was devastating news. Earlier in this narrative I referred to an inner feeling that I would survive the war in Europe. But now I had just as strong a feeling that I would not survive the invasion of Japan. Judging from what we had learned of the costly nature of such recent battles as Iwo Jima, and given the rumors that higher authorities expected as many as a million casualties in the invasion of Japan's home islands, there was no room for optimism. In three campaigns in Europe, surely I had used up all the luck fate had allotted me. It was not that I failed to recognize a duty to help end the war with Japan, it was just that I thought it fair for infantry to change places with some of the rear echelon forces.

In July the division began training for duty against Japan. Some men went to special schools for instruction in Japanese tactics and other useful matters. They were to return and instruct the rest of us. As the squad's gunner and assistant leader, I helped the newer men and the transfers in learning to use the anti-tank gun.

In mid-July a regiment. of the 1st Division relieved the 311th and we moved to a smaller area of responsibility north of Kassel. We made the move north by truck, traveling part of the way on the autobahn that ran northeast of Kassel. We came up the east side of a river big enough and pretty enough to be impressive. This, I learned, was the Weser which ran northwest through Bremen and entered the North Sea at Bremerhaven.

Our company convoy stopped opposite the small town of Veckerhagen. Using a ferry that carried no more than two vehicles at a time (only one, if it towed a gun or trailer), we crossed the Weser. When I say that the ferry resembled one that at one time crossed the Current River at Owl's Bend in southern Missouri, my family will get the picture!

Veckerhagen would be my army home for the next four months. Cannon Company occupied another small town a short distance down the road, and other companies of the 311th were scattered all around the area. In order to provide quarters for our company several families had been ordered to leave their homes and move in with relatives and friends. Our squad had a nice house to itself, and the rest of the platoon was in adjoining houses. I got my choice of a neat little bedroom just large enough for two cots and a dresser. We had water in the house for wash basins, but a call of nature necessitated a trip to a one-holer out back. Since this was all I had known for most of my life and all of us had extensive experience with slit trenches, this posed no problem.

Many of the townsmen were farmers who had small fields and pasturage for their animals just outside the town. The farmer who owned our house had a small barn and sheds for his animals just back of the house, not attached as I had found in Belgium. He carefully collected all the animal waste for use on his fields. Using a tank on a wagon, which soldiers named the "honey wagon" or sometimes the "cognac wagon", he hauled liquid refuse out for distribution. It impressed me that German farmers wasted nothing.

With the exception of a saw mill, there was no other industry in the town that I remember. The mill I recall because of my acquaintance with a teen aged boy, Werner, who was proud when he got a job handling lumber.

As a small and rather out of the way place, Veckerhagen showed no outward signs of war damage. Germany experienced so many military casualties, however, that within most families there must have been great loss. The outlook was both bleak and uncertain for many Germans that summer and fall of 1945. But at least many of the people of Veckerhagen could grow their own food. Some of the less fortunate families soon learned that if they sent their children around with buckets and other containers at our meal time, they would be given the surplus food from the mess line. I would have been glad to see food go to needy people anyway, but at the time I had no other use for much of my share. My stomach still rebelled against much of the preparations of our cooks. By the this time I was probably a good 20 to 25 pounds lighter than when I arrived in Europe.

Our government began issuing occupation marks in 1944. By providing goods and services to occupying soldiers, some of the town's inhabitants were paid in these marks. Many of us, for instance, went regularly to a Veckerhagen barber. Living near our platoon was a man with carpentry skills. He crafted a considerable number of small wooden boxes and sold them to soldiers for shipping souvenirs and other items home. I received official authorization to send a Mauser rifle home as a war souvenir. After I had disassembled it, the carpenter made a neat box for shipment. Using blue and silver metallic thread, another man fashioned an attractive Combat Infantryman Badge to be sewn on a uniform jacket or shirt.

1st Squad, 3rd Platoon, AT Co. 311 Inf. Rgt. (1st row, kneeling from left: B. Parsons, B. Young, and W. Horne; 2nd row, standing from left: T. Randazzo, R. Pooley, J. Quinn, H. Lewis, L. Breeze (me) and D. Hildebrand. At Veckerhagen, Germany. Summer, 1945.

With a full company of soldiers in town, the purveyors of drink could always count upon a ready market. A modest amount of wine sufficed for me, but several fellows in the platoon liked German beer. I found the taste very displeasing and one of my friends acknowledged you had to work at learning to like it. Never being one to do things just because others did, my response was "Why bother?" Besides, I explained, it reminded me too much of a natural product I used to see flowing from our horses. There was a brewery in a nearby town and on one occasion some platoon members purchased a keg of beer. A few of the fellows got a good buzz from drinking, but after our North Carolina mountain boy left us, I do not recall any of them getting thoroughly sloshed. Frequently he imbibed overly generous quantities of schnapps distilled from potatoes. Invariably it left him with a monumental headache, and he would go around inquiring if anyone had an "aspreen tablit." For him to repeat this behavior at every opportunity made no sense to me, but then army life had already taught me that a lot of human behavior defies good sense.

In July we had a momentary break in training with an opportunity to see a USO show featuring Bob Hope. The locale was in a large open field somewhere near Kassel. Thousands of soldiers were trucked in from all over the 78th area, so many in fact that our unit ended up quite some distance from the stage. Perhaps I went expecting too much, but I was not impressed with Hope's performance. On the other hand the bug-eyed comedian that accompanied him, Jerry Colonna, provided a humorous note and Ingrid Bergman added a bit of glamour.

Near the end of the first week in August the whole company began listening eagerly to the radio at every opportunity. We learned that on August 6 a single bomb of a totally new type (referred to as "atomic") had utterly devastated the Japanese city of Hiroshima. The Japanese ignored a demand to surrender unconditionally, and on August 9 a second bomb was dropped at Nagasaki. As we listened to optimistic newsmen, it seemed to us that an unbelievably miraculous weapon might keep us from involvement in a bloody invasion of Japan. On the evening of August 14, 1945, I wrote to my parents: "Well, thanks be to God, it looks like good news at last. It isn't official from Washington yet but I think the Japanese have surrendered."

Feeling as I had since learning that the 78th was to help with the conquest of Japan, I looked upon the splitting of the atom and the creation of the bomb as a miracle weapon that most probably saved my life. Many decades later I still support President Truman's decision to drop the bomb. I have no patience with those revisionists who, safely removed in body and time, pull events out of their historical context to condemn a president who, unlike his critics, experienced war close up. As one who both lived the events of the time and studied history professionally, I remain convinced that the president's action, terrible though it might be, saved the lives of hundreds of thousands of Japanese people, to say nothing of multitudes of GIs.

In my letter home the next evening (August 15) I could write with more assurance of the good news even though it still had an almost "too good to be true" quality about it: "Oh, Happy Day. This is it, the day we've hoped and prayed for so long. Isn't it wonderful that we have peace again. It doesn't seem possible that the war can be all over. It seems like a dream which we will wake up from."

Now that I could begin to think about getting out of the army, I thought it prudent to urge my parents to be patient. In May, 1945, the War Department prepared a demobilization plan based upon a point system. Each enlisted soldier was issued an Adjusted Service Rating (ASR) card. In my case this included one point for each month of service credit, a point for each month of overseas duty, and five points for each battle participation star (the Ardennes, Rhineland, and Central Europe) for a total of around 57 points at the time. This was a good number, but far from enough to get me home soon. So I wrote:

> I hope that now you won't get too built up on my getting home soon. By this time you know how the army operates and besides there are a lot of men to move out of Europe. I just now heard that by the next 30 days the redeployment system here in Europe would be completely reversed so that high pointers could get shipping priority. [over those previously marked to go fight the Japanese] (8/15/45)

On August 28 American troops began landing unopposed in the home islands of Japan. On Sunday September 2, 1945, the Japanese signed surrender documents aboard the U.S.S. Missouri in Tokyo Bay. V-J Day had arrived, and finally the war was over.

Following the Japanese surrender and the end of a need for combat training, we were given more opportunities for recreation and entertainment. Jack Benny brought a show to a stage set up on the grounds of an imperial castle near Kassel. I found him more entertaining than Hope. A singer, Martha Tilton, was with him as well as some other good entertainers, including a harmonica player, whose music I enjoyed very much. His name was Larry Adler, and later I read that he got into trouble with the House Un-American

Activities Committee in the midst of our Red-hunting paranoia at the onset of the Cold War.

On another occasion I saw a small, but very good, European circus that had survived the war. As a Missourian, I was impressed when their band played the "Missouri Waltz", evidently as a tribute to President Truman.

Plays and musical shows sometimes came to Hofsgeismar, site of division headquarters, and if the company sent in a truck, I usually jumped aboard. Several evenings a week a truck would be available to go to a movie in Hofsgeismar, or to the Red Cross canteen there. The latter was a good place to visit, drink coffee, eat doughnuts (which my stomach now accepted!), and often watch some kind of entertainment.

Athletic equipment was made available, and I spent a lot of time playing softball. A few of the more avid hunters in the company had an opportunity to go on organized parties to hunt, among other things, wild boar.

Education programs were established and I spent some time trying to learn a little German. It was very frustrating to discover that I had neither the ear nor the aptitude for a foreign language. While I learned to count and read simple words in German, it seemed obvious my ears would never separate and distinguish sounds well. At the time I thought it might be attributable to the damage done, especially to my left ear, by the explosion of too many 88's around me. This may have been worsened by a hereditary defect, for later I realized that my father often had trouble separating sounds as he grew older.

Our chaplains conducted services in a local church, and I often attended the Protestant service led by a man with the interesting name of Albert Casebeer. Before we left Hersfeld, a very moving memorial service for our fallen comrades of the 311th was held in the church.

Uncle Ruphard Griner wrote to give me the address of his son Roy, who was with the Canadian Army in the British zone of occupation. If first cousins, one American and one Canadian, could meet for the first time somewhere in Germany, I knew it would mean so very much to my mother and his father. Before we could make a connection, however, Roy was sent back to England in preparation for shipment home.

According to War Department regulations, "The Bronze Star Medal is awarded to any person who, while serving in any capacity in or with the Army of the United States, on or after 7 December 1941, distinguishes or has distinguished himself by heroic or meritorious achievement or service not involving participation in aerial flight, in connection with military operations against an enemy of the United States."

Only when a list of regimental recipients came out in the fall of 1945 were many of us in the company aware that Captain Gapen had recommended several men to receive the Bronze Star Medal, based on meritorious achievement or service. Although a couple of my private first class friends were on the list, most were platoon leaders, platoon sergeants, and squad leaders. Other than the printed list there was never any public acknowledgment, no formal presentation. Nor do I know whether any of them had the actual medal in hand. In many cases medals and awards were mailed to the recipient following discharge, some had to be requested from the War Department, and some people waited years to receive them.

The above prelude is offered in an effort to place into understandable context my absolute astonishment during a company formation in the third week of August, 1945. Sgt. Hildebrand came back from a meeting and told the squad we were all to appear in dress uniforms for a company formation in the late afternoon. Then he pulled me aside and advised me to look especially sharp, for the captain had something to give me. He left me wondering what it was all about, but when he smiled broadly, I knew it did not mean trouble.

After calling me out of ranks and to the front of the whole company, Captain Gapen read a few excerpts from an official-looking piece of paper. The citation read:

By direction of the President, under provisions of AR600-45, dated 22 September 1943, as amended, the Bronze Star Medal is awarded to: Private First Class <u>Lawrence E. Breeze,</u> 37242203, Anti-Tank Company, 311th Infantry Regiment, for heroic achievement in connection with military operations against the enemy on 11 March 1945 in Honnef, Germany.

Some details followed and at the bottom of the page was typed: "By Command of Major General Parker", and it was made official by the signature of the 78th Division's adjutant general.

After reading the citation, the captain presented me with the beautiful medal. A handsome box came with it along with a ribbon for my army uniform and a lapel pin for civilian dress. Seldom have I worn the latter.

Pleased as I was to receive such recognition from my commanding officer, it was also a little embarrassing. Better than anyone else I knew it was an exaggeration to describe my actions as "heroic", but the captain did not stop with the formal presentation. He sent me to Grebenstein, Germany, where the regimental newspaper, *Timberwolf,* was published.

The paper included in each issue what was called "Heroes' Corner", generally featuring one Silver Star recipient and two Bronze Star winners. The paper's artist drew sketches of the men to accompany an article describing the action. Thus my picture (not a very good likeness but he did catch the distinctive Griner nose) and accompanying article entitled "Assumes Command of Anti-Tank Gun Squad," appeared in the issue of November 3, 1945. At the time the best thing to come out of it all was the additional five points to my ASR, thanks to the medal. This gave me a chance at an earlier departure for home.

For a short time in the late summer of 1945 I had hopes of getting to England, not for a stop on the way home but to do farm work. With so many of their men still scattered all around the world, apparently the English were concerned about a manpower shortage for harvest work. Word came to us that they might seek help among nearby American soldiers with farm experience. Indicating my readiness to volunteer for such a mission, I looked forward to the venture with great anticipation. I have always regretted that nothing ever developed from what could have been an exciting and enriching experience for a young man who, as it turned out, would become an ardent Anglophile and professor of British history.

At some point that fall I heard there was a good chance for my promotion to corporal. For several months I had served in a position normally held by corporal rank, but with an overall surplus of noncoms in the company, I never expected to get the stripes. At last perhaps there was a shot at them, especially as some older noncoms had left on points. It did not happen.

With the end of any need for the 78th Division in the Far East, it was redesignated as an occupation force (Category I). Subsequently we learned that sometime that fall the division would go to Berlin. Divided into four sectors (American, British, French, and Russian), the capital city of the Third Reich was supposed to be jointly controlled. It was meant to be a symbol of Allied unity. Unfortunately Berlin was located in the Russian zone over a hundred miles from a Western zone. The absurdity of it all was that no military corridor had been provided for Western troops and supplies to get to Berlin. We could get there only by Russian "permission" for the use of a land route through their zone. The workability of this arrangement would be a test of Russian trustworthiness and one they would fail abysmally.

Except for those men involved in the transport of slave workers into the Russian zone mentioned earlier, our company had no experience with the Russians. When we got to Veckerhagen, the Russian zone was several miles east of us. To my knowledge none of my company had any close contact with them. But I began to hear disturbing stories that where the British and Russian zones came together north and east of us, the Russians sometimes behaved more like unfriendly forces than wartime allies. One of the noncoms in my platoon became acquainted with a British officer, who was charged with patrolling a road that ran close to the Russian area. Through him we learned that whenever his men came near a certain point, the Russians frequently fired upon them. It was an infuriating situation but also very worrisome to the officer, for higher authority still hoped it was possible to get along with the Russians and would not welcome a disturbing incident.

It was considered an honor for a division to be chosen to represent the American occupational presence in Berlin. In going there the 78th would replace the well-known 82nd Airborne Division. In mid-November a large part of the division began moving in motor convoy to Berlin. It transpired, however, that the 311th would not make the move. The regiment remained behind in the Hofgeismar area and prepared for an eventual move north to the Bremen-Bremerhaven enclave where it would replace the 29th Infantry Division in the occupation of what had been Nazi Germany's number one port.

By this time the various divisions were busily calculating point totals and shuffling personnel. The significant one for me came on November 20th. On that date the 29th sent several hundred men with less than 60 points to the 78th in exchange for men with 60 points or more. With 65 points, I was soon on my way to the 29th in northern Germany.

Chapter Thirteen

The 29th Division and Home

Known as the "Blue and Gray," the 29th Infantry Division had landed at Omaha beach on D-Day, June 6, 1944. Now this veteran outfit was slated to return to the States, and I was happy to join its AT Company, 115th Infantry Regiment. Upon arrival in Bremerhaven, I found they did not have a firm departure date.

The waters approaching the great port had been heavily mined and our navy, apparently making some use of experienced German naval personnel, was still in the process of clearing a safe passage through the harbor. Anxious though we might be to start home, no one wanted to risk hitting a mine before we even left German waters! Naturally the exchange of information, picked up through various contacts during the day, dominated the nightly mess hall conversation. Typical of much army talk, it was a jumble of fact and rumor.

Once the harbor had been cleared of mines, we waited impatiently for our ship to come in. Actually we needed several ships, especially if they were Liberty ships, to transport the whole division. Speculation was rife and rumor abounded. I do not know how many times someone would return from his daily wanderings with the word that a ship was due in the next day. It did not appear, of course, and this pattern was repeated endlessly.

Meanwhile we performed some limited duty and tried to find ways to pass the time. We were stationed in what I recall as some kind of naval complex. There were some important facilities to guard as well as some warehouses containing food and supplies.

I bunked in a room with a half dozen or so other members of the platoon. Other than some limited guard duty, our time was generally our own. There was enough sleeping time to make even Mort Walker's Beetle Bailey happy. The problem was we all soon caught up and became a room full of insomniacs, unable even to sleep well at night. All agreed it was an unexpected and disgusting situation. Until recent months every one of us had gone through a long period of limited opportunity for decent sleep. We had been cramped, cold, sometimes damp, and often afraid. How blessedly wonderful it would have been just to sleep and sleep without interruption. Now that this opportunity had been granted to us, we were all wide awake. It was a good thing the group was congenial, otherwise we would have gotten on each other's nerves.

No doubt it was highly unusual in a group, but the others in the room shared my lack of enthusiasm for card games. One or two enjoyed solitaire and got me interested in that. Among my possessions somewhere is a pack of cards that helped me pass a lot of time in Bremerhaven. Pocket books were very popular at the time, and we read all those that came our way and wished for more. One of the assistant squad leaders in the platoon was very sports minded, and he organized a company basketball team. I played on it and we competed against teams from other units in the regiment. Movies were shown at a makeshift theater, but we got only one new film a week. With nothing better to do, we might see each picture several times.

Sometimes I felt the need to go for a solitary walk. On one occasion I followed the railroad line away from the inhabited area. Keeping with the tracks I figured even I could not get lost. In that area the countryside was very flat, and in one place I came across something new to me: a peat bog. No one was working in it that day, but I got a good look at the interesting brown-colored formation from which slices of turf had been cut,

The 311th Regimental Combat Team arrived to take over occupation duties in the Bremen area. I was pleasantly surprised to run into Sgt. Hildebrand and other familiar faces from my old third platoon. They were surprised to find me still around, for they expected me to be on the way home.

As the month of December wound down, it became apparent I would spend my fourth Christmas in the army and my second in Germany. At least this was bound to be a vast improvement on the previous one! It turned out to be very different from any other I have ever experienced and in a most satisfying way. We decorated the company mess hall with everything we could find to make it look like Christmas. Our cooks prepared lots of turkey and all that went with it, and baked lots of goodies. Then we invited a lot of children to a Christmas party. We did not have presents to distribute but we gave plenty of hard Christmas candy. The children were well fed and happy, and we felt like the Christmas spirit had truly visited us.

With the beginning of the new year, a ship finally came in for us. Carrying our duffel bags, we marched to the dock eager to begin our much anticipated journey home. Our vessel was one of the mass produced Liberty ships, built in this case to serve as a troop transport. It differed drastically in size, condition, accommodations, and just about everything else from the *Carnarvon Castle*. But hopefully it would stay afloat and could get us to New York.

We were the only infantry company to board the ship. Artillery batteries and miscellaneous units from elsewhere in the 29th made up the rest of the list. Informed that our company would serve K.P. duty for the whole trip, we grumbled about the typical abuse of the infantry. In actuality it worked to our advantage because we got our choice of food and easy access to the good things such as ice cream, generally unavailable or in short supply to others on the ship.

Our company was settled in the ship's midsection which, given the rough crossing we had, was the best possible location. Again, did the infantry just luck out, or was it given its due as the so-called "Queen of Battle?" We were crowded into close quarters with bunks in four tiers set very close together. Luckily no one around me seemed to suffer from claustrophobia. By comparison I remembered the *Carnarvon Castle* as downright spacious.

Once the ship had passed through the area cleared by the mine sweepers and was well into the North Sea, I relaxed and figured we were safely on our way. Sometime that night we entered the Strait of Dover and were told that a light off the starboard side was Dover. It was too dark of course to see the famed chalk cliffs or to look for the bluebirds of the popular wartime song. Entering the English Channel we thought the sea was rough. Probably so, but in comparison to what we were about to get into, it was relatively calm.

Moving on into the Atlantic Ocean, the ride got progressively rougher. While I did not keep a written record of the trip, we must have been about three days out of Bremerhaven when we ran into a fierce winter storm. From our position below deck, it felt as though the ship was being tossed about like a toy. It was very disconcerting and caused us a lot of anxiety.

Two or three times in the next several days I ventured out on the top deck. Clutching something sturdy and hanging on for dear life, I was very careful to stay away from the outside rail. On my first trip up top, I remember being astonished, awed, and very alarmed at the sight before me. It seemed impossible that waves that high did not swamp the ship. The deep trough between waves resembled the valleys between the hills back home. Just when I thought water would surely overwhelm us, the bow rose up in the air to a perilous angle as though taking to the sky. Then surmounting the wave, it came down and for an uneasy moment appeared to be diving into the sea. At that point the stern came up, then when the bow rose upward again the stern came down. Below decks, the effect of this was very jarring and noisy, creating in my mind the image of propellers running over large logs before they settled firmly into the water.

Being on deck gave me a keen appreciation for our company's midship location. We rose and fell with the ups and downs of the ship of course, but the men both fore and aft had it much worse. They rose very high and then fell very low, with plenty of rolling action to port and starboard to go with it. After the first day of the storm, we became aware of declining numbers coming through the chow line. Eventually few men showed up from the sections far forward or far aft. From all accounts they were not only too sick to eat, they were too miserable to care much whether they lived or died. I still shudder to think what a dreadful mess it must have been in those crowded quarters.

A few men in our company became seasick, but the majority of us kept going and eating well. I remembered the advice of a British sailor on the *Carnarvon* on that point. Many of us were grateful at this time to be on K.P. where we got our choice of good food. Besides, with few of the other outfits eating, our work load had been greatly reduced. Thankfully no one in my immediate bunking area became ill. That would have made it difficult for the rest of us to maintain a steady stomach. Remembering how often as a boy I had been sick to my stomach, I was especially thankful, even proud, to ride through the storm in such surprisingly good shape.

Duty in the galley offered another unexpected benefit. It enabled me to keep busy and occupy my mind with something other than the perils of the voyage. Back in our bunk area time could really drag, and the pooling of collective uneasiness did not make for much rest. One of the men in the company had a mandolin and was quite good with it. When he could be persuaded to play, a few others would sing and it brightened spirits and elevated the mood of everyone.

A large map of the Atlantic hung on the wall in the galley area. Each day a member of the crew stuck a pin in it to show our progress. As the ship fought its way slowly westward, there were days when the pins seemed to remain very close together. The open space to be covered with pins remained discouragingly wide. At last the storms abated and we began to cover more distance each day. But just when it appeared one more pin would put us into New York, the ship broke down! A couple of days or so later, we limped into New York Harbor. It had taken at least two weeks to make a voyage we had been told should take several days less than that. I was thankful to see the Statue of Liberty again, and this time from the right direction, coming home!

Earlier on the voyage we had been given forms to prepare a telegraph message to our families saying we had arrived back in the States and would be home in a few days. Once off the ship we were taken to a nearby military base.

The name and exact location I no longer remember. On the way there we were promised a meal appropriate for returning soldiers. As anticipated, it turned out to be steak, and for army food, quite good.

After the meal, we were sorted out according to assigned discharge centers. Instead of being sent back to my induction center at Ft. Leavenworth, I was to be discharged at Jefferson Barracks. Thus before the end of the day I was on a troop train bound for St. Louis.

At the Barracks our group from Europe joined a bunch of men just in from the Pacific. All of us were hustled from station to station, turning in things, providing information, completing forms, learning about veteran benefits, and taking the army's final perfunctory physical exam.

We were given an opportunity to take up the payment of premiums that would keep our life insurance policy in force. As a single man and with no immediate plans to change that status, I gave it little consideration and simply opted out. Acquiring dependents and responsibilities a few years later, I regretted my quick decision.

All of us were required to listen to a spiel from a noncom, who probably never got within a thousand miles of the real war and was assigned to persuade us to sign up for Army Reserve. Not appreciating that his captive audience was comprised heavily of combat infantrymen from both theaters of operation, he made the mistake of trying to sell us on the advantages of staying with something for which we were already trained! After his words were received with several derisive hoots, he surrendered and let us move on to our next station.

Having made all the rounds required of me and drawn the last of my army pay, I received my discharge papers. In addition to the all important paper itself, there was a wallet size copy of it. A paper entitled "Enlisted Record and Report of Separation" noted that I had been awarded a Combat Infantryman Badge; a Bronze Star Medal; three small bronze battle stars for the Ardennes, Rhineland, and Central Europe campaigns; and the Good Conduct Medal. It noted that I was entitled to wear the American Theater campaign ribbon, the European African Middle Eastern

Theater campaign ribbon (the three small bronze stars to be worn on this ribbon); the Victory ribbon; and two overseas bars. It showed I had a lapel button for use on civilian clothing to show that I had served my country. This button soon acquired the forbidding nick-name of "ruptured duck", and I doubt that many of us ever wore it.

A few months after discharge I received by mail the Army of Occupation Medal with a clasp indicating service in "Germany." Years later I learned that with service in both France and Belgium in 1944, I was entitled to medals struck by the governments of these countries in acknowledgement of such service, and made arrangements to add these to my collection. Later still, I learned that, having been awarded the CIB, I was entitled to an oak leaf cluster for the Bronze Star, and added this too.

The discharge papers included a "Separation Qualification Record." This information was intended for the veteran to present to prospective employers, representatives of schools or colleges, or to use in any other beneficial way. The description of my infantry skills and experience hardly could be helpful in anything I might want to do, but the information on my ASTP courses in the fundamentals of engineering at UNH were more likely to be helpful.

Having given me an honorable release from its service, the army took me to Union Station in St. Louis and said, in effect, that my life was again my own. With my discharge papers tucked securely in my pocket, this time I purchased a one-way ticket to Lock Springs. Boarding the Wabash train, I began the last leg of my long journey. There were several other soldiers, all newly discharged, in the coach.

Sometime after midnight the train made its stop in Chillicothe. A little later we passed just south of where, as a boy, I used to watch the trains and think how wonderful it would be to get on and ride to distant and exciting places. Then we were in Lock Springs, and there my parents were waiting to take me home.

Less than fifteen miles separate Chillicothe and Lock Springs. Yet as a measure of what had happened in my life and how it had been changed, the bus station of the former, where sorrowful parents dropped me off on a gray November day in 1942, seemed a world away from the railroad station in the latter where thankful parents met me on a cold January night in 1946.

Picture Gallery

Reunions

Squad members at the 78th reunion, St. Louis, MO, 1994. From the left: D. Hildebrand, B. Parsons, L. Breeze (me), L. Rifenberrick.

The first meeting since 1945 with the author's AT Co. commander, Capt. John Gapen: "You can call me John now, Larry."

Frank Galloway and I, roommates at UNH met again in 1991. This was our first time together since we were separated at Camp Pickett in the Spring of 1944.

Picture Gallery

Europe Revisited

Many of the 311th fallen were brought to Henri Chapelle Cemetery, Belgium In the immediate foreground is the grave of James L. Ford.

Some of the 311th fallen were taken to the Netherlands Cemetery, Margraten. The grave in the immediate foreground is that of Christian J. Gabriel.

Henri Chapelle Cemtery. Both Richard Meade and Guy Walker initially rested here, but were "repatriated" to home cemeteries after the war.

Reading the 78th Inf. Div. plaque on the River Wall at Remagen, June 2000.

The west towers of the bridge today. Part of the war memorial there. Remagen, June 2000.

My son, Daniel, and my wife, Alice, pose with me in front of the west towers at Remagen.
June 2000.

Epilogue

My memoir began as an effort to tell my children about my experience as a soldier during the Second World War. It seems appropriate to follow with an attempt to show how the experience affected me.

All Americans, no matter their place or role, were affected in some way by that war. Those of us who served in some branch of the armed services were affected by a broad variety of experiences. These could range from pleasant, enriching, and absolutely awesome to unpleasant, difficult, barely tolerable, frightening, and downright horrendous. I ran the gamut of these experiences. I, who had never been far from the home farm, traveled from mid-continent to the Pacific coast and back across to the Atlantic coast. I sailed across the Atlantic and spent time in several European countries. Training with an armored division was followed by a marvelous opportunity to study pre-engineering in a New England university. And finally I became part of an infantry division with combat experience in three historically significant campaigns.

"Innocent" seems an apt description for me when I left the Chillicothe bus station in the late fall of 1942. No doubt it could apply equally well to countless numbers of young men and women who went to war from small communities. Given the nature of my farming and small town community, and my limited contacts (mostly through reading) with the world beyond, the term fit me well.

Socially conservative and homogeneous in ethnic (Anglo-Saxon) and religious (strictly Protestant) background, and with shared experiences, commonly held values, and the narrow views of a small place, my home community served as an insulating force against the lures and temptations of an outside world.

To outsiders, our community of Lock Springs-Sampsel must have appeared a social backwater. It did not possess a tavern, a dance hall, or even a pool hall. The few men inclined to an occasional drink (unthinkable for the women) did so on the sly. Public inebriation would have disgraced a family. There was a strong work ethic and excess energy, especially in growing boys, was channeled into sports, fishing, hunting and generally harmless pranks, and especially at Halloween, creative mischief. Any kind of violence was rare, and crime against person and property practically unknown in this church going community.

The war took me out of this provincial setting and introduced me to people, places, and experiences that broadened my outlook and enriched my life. Arriving in California for my first assignment, I was, thrown in with men from different backgrounds, national origins, religions, interests and in some cases, moral values. Moving on to other postings, I encountered this same diversity. But we were all in the war together, and living and working together became a learning experience for all. Certainly it was a growing experience for someone of my limited background, and I came home with a firm conviction that people should make a genuine effort to understand each other no matter the outward appearing differences. Beneath it all, we could find mutually beneficial results in cooperative understanding.

It became a point that figured importantly in my study of history and ultimately in my efforts to interest others in history. In a devastated Europe I had seen the terrible consequences of the inability of people to live with neighbors who appeared different. When I left Europe in 1946, I despaired that people there would learn from lessons offered by the war. But later as I began to study and teach modern European history, I was heartened by signs of understanding and cooperation beginning with the small Benelux nations and followed by genuine efforts on the part of old enemies, France and Germany.

Moving by train from one assignment to another and on furlough home, I had an opportunity to see more of our country than I had ever dreamed possible. Trying to make the most of it as I passed through the strange and colorful landscape of the Southwest, crossed the majestic mountains of the West, traveled the length of the rich agricultural heartland of America, witnessed the vibrant industrial activity in the cities of the upper Midwest and East, spent some time in the nation's largest city, studied in a small New England town, and trained in the heart of the Old South, I got an informal education in the geography, people, and resources of our vast and richly diverse nation.

From boyhood I had been enchanted with history, and my experiences in the war nourished this interest. The simple act of training in hills neighboring the California gold fields of 1849 or passing along the Potomac and through Harper's Ferry (John Brown's raid, 1859) made me feel close to history. Even though often thoroughly miserable in France and Belgium in the late fall of 1944, I found some satisfaction in the atmosphere of history exuded by the area.

After the frustration of ailments and other signs of physical weakness in my younger years, it was a confidence builder to get through the war years with only a single sick call. And by a combination of incredible luck and the unseen hand of fate, unlike the other less fortunate men in the squad that entered combat together, at no time did I have to be evacuated to the battalion aid station.

The deaths of combat buddies, the wounding of others, and my own narrow escapes, left an enduring impression on the way I viewed life. Problems and troubles could still be very serious but they would forever be seen on a different measuring scale from that viewed by young innocence. There would be a lingering sadness over the loss of friends throughout the regiment. Yet even in this there would be something indescribably special about the memory of comradeship unlike any other.

When I returned to the Lock Springs-Sampsel community in 1946, innocence was long gone. I have always been grateful that the solid family and community environment in my background allowed me to select from the best of what the outside world offered and avoid the worst. An opportunity to earn the equivalent of a year and a half college credit while still fulfilling my military obligation proved an unexpected bonus. Then there was an eye-opening informal education in travel, history, places, and people. I returned home with a greater understanding of people, considerably more tolerance, firm convictions of right and wrong, a revulsion for extremism in any form; and after seeing what happened in Europe when fears and prejudices were manipulated for terrible purposes, a strong feeling for truth, fairness, and justice. My good character survived the test of war, and undoubtedly became stronger for it. My approach to life in the post-war world would be low key and temperate.

In retrospect it seems evident that my experience during the war had prepared me quite well for a career in history. When it came time to take advantage of the educational benefits offered by the G.I. Bill, however, my goal was to resume the study of engineering.

Once again fate intervened and a letter of acceptance to the University of Missouri engineering school never reached me. With enrollment time drawing near and no word from the engineering school, I got on the bus and seventy-five miles down the road from home entered a small liberal arts institution, Missouri Valley College.

Seeing two interesting looking history courses available, I enrolled in both. In so doing, I came under the influence of a brilliant woman, Dr. Belle Campbell Huff, the most demanding, stimulating, and inspiring teacher of all my college years. When, at the end of the semester, a letter from the University of Missouri engineering school reached me with an inquiry as to why I had not enrolled, I was already hooked on history and the goal of a college teaching career.

Surely it was meant to be. My decision led to a most satisfying and rewarding life. In a career of nearly forty years of college teaching, I enjoyed the association with hundreds of students and dozens of wonderful faculty colleagues. But above all else, I am thankful that fate set me on a course to meet the woman who has been my wife of fifty plus years. She was a student in my first class in my first full-time college teaching position.

And it all began when an innocent young man left farm and home for military service in the Second World War.

Dr. Breeze at the podium

About Larry Breeze

Dr. Larry Breeze was born near the small community of Sampsel in Livingston County, Missouri, on June 3, 1922. By his own definition "an innocent Missouri farm boy," he entered military service in November of 1942 and was discharged in January of 1946. Innocence was lost in the Battle of the Bulge, at such places as Drachenfels, Wuppertal, Euskirchen and Remagen.

When he returned home he wanted to pursue a career as a civil engineer, but his acceptance letter from the University of Missouri never reached him and he enrolled at Missouri Valley College where a professor of history changed his career goals. As a result of this inspiration, he received an M. A. in history in 1951 and a Ph.D. in European history in 1960. He taught at Jacksonville University in Florida until 1966 when he moved to Southeast Missouri State University. There, until retirement in 1989, he taught a wide variety of courses in European history concentrating upon modern British history. There he did what professors of history did at the time—deliver papers at history conferences, publish articles, and write academic books. But, most of all, he served as a teacher, gentle, caring, dignified, and scholarly.

Larry and Alice, his wife of fifty-five years, have two children, Alison and Daniel, and continue to live on Missouri Street in Cape Girardeau, Missouri, within easy walking distance of Southeast Missouri State University.